D1376405

DEFENDING MOTHER EARTH

DEFENDING MOTHER EARTH

*Native American Perspectives
on Environmental Justice*

edited by

Jace Weaver

ORBIS BOOKS

Maryknoll, New York 10545

The Catholic Foreign Mission Society of America (Maryknoll) recruits and trains people for overseas missionary service. Through Orbis Books, Maryknoll aims to foster the international dialogue that is essential to mission. The books published, however, reflect the opinions of their authors and are not meant to represent the official position of the society.

Copyright © 1996 by Jace Weaver

Published by Orbis Books, Maryknoll, New York 10545-0308

Queries regarding rights and permissions should be addressed to:
Orbis Books, P.O. Box 308, Maryknoll, NY 10545-0308

Cover art: "Mistissini Marches for Oka" by Glenna Matoush (Anishinaabe/Cree)

Manufactured in the United States of America

Ediset by Joan Marie Laflamme

Library of Congress Cataloguing-in-Publication Data

Defending mother earth : Native American perspectives on environmental
  justice / edited by Jace Weaver.
        p. cm.
    ISBN 1-57075-096-3 (alk. paper)
    1. Indians of North America–Social conditions. 2. Indians of
  North America–Civil rights. 3. Indian philosophy–North America.
  4. Human ecology–North America–Philosophy. 5. Environmental
  degradation–United States. 6. Environmental protection–United
  States. 7. United States–Environmental conditions. 8. United
  States–Ethnic relations.   I. Weaver, Jace, 1957-
  E98.S67D44   1996
  305.897'073–dc20   96-21203
                                                                                CIP

For K.L.,
my greatest defender and my greatest critic.
I hope she recognizes herself in this.

We believed in a power that was higher than all people and all the created world, and we called this power the Man-Above. We believed in some power in the world that governed everything that grew, and we called this power Mother-Earth. We believed in the power of the Sun, of the Night-Sun or Moon, of the Morning Star, and of the Four Old Men who direct the winds and the rains and the seasons and give us the breath of life. We believed that everything created is holy and has some part in the power that is over all.

Carl Sweezy (Arapaho)
(c.1881-1953)

Man's heart away from nature, becomes hard; [the Lakota] knew that lack of respect for growing, living things soon led to lack of respect for humans too.

Luther Standing Bear (Lakota)
(c.1868-1939)

JOB'S GARDEN

The difference is wide
  between North and South.
They sat side by side
  to change our ways.

They did not know our feelings.
They took away our lands.
They said it was not wrong.

In the hills stood the pines.
Mighty rivers flowed on.
We were free
  to hunt the fair mink of the land.

Fast rivers guided the voyageurs,
  the adventurers of long ago.
They sang of great rivers,
  the easy riches of the fur trade.

Now the surrender of rivers
  lays Job's garden in ruins.*
Nothing is sacred
  in Job's garden now.

Margaret Sam-Cromarty
May 13, 1995

---

*The reference here is not to the biblical Job but to Job Bearskin, the subject of a documentary entitled "Job's Garden." Bearskin, a Cree trapper, was a witness in court proceedings to block hydroelectric development at James Bay, Québec. Testifying about the impact dams on the La Grande River would have on his livelihood, he stated, "It can never be that there will be enough money to help pay for what I get from trapping. I do not think in terms of money. I think more often of the land because the land is something you will have for a long time. That is why we call our traplines, our land, a garden" (Boyce Richardson, *Strangers Devour the Land* [Post Mills, Vt.: Chelsea Green Publishing, 1991], p. 121).

Contents

Foreword

RUSSELL MEANS

All too often we concentrate only on the problems, the devastation brought upon us by over five hundred years of colonialism. This book and the conference that led to it went beyond that. I think we should be very happy and proud that we are still Indian people. We're still alive, and we're still resisting. We still have respect for the earth. We have traditional knowledge and values that are superior to anything in Western, "scientific," industrialized culture. Yet industrial society neither understands nor wants our knowledge and our values. That is sad, and we should feel pity for it.

Many years ago my uncle, Matthew King, told me, "You have to remember that the White man is like a little child. You have to have patience with him." But patience won't bring back the redwood trees once they're chopped down. Patience won't breathe life into rivers once they're poisoned and dead. Patience won't restore the earth when its skin has been torn, and it has been raped by strip mining. In Canada, corporations are cutting down Arctic forests that will never grow back. They're sowing the earth with DDT and Agent Orange. They're threatening to destroy James Bay. In Mexico, NAFTA already has killed or displaced thousands of Native peoples and threatens to kill the Mayan corn economy. From Tuktoyaktuk, Northwest Territories to Tierra del Fuego, Native America is under assault, and the destruction is disguised in Orwellian doublespeak. It calls the destruction of Chippewa wild rice crop, "rendering their subsistence usages less than effective" and labels leaking nuclear waste transported across Indian land "materials shipped in a partially unshielded condition." It calls making the Black Hills or Four Corners unfit for human habitation because of mining and industrial wastes designating them as "national sacrifice areas."

Industrial society is wearing itself out. We need to talk to White people patiently in terms they will understand. In capitalist economics, one of the first principles taught is never to spend capital. Corporations need to be made to see that they're losing their capital. They are spending their capital because the human species is the only living thing that is literally consuming the environment. If we put it in the crass terms of Western business, perhaps they will slow down and take another look. There is a Cree saying that I keep on my desk. It says, "Not until you have poisoned the last root, not until you have poisoned the last fish, not until you have poisoned the last animal—only then will you find out that money is worthless."

Jace Weaver raises the question of whether it isn't presumptuous of human beings to speak of "defending" Mother Earth. I don't believe we should be too concerned about the semantics of the English language in this book. We are the children of the Earth. She is our Mother, and it's our right and duty to protect her. There are forces in the universe beyond anything Europeans can imagine. From our traditional ways, we know that we do not have the right to degrade our Mother and that we must live in harmony with all creation. The Europeans' lopsided emphasis on human beings at the expense of the rest of the created order and their presumptuous assumption that they are somehow outside the chain of interrelatedness of all things have led inevitably to imbalance and disharmony and will result in a readjustment that will cut arrogant human beings down to size, give them a taste of that ultimate reality that is beyond their ability to manipulate or control, and restore balance and harmony. If humanity keeps abusing Mother Earth, she will retaliate, and her abusers will be eliminated. As this book points out, many of our prophecies tell us that.

I strongly believe in the power of mothers. If we have anything to convey to non-Indians, it is the true sense of this power and its sacredness. If the feminist movement, or society in general, is to stop violence against women, it first will have to stop the initial rape and violence against our Mother Earth.

I was blessed to witness the births of my last two children. It is the most awesome thing in the world in which to be able to participate. I think back to those experiences. I think about how their mother took them in her arms and began the nurturing process. I think of the power that possesses and know that is where the change must start. If industrial society is to change, it's going to have to come from the mothers, and it must start with respect for Mother Earth.

It is our desire to defend our communities and our Mother that makes sovereignty guaranteed by treaties the number one demand of indigenous peoples. We won't get sovereignty simply by continually asking for it. It must be implemented. Dependency is killing us, so that we become our own enemy. Some of our people talk about our inherent right to welfare, but that is part of the death dance of dependency. Our treaty rights do not include the right to food stamps! Our right is to have gardens again! Our right is to have a clean environment on land that *we* control, where we can hunt, and fish, and gather foods and medicines without fearing that they are too polluted with toxins for us to eat or to use. As John Mohawk has said, "If you want to be sovereign, you have to act sovereign." The American Indian Movement showed that in the 1970s, and Canadian First Nations showed us again at Oka. The case studies in this book demonstrate the need for Indians to undertake their own hearings on the environmental genocide of indigenous peoples and present the findings to national governments and the United Nations. We can't wait for others to do it for us. If we want to be sovereign, we have to act sovereign.

We are fond of saying that in any action we take we must look to the effect of that action to a minimum of seven generations into the future. That is what our ancestors did. In making treaties, in spite of the duplicity and treachery of the business interests, governments, and armies with whom they dealt, they looked ahead and tried to protect seven generations. We are now living in the seventh generation after the treaty period. In fact, we are toward the end of it. Now it is our responsibility. We must find the method that our ancestors found to ensure the safety and livelihood of our nations seven generations from now. We cannot do it simply by going to international conferences or by using band-aid approaches to global, systemic problems. We all want what is best for our people. We all need to work together—educated and uneducated, urban, rural, and reservation Indians—to save our people, our lands, and the planet.

Indigenous people have engaged in resistance for more than five centuries. We should feel proud that after five hundred years we are still Indian people. Despite the fenced buffalo and the disappearing salmon, we're still here. Ultimately, I don't care what industrial society does. I don't care if there is finally just one Indian village left high in the Andes, or deep in the Amazonian jungle, or up in the Arctic. We're going to survive. I think that alone is hope for the era in which we live. This book contributes to that survival.

Preface

JACE WEAVER

From March 16 to March 19, 1995, an extraordinary conference took place on the campus of the Iliff School of Theology in Denver, Colorado. The North American Native Workshop on Environmental Justice brought together a small group of concerned persons from Canada, the United States, and Mexico to discuss the ecological issues confronting the indigenous peoples of the continent. Limited to Natives, the gathering included scholars, activists, and scholar-activists. Participants represented twenty tribal backgrounds and a spectrum of religious practice from traditional to Christian. The majority were women. The ensuing discussions were both productive and broad in scope. In addition to discussion of specific environmental concerns, links were made to such far-ranging events as NAFTA, the Mayan rebellion in Chiapas, and Québecois separatism.

George Tinker first approached me to ask if I would organize such a conference in September 1994, while he was a visiting professor at Union Theological Seminary in New York. It was to be sponsored by the World Council of Churches, which was conducting a series of consultations around the world on the meaning of the affirmation "Creation As Beloved of God" for various cultures. North American reflections were being coordinated by the Boston Theological Institute. Originally, we had been asked to take part in the meetings being organized by B.T.I. We, however, declined. Those involved in the environmental movement are overwhelmingly White. Both George and I previously had spoken and participated at conferences planned by one or another of the organizations making up the loose-knit movement. We had experienced firsthand the marginalization of indigenous concerns at such meetings, and we had no desire to once again be token presences at largely non-Native gatherings. Instead, we proposed an all-Native workshop, which would assemble some of the people working on the grassroots, national, and international levels, to address the wide range of environmental problems facing Native communities.

When I agreed to undertake the task, I never dreamed that getting twenty people into the same room would be such a difficult job. Because Native environmental activists are relatively few when compared to their non-Native counterparts, their schedules often resemble a frenzied swirl of constant meetings and travel. Calendars fill up quickly. Funding is in critically short supply. In the end, however, we assembled a fine panel, representing the major concerns affecting Native peoples. I want to thank those who participated in the workshop: Margaret Sam-Cromarty (James Bay Cree), William Cromarty (Ojibway), Josh DiNabaugh (Cheyenne River Sioux), Thom White Wolf Fassett (Seneca), Donald Fixico (Shawnee/Sac and Fox/Muscogee/Seminole), Duane Good Striker (Blood), Norma Kassi (Gwich'in), Anne Marshall (Muscogee), Russell Means (Oglala Lakota), Glenn Morris (Shawnee), Gabina Pérez Jiménez (Mixtec), Sage Douglas Remington (Southern Ute), Dale Ann Frye Sherman (Yurok/Karok/Tolowa/Hupa), Andrea Smith (Cherokee), Justine Smith (Cherokee), Grace Thorpe (Sac and Fox), George Tinker (Osage/Cherokee), Jackie Warledo (Seminole), and Phyllis Young (Standing Rock Sioux). They made my job much easier through their flexibility, willingness to remake schedules to accommodate one another, and unfailing good humor.

The presentations made at the workshop form the nucleus of this volume. Not all those who participated delivered papers. They did, however, take part in the discussion surrounding them. Their comments are reflected in the final edited product. Because of multiple conflicts, Don Fixico was unable to be present for the meeting. He nonetheless sent along his thoughts for inclusion in the discussion and worked these into the article included herein. In addition, the pieces on environmental law and population control grew out of interchanges at the workshop, though there were no formal presentations on these topics. Russell Means, Thom Fassett, and "Tink" Tinker graciously agreed to provide a foreword, afterword, and a theological reflection on the proceedings (chapter 10), respectively.

As William and Margaret Cromarty reminded those of us at the conference, we are not Moses coming down from Sinai with the Ten Commandments of Environmental Protection. Indians have been stereotyped far too long by the environmental movement as those with the mystical, ancient wisdom that alone can save the planet. Rather, we presented and represented the honest and extremely difficult struggles of indigenous peoples to meet ecological challenges confronting them. Though traditional knowledge and ways play an important part in these battles, so do all the tools of technology, modern modes of communication, and the simple investment of time and sweat. It also must be noted that the conference did not (nor does this volume) address every environmental issue affecting Natives in the Americas. For example, we did not address, or addressed only obliquely, issues as diverse as development on the Atlantic coast of Nicaragua, the petroextermination of the Huaorani and the destruction of the Amazonian rainforests, and toxic pollution in Oklahoma. We have, however, provided a representative sample of a multiplicity of problems, discussed by persons who are intimately involved.

In any project of this kind, there are numerous persons to be thanked. I want to thank Martin Robra of the WCC, which provided major funding for the workshop; Rodney Peterson of B.T.I., who served as our liaison with the WCC on some issues; Robert Ellsberg of Orbis Books, who committed to the project at an early stage, before the conference even occurred; Riverside Church in New York, who, through funds from the Danforth Foundation, provided support for the writing of this book; and Lisa Doucet and Teri Desjarlais of *Native Journal* for their input and cooperation. In addition to persons already named, I want to thank some of the many friends who read all or parts of the manuscript: Diane Glancy (Cherokee) of Macalester College, M. A. Jaimes-Guerrero (Yaqui/Juaneño) of San Francisco State University, Thomas King (Cherokee) of the University of Guelph, Gerald Vizenor (Anishinaabe) of the University of California, Berkeley, and Robert Warrior (Osage) of Stanford University. Special thanks goes to Glenna Matoush (Anishinaabe/Cree) for generously consenting to the use of her wonderful painting "Mistissini Marches for Oka" (depicting her people's support for that sovereignty and land-rights struggle) on the cover. Thanks as well to Teri Carey (Cree), who transcribed hours of taped discussions from the conference and put them into a more usable form. I want to thank Philip Bankwitz, distinguished professor of history emeritus of Trinity College, for opening his farm in old Pocumtuk territory, where much of this manuscript was edited. Finally, I also want to thank my friend Homer Noley (Choctaw) of the School of Theology at Claremont, and Delores Williams and my advisor, James H. Cone, both of Union Theological Seminary, whose counsel and unswerving support for me have gotten me through many difficult days.

It often seems that those Natives who work for environmental justice are beating with bare fists on stone walls. Many burn out and give up. Perhaps through the workshop and this book, they have had their strength renewed just a little to continue the struggle. For those non-Natives who read this work, we all hope that they will take away a better understanding of the pain and hope of this continent, which has experienced an exploitation not only of human and natural resources, but of the spirit as well.

Introduction

Notes from a Miner's Canary

It had been several years since he had heard the wild turkeys flying up to roost along the creek, and he could scarcely remember what the howl of a wolf was like. The crows going to roost did not fly raucously over his father's house any more, but sometimes, if he happened to be awake, he could hear in the ringing silence of the morning before dawn the long, quavering chant of death from the hills across the valley. . . . Away from the activity of Progress which had become so important, he felt a pleasure which seemed to be absent when he was in town. On the few occasions when the pounding hoofs of his pony flushed a small flock of prairie chickens, he would come to the realization that he didn't see them in large flocks any more; that it had been years since he had heard the familiar booming carried across the April prairie. When he came to little black-jack-covered ravines that reached out like feathered fingers into the prairie, he didn't seem to miss the band of deer bounding away; their white tails bobbing and seeming to float away among the black boles of the trees. Had he seen one lone frightened buck, he might have missed the band, but there were no more deer, and he was not acutely conscious of their absence.

–John Joseph Mathews (Osage)
(1895-1979)[1]

When I was growing up in Oklahoma, not that far from where Chal Windzer, John Joseph Mathews's fictional alter ego, experienced this personal silent spring, wolves were only a memory, but one could still find wild turkeys in the woods and fields. I remember cold, foggy mornings when I would go hunting for the wily birds with Bill Kenney, wearing a big, brown/drab hunting coat that had belonged to my grandfather. Today turkeys are less commonly spotted, not due to hunting but because of urbanization and the "activity of Progress" about which Mathews wrote. In a small museum in Cheyenne, Oklahoma, I remember seeing the last cougar spotted in the area, stuffed and mounted. As a child, I once saw the skeleton of Chief Black Kettle[2] in a glass case

1

at that same museum. It had recently been transferred there from the window of the local newspaper office.

In "The Man Made of Words," his meditation on tradition, reality, and imagination, author and poet N. Scott Momaday (Kiowa/Cherokee) advises,

> Once in his life a man ought to concentrate his mind upon the remembered earth. . . . He ought to give himself up to a particular landscape in his experience, to look at it from as many angles as he can, to wonder about it, to dwell upon it. He ought to imagine that he touches it with his hands at every season and listens to the sounds that are made upon it. He ought to imagine the creatures that are there and all the faintest motions of the wind. He ought to recollect the glare of noon and all the colors of the dawn and dusk.[3]

There are many places in my landscape of memory, but when I cast my mind back it inevitably runs to western Oklahoma, where I was born.

There is a bald knob there on the Oklahoma prairie. In the glare of a hot summer sun, horned toads and boomers scuttled across its surface of soil, gypsum, and patchy grass. On clear nights coyotes stood on its lowrise promontory and talked to the moon. Sitting on it, you could watch Oklahoma thunderstorms coming from a long way off, rolling across the open ground like the dust clouds of the thirties. I sat on that hill one spring night during such a storm. Thunder rumbled in tympanic drumrolls, punctuated by sharp crescendos. Flashes of lightning made the red dirt glow and lit up the night like bright midday. The wind whipped around my body, beating me from eight different directions. Ozone-rich air smelled like rain.

That hill is nothing special. It is like hundreds of others throughout the state. A few hundred yards from this particular one, wavelets of Foss Reservoir lapped at its shore. Foss was created by construction of what we were told was the world's largest earthen dam, one of many lakes brought into being by damming all but one of Oklahoma's free-flowing rivers in an era when the state was a veritable playground for the Army Corps of Engineers.

Oklahoma is Indian Country, and throughout the Americas, Indian Country is under attack. Felix Cohen, the modern founder of federal Indian law, declared, "The Indian plays much the same role in our American society that the Jews played in Germany. Like the miner's canary, the Indian marks the shift from fresh air to poison gas in our political atmosphere; and our treatment of Indians, even more than our treatment of other minorities, marks the rise and fall of our democratic faith."[4] This is nowhere more true than in the environmental arena. As Indian lands are assaulted, so are Indian peoples. The same mentality that allows the remains of a victim of genocide to be displayed for public approbation in a newspaper office window or a museum case permits the destruction of Indian lands in the service of some supposed greater public good. Environmental destruction is simply one manifestation of the colonialism and racism that have marked Indian/White relations since the arrival of Columbus in 1492. As Donald A. Grinde, Jr. (Yamasee) and Bruce Johansen observe, "Native America today provides a virtual catalog of environmental destruction."[5] Signs of devastation "can be seen in nearly every quarter of Indian country— in the Navajo Four Corners region, the coal strip-mining operations on Cheyenne and Crow Lands in Montana, Pyramid Lake in Nevada, the Arkansas River-bottom ripoff in eastern Oklahoma."[6] They are evident in proposals that would turn Indian lands into dumps for toxic and nuclear wastes and in the NAFTA-engineered collapse of the Mayan corn-based economy.

It is, however, one of the ironies of the colonial relationship that even as Native lands and peoples are destroyed, they are also idolized and idealized. Non-Natives in the Americas have always exhibited a strange attraction-repulsion relationship toward the indigenes of this hemisphere. Thus in Guatemala, while officially there are *no* Indians, 70 percent of the population is Native and twenty-five different languages are spoken; colorful Mayan pageants provide a valuable source of tourism.[7] Mexico prides itself on being a nation totally comprised of *mestizos,* mixed-blood people who are neither Indian nor European but both at once. Yet Indians rank at the bottom of the social order.[8] In the United States, Oklahoma can trumpet that "Oklahoma is Native America," while the Indians whose heritage it celebrates are discriminated against and marginalized.

As awareness of the dimensions of the environmental crisis facing the planet grew in the 1970s, Indians were convenient symbols of ecological harmony. In his new edition of *God Is Red,* Vine Deloria, Jr. (Standing Rock Sioux) describes the period, "Finally the ecologists arrived with predictions so chilling as to frighten the strongest heart. At the present rate of deterioration, they told us mankind could expect only a generation before the species would finally be extinguished. How had this situation come about? Some ecologists told us that it was the old Christian idea of nature: the rejection of creation as a living ecosystem and the concept of nature as depraved, an object of exploitation and nothing more."[9] He states,

> The collapse of the Civil Rights movement, the concern with Vietnam and the war, the escape to drugs, the rise of power movements, and the return to Mother Earth can all be understood as desperate efforts of groups of people to flee abstract articulations

of belief and superficial values and find authenticity wherever it could be found. It was at this point that Indians became popular and the widespread and intense interest in Indians, as seen in the fantasy literature and anthologies, seemed to indicate that Americans wanted more from Indians than they did from other minority groups. For many people the stoic, heroic, and noble Indian who had lived an idyllic existence prior to contact with whites seemed to hold the key to survival and promised to provide new meaning for American life.[10]

The image of Indian actor Iron Eyes Cody (Cherokee) shedding a single tear for the polluted earth became emblematic. A fraudulent version of a speech delivered by Chief Seattle (Duwamish) in 1854 became the desiderata of an entire movement.[11]

Euro-Americans have always looked at Indians in some distorted funhouse mirror, gazing upon them and seeing whatever they most desire. For many worshipful Whites, Indians were the first environmentalists. For Jay McDaniel, a professor of religion at Hendrix College, they were the first American "bioregionalists."[12] Though counseling hearing Native objections to appropriation of their religious traditions, he nonetheless offers selected "spiritual lessons" from Native America, drawing, from among other sources, on the as-told-to autobiographies of Mary Crow Dog and John Fire Lame Deer.[13] Similarly, theologian Geoffrey Lilburne notes the "arrogance and romanticism" that have colored relations between Europeans and Natives in North America but nevertheless proceeds to discuss the centrality of land to the spirituality of aborigines in Australia and the United States "to understand the viability and relevance of their adaptation to this land."[14] McDaniel and Lilburne do not, however, deserve such singling out. They are merely examples—and far from the worst—of environmentalists and ecologians who point to Native peoples, not so much to learn from them as to buttress their own positions and beliefs.

One strain of this stereotype of Natives as "environmental perfectionists" holds that they did not *use* the land, existing on it as in some ecological stasis box and leaving no tracks or traces of their presence. This seemingly affirmative, if highly romantic, vision in reality contributes to the exploitation of Natives and their land. It denies Indian personhood and erases Natives from the landscape where they lived for countless generations before the advent of European invaders. Having thus "ethnically cleansed" the continent, the conquest can then be justified.[15] Natives become nothing more than stewards of the land, preserving the land intact and holding it in escrow from the foundation of the world for the colonizers who would come later.[16]

Not all environmentalists, however, pretend to hold American Natives in such high regard.

"Radical ecologist" George Weurthner of the environmental organization Earth First! argues that "far from having achieved spiritual traditions predicated on an understanding of natural harmony and balance, ancient American Indians were really the 'first environmental pillagers.'" This flat reversal of even the most elementary meanings of native tradition is then "explained" as Weurthner wanders through a self-contradictory and wildly convoluted monologue in which he saddles North American indigenous societies with everything from the extinction of the wooly mammoth to desertification of the Sonora. That he deviates from logic, known fact, and even plain common sense while making his "case" does nothing to deter his stream of bald assertions.[17]

Similarly, Dave Foreman, the Earth First! political leader, has pronounced Native peoples "a threat to the habitat" and told ecologists and New Age adherents actively to resist their land and water claims.[18] On a more scholarly level, anthropologist William Starna terms the belief that early Natives possessed an environmental ethos "pan-Indian mythology."[19]

Historian Calvin Martin seems to adopt the image of the Indian as ecoterrorist, maintaining that Natives had an "underlying spiritual motive" for attempting to exterminate animals in service of the fur trade. He contends that at the time of European contact, the Cree, for example, were in a state of war with beavers and bears and that the indigenes were operating under a divine injunction to kill them. He bases this thesis on the testimony of two White fur traders, David Thompson and Alexander Henry, the latter of whom was an "*adopted Ojibwa*."[20] In this primordial warfare, access to European technology tipped the balance of power in favor of the Native, and "nature, which had once rejected his supplications and frightened him, now lay prostrate at his feet."[21] Martin contends that millions of dead beavers give silent testimony against "any argument that native peoples generally held nature to be sacred and that most native peoples took from nature only what they needed."[22]

As a historian, Martin has argued that modern non-Natives must not assume that the worldview of Natives was the same as that produced by the Western Enlightenment or that Natives operated from the same motivations as their Western counterparts.[23] Here, however, he employs that difference in frames of reference as a club with which to bludgeon the indigenous peoples. He depicts Indians as scared of the very environment in which they lived, reflecting more the European alienation from nature than Native thoughtworlds.[24] Despite his own evidence to the contrary, he virtually ignores the dislocations caused in Native society by invasion and the fur trade before large-scale killings of fur-bearing animals occurred. Inadvertently or by design, he absolves non-Natives of culpability in these dislocations when he points at the pre-existing spiritual warfare between humans and animals. In fact, many tribal traditions preserve stories of such antipathy. The Cherokee, for instance, tell of a council of animals in which animals, fearing overpopulation by humans, invent disease; plants, however, overhearing the animal plot, devise medicines to counteract the various contagions.[25] Martin's own data illustrate the fact that, beyond economic dislocations creating incentives to participate in the trade, Native destruction of animal populations was a means for them to come to terms with epizootics and their potential impact upon humans.[26] Martin points to the romanticized stereotype of eco-harmonic Natives manufactured by the environmental movement and concludes that modern society has little, if anything, to learn from indigenous cultures. He writes,

> Even if we absolve him of his ambiguous culpability in certain episodes of despoliation, invoking instead his pristine sentiments toward Nature, the Indian still remains a misfit guru. Even if he were capable of leading us, we could never follow him. The Indian's was a profoundly different cosmic vision when it came to interpreting Nature—a vision Western man could never adjust to. There can therefore be no salvation in the Indian's traditional conception of Nature for the troubled environmentalist. Someday, perhaps, he will realize that he must look to someone else other than the American Indian for realistic spiritual inspiration.[27]

In contrast to Martin, Dennis McPherson (Anishinaabe) and J. Douglas Rabb point to just such an environmental ethic among the Great Lakes Natives. Discussing McPherson's own Ojibway people, they note that hunters offer gifts to the creatures they hunt in a complex and reciprocal system of barter in which the animal (considered an "other-than-human person") gives its life to sustain humans in exchange for the gift. Not to offer gifts in exchange would be to bring shame on the hunter. They write,

> Is it not also the case that members of the [tribe] would bring shame upon themselves if they stood by and did nothing while the habitat of those other-than-human persons with whom they exchange gifts is threatened or destroyed? After all, it is through the exchange of gifts that one maintains one's membership in Ojibway society. Are not these other-than-human persons with whom they exchange gifts members of that society and entitled to the same respect and help accorded to any other member of the community? There is, we suggest, a moral obligation to pro-

tect the habitat of the moose, the beaver, the muskrat, and the lynx; the habitat of geese, ducks, grouse and hare, not just because members of the [tribe] wish to continue hunting and trapping, but because these other-than-human persons are also members of Ojibway society.[28]

They note that similar attitudes are found in most Native cultures, and I believe the studies in this volume bear them out.

In reality, modern Natives and their ancestors are neither saints nor sinners in environmental matters. They are human beings. The Americas were no Edenic paradise. "People sometimes went hungry . . . ; wars were fought, and people died in them. Occasionally, a native civilization overtaxed its environment and collapsed."[29] Grinde and Johansen state, "Occasionally, in pre-Columbian times, native urban areas taxed the local environment (e.g., by overgrazing and razing the forests). Like all societies, those in pre-Columbian America faced the question of how to utilize land for purposes of survival. Indians manipulated the environment to improve their material lives."[30] The general consensus today, however, is that, given pre-contact population numbers, Native peoples could have wrought much more environmental damage than was the case.[31] Again according to Grinde and Johansen, "While mistakes were made, the fact that Europeans found the Western Hemisphere to be a natural treasure house indicates that misuse of the environment was not frequent or sustained over long periods of time."[32] Likewise, some contemporary Indians have demonstrated themselves capable of making devastating choices for the environment. Others try to live a life that is in harmony and balance with the natural order. Their task is complicated, however, by powerful systemic forces arrayed against such ethical choices.

For Natives, living within the bounds dictated by creation and the environment was not a product of some abstract ecological ideal. Rather, it was necessitated by the need to understand and adapt to the diverse environments in which they found themselves in order to survive. As Marcos Terena (Terena) puts it, "Indigenous man has been able to decipher the greatness of nature and set down a code of life 'civilized' man could never understand, whether in its materialistic or spiritual aspects."[33] In traditional Native education, the environment was the textbook and animals the teachers. The seasons became the calendar. The people's needs were the clock they worked by, and their senses and imaginations were their tools of survival.[34] Natives therefore learned to practice reciprocity and natural conservation techniques in order to ensure ample resources for themselves and their progeny.[35] They learned to distribute their populations over areas of sizes and types to sustain them. They learned not to ask for or take more than could be used, else misfortune occur. Among the Natassinan Innu, for example, traditional religion is based on a belief in animal masters. When they hunt, the Natassinan must show respect for these masters. They place the bones of caribou, bear, marten, mink, and other creatures on tree platforms so dogs cannot get them. They do not overhunt or overtrap areas where animals are scarce. If they do not show respect in this way, they understand that the animal masters will get angry and punish them by not giving them game in later seasons.[36] In like manner, George Blondin (Dene) states, "The land, and all it provides for our people has been the very spirit of the Dene way of life. From the land came our religion . . . from the land came our life . . . from the land came our powerful medicine . . . from the land came our way of life."[37] The Native hunter, then, is "not just participating in a purely mechanical subsistence activity, but is engaged in a complex of meditative acts, all of which—whether preparatory prayer and purification, pursuit of the quarry, or the sacramental manner by which the animal is slain and subsequently treated—are infused with the sacred."[38]

This need for collective survival led Native peoples to an emphasis on community. Such an emphasis, as Vine Deloria points out, means that "Indian tribes are communities in fundamental ways that other American communities and organizations are not. Tribal communities are wholly defined by family relationships, whereas non-Indian communities are defined primarily by residence or by agreement with sets of intellectual beliefs."[39] Community is thus the highest value among Native persons, and fidelity to it is the highest responsibility. Jeanne Rollins (Swinomish) vividly captures this sense of community and its connection to living in harmony with the environment when she writes:

> We are a people who live in community closely to one another. Our way of life centers around a brotherhood that is permanent—deeply observed and deeply offended. . . . The Indian way is to live with nature, not against it. It is important to maintain a compatible and working relationship with all living things. Whatever one holds sacred is to be respected. . . . A sense of group responsibility is evident especially in our upbringing and discipline. For instance, a household without a father image is given one by another member of the community who may or may not be related. As the fruits of the womb are shared within the community so too are the fruits of our Mother, the Earth. Each and all must be cared for. In the past we were taught our responsibility for this, and today we must continue on if we are to survive and be liberated as a people. . . . It is our responsibility to provide for the good for all the community and to have respect and reverence for all of creation.[40]

As Rollins alludes, this way of life led to an understanding of nature as an organic entity. The environment in which traditional Natives live is impassive and dispassionate, but it is also alive and nurturing. Many times, in widely diverse parts of the Americas, this personified world was envisioned as female. A pre-Columbian Mixtec codex from central Mexico, for example, shows humanity emerging from the earth depicted as a womb.[41] Isidore Kochon, a Dene from Western Canada, states, "The land fed us all even before the white people ever came to the North. To us she is just like a mother that brought up her children."[42] Among the Quechua of Peru, the world is revered as *Pacha Mama*, Mother Earth.[43] Such examples could be reproduced from numerous tribes in various periods of history.

Recently some scholars have disputed the antiquity and authenticity of this concept, central to many Indian peoples and to this volume, of Mother Earth. Sam Gill, in *Mother Earth: An American Story*, argues that the concept is largely invented, the product of scholars and other observers and of Native interaction with Europeans. He writes, "While I have been able to find a number of tribal traditions that make references to the earth in personal and kinship terms, there is an absence in the vast literature on North American tribes of any identification of the earth or the spiritual personification of the earth as a *major goddess*. Not until the twentieth century and then for the most part not until mid-century is there any extent of clear reference to Mother Earth made by native peoples."[44] He goes on to state, "It seems that Mother Earth as a major goddess of the Indians of North America is a reality, but that she has become so only during the twentieth century."[45] For Gill, "Mother Earth is a central figure in that long saga in which Americans of European ancestry have attempted to define and create themselves as Americans." She is also mother to Indians, but "she has become so only recently and then not without influence from Americans, with their thirst for land and their need to define themselves in terms of likeness and contrast with those they imagined to be 'the Indians.'"[46] John Bierhorst writes,

> In contemporary Indian thought, especially in North America, some voices are skeptical of this mute, passive earth mother, creative in only the physical sense. At the same time there persists an age-old awareness of the idea's political—and moral—value in the continuing struggle for ownership of the American land. In other words, the image of mother earth is useful and deep-seated, even if, in modern contexts, it is too often sentimentalized and oversimplified.[47]

For Bierhorst, then, Mother Earth is little more than a political expediency.

To be sure, not every Native culture in the tremendous diversity of the Americas conceives, or conceived, of the earth in feminine terms, as Bierhorst demonstrates.[48] Likewise, it is undoubtedly correct that the idea of Mother Earth has been interpreted and reinterpreted so that it is difficult, in many cases, to retrieve its original indigenous significance.[49] Increasing pan-Indian discourse has both spread the concept and broadened its meaning. Scholars such as Gill and Bierhorst, however, diminish its importance for Indian peoples when they ignore evidence that the fundamental notion is both ancient and widespread. Deloria has traced references as far back as 1776, when Cornstalk (Shawnee) attempted to persuade the Iroquois to ally with the colonists during the Revolutionary War by arguing, "For this Big [Turtle] Island being our common Mother, we and they are like one Flesh and Blood."[50] And Grinde and Johansen discuss a seventeenth-century reference attributed to Massasoit, the Wampanaog chief who befriended the Pilgrims: "What is this you call property? It cannot be the earth. For the land is our mother, nourishing all her children, beasts, birds, fish, and all men. The woods, the streams, everything on it belongs to everybody and is for the use of all. How can one man say it belongs only to him?"[51] Both references are well before the 1805 statement of Tekamthi ("The earth is my mother–and on her bosom I will repose")– the earliest statement cited by Gill and one of the first generally pointed to in discussions of the concept of Mother Earth[52]–and probably too early to have been corrupted in the manner Gill delineates.[53]

The Americas' indigenous nations are possessed of an incredibly rich diversity of histories, spiritual traditions, and cosmologies. Despite a view in the dominant culture that tends to homogenize all Natives, there is no such thing as a monolithic Native American experience. At the time of contact, there were probably around two thousand different tribes inhabiting the North American continent. Today there are approximately six hundred. No single ethnicity can encompass the four hundred different ethnicities, eight major language groups, and three distinct racial strains usually lumped together under the collective label Native American or American Indian.[54] This multiplicity of peoples developed distinctly different understandings of the Creator, the creation of the world, and its destiny.

The Cherokee revere a supreme being and creator called Yowa, a deity whose name was so sacred that originally it could be spoken aloud only by certain priests.[55] Yowa is a unity of the *cho ta auh ne le eh*, the three Elder Fires Above, but these, in turn, are always and forever unanimous in thought and action. They are merely aspects of a single mind, manifesting itself in multiple forms. Through the fires, Yowa undergirds and permeates all creation with his will, love, and intelligence. The process is not static but dynamic. Creation is viewed as ongoing throughout all life.[56]

Navajo artist Carl Gorman describes his people's view of ultimate deity:

> It has been said by some researchers into Navajo religion, that we have no Supreme God, because He is not named. That is not so. The Supreme Being is not named because he is unknowable. He is simply the Unknown Power. We worship him through His Creation. We feel too insignificant to approach directly in prayer that Great Power that is incomprehensible to man. Nature feeds our soul's inspiration and so we approach Him through that part of Him which is close to us and within the reach of human understanding. We believe that this great unknown power is everywhere in His creation. The various forms of creation have some of this spirit within them. . . . As every form has some of the intelligent spirit of the Creator, we cannot but reverence all parts of the creation.[57]

The Maya understand that time and space are primogenital gods. Nature is the superior force from which emanates that power that gives direction to life and all beings. All nature is animate and alive, and earth and water are superior to all other elements of nature because they are the origins of life. Every animal, river, and stone has its own *nahual* or "divine personification."[58]

Among the Sioux, Wakan-Tanka is both supreme being and the totality of forces in creation. It is everything and yet above everything. It has the power to create and the power to destroy. It is this that makes it great and sacred.[59] Wakan-Tanka is often translated into English as Great Mystery, but is better, though still inadequately, rendered Great Mysterious. Norma Kassi, of the Gwich'in people of the Dene Nation, discusses the Great Energy in similar terms:

> We have a powerful sense of interrelatedness from the Creator that we always pray to. We pray to Mother Earth, we pray to the mountains. We pray to the Moon as our Grandmother, and to the Sun as our Grandfather. We pray to all the waters that feed us and nourish us all the time. That's what we pray for. Those are the greatest creators. The energy they all give off makes up the ultimate Great Energy. There is no man attached to it, nor is there a woman—though perhaps it is more closely a woman. Those are the energies that we give to each other, that we pray to, that we give thanks to. Energy directed to each other has the power to make things happen.[60]

While there are commonalities among these descriptions of ultimate reality, traditional Native religions and their accompanying worldviews are actually quite varied. Religions of different tribal groups are often as different from one another as Christianity is from Buddhism. These differing understandings of the Creator inevitably reflect themselves in differing accounts of creation itself. Such understandings are also very different from the Jewish and Christian accounts contained in the Bible.

In the Cherokee creation myth, for instance, there is no concept of a *creatio ex nihilo*. There is no interest shown in the creation of the cosmos. The materials of creation are already present.[61] Similarly, in the story of Corn Mother, the most important Cherokee aetiological myth, corn springs from the fecundity of her own body.[62] The world and "all living things" are both preexistent. In the earth origin story, even the mud with which Water Bug creates the land mass is already present, under the water, waiting only to be brought to the surface. Rather than a grand tale of cosmic creation, as in Genesis, it is a story of the fashioning of the land. As for Augustine, there is no questioning what existed before creation, and there is no asking what the Creator was doing before creating occurred. In one account of the myth, the storyteller professes ignorance as to who made the first animals and plants, though they are certainly under the care of Yowa. Further, although ostensibly an account of the making of all the earth's lands, it is in actuality a story of the making of Old Cherokee Country in what is now the American Southeast. After the land is created, the animals above in *Galun-lati* are anxious to get down to earth and send Buzzard to survey it. Though he flies over all the earth, the story focuses on his weariness when he reaches the future home of the Cherokee. As he tires and flies closer to the earth, his wingbeats carve out the Smoky Mountains.[63]

The Cherokee, like other Native peoples, are spatially rather than temporally oriented. Their culture, spirituality, and identity are connected to the land—and not just land in a general sense but *their* land. The act of creation is not so much what happened *then* as it is what happened *here*.[64] Thus, when Indian tribes were forcibly removed from their homes, they were robbed of more than land. Taken from them was a numinous landscape where every mountain and lake held meaning. For example, the Cherokee word *eloh'*, sometimes translated "religion," also means, at exactly the same time, history, culture, law—and land.[65] Because of these intimate interrelationships, relocation was an assault upon Native culture, identity, and personhood. Ray Sonfrere (Dene) summarized these connections when he said, "I need and love the land I was born and raised on. Many people find meaning in different things in life. Native people find meaning in the land and they need it and they love it."[66] Salvador Palomino (Quechua) puts it somewhat differently: "The Earth, our Mother Earth, has always been part of our collectivity. We belong to her, she does not belong to us. Land and community are the souls of our peoples."[67]

This spatial aspect of Native worldviews must not be underestimated. Mircea Eliade points out that what he calls "primitive man" sees himself as related to the cosmos and to the land, whereas "modern," Western humanity sees itself connected only to history.[68] This difference is closely related to "fall/redemption" theology. Both American Joseph Epes Brown and Brazilian Leonardo Boff observe that Western religions lack a metaphysics of nature. Boff, in *Ecology and Liberation: A New Paradigm*, notes, "The dominant trend of Christian reflection has not taken . . . creation to any profound level of consideration. For historical and institutional reasons, there has been much more consideration of redemption." He states that "redemption presupposes a drama, a degeneration of creation, a failure of human vocation that has affected all human beings and their cosmic environment."[69] Vine Deloria also notes the role of "the Christian idea of a complete alienation of nature and the world from human beings as a result of Adam's immediate postcreation act in determining the Western and Christian attitude toward nature."[70] In contrast to the view of dominant streams in Jewish and Christian thought, for Natives, creation never "fell" and so is in no need of redemption. Given the grimness bred by Western thinking against both humans and the environment, it may be that the true nature of the fall of humanity is to be condemned to live only in history. Deloria highlights this dichotomy between Native religions and Christianity in their views on creation, stating,

> Both religions can be said to agree on the role and activity of a creator. Outside of that specific thing, there would appear to be little that the two views share. Tribal religions appear to be thereafter confronted with the question of the interrelationship of all things. Christians see creation as the beginning event of a linear time sequence in which the divine plan is worked out, the conclusion of the sequence being an act of destruction bringing the world to an end.[71]

This is not to imply that there is no temporal element in Native cultures and spirituality. All tribes preserve stories of their histories. Many tribes maintain elaborate "winter counts," recording and naming the years after the most significant events occurring in them. It is merely to say, as George Tinker (Osage/Cherokee) points out, that the temporal is subordinate to the spatial. Further, time is most often not linear but cyclical, mirroring the rhythm of the seasons and reinforcing "one's individual and collective connectedness to the immediate environment."[72]

Many tribal traditions possess a strain of eschatology in the form of end-time myths and prophecies.[73] In keeping with the cyclical nature of time, however, in such myths and predictions, eschaton is usually not an *ekpyrosis*, a cataclysmic end to creation. Rather, it is most often, though again not universally, an event leading to *metacomesis*, the periodic renewal of the world. Eschaton is therefore the mirror image of creation. Beginning and end are homologues with "eschatology, at least in certain aspects, becoming one with cosmogony."[74] Cosmology triumphs over chronology.

Since contact, many of these myths have become, to use William McLoughlin's term, "fractured," reflecting contact with Christianity and the pressures exerted upon Native communities by invasion and colonization.[75] Prophecies of impending disaster have taken on more urgency and, as the ecological crisis has intensified, often have a distinctly environmental element. Asa Primeaux, Sr. (Yankton Sioux), a traditional pipecarrier and a peyote singer, points to the continued use of the earth in a non-sacred way and says, "Getting everything out of the earth, the gas and the oil, is making the world hollow, off-balance. One of these days the gases will be ignited and they will blow up the world."[76] Besides the Lakota/Dakota, tribes as diverse as the Dene, Wintu, Chiricahua Apache, Hopi, and Zuñi have prophecies of catastrophic collapse linked to environmental devastation.[77] The Nisqually of Puget Sound link destruction to overpopulation, followed by consumption of all fish and game and resulting in cannibalism.[78]

As Grinde and Johansen write, "The environment is a mirror that reflects cultural values."[79] Many Natives concerned, as Deloria points out, with the interrelatedness of all things view the created order and see in the fact that humanity is last in the economy of creation that humans are the youngest. The earth and all the rest of creation are thus elders who care for humanity, from whom it can learn, and whom it must respect. In linear, temporally oriented Christianity, humanity's place in the creative chain is considered proof that humans are called to dominate and subdue all that came before them. The biblical injunction of Genesis 1:28 is for human beings to "be fruitful and multiply, and fill the earth and subdue it; and have dominion over the fish of the sea and over the birds of the air and over every living thing that moves upon the earth."[80]

This dominion theology has been at work in the Americas from the onset of colonization. In 1782 French settler J. Hector St. John de Crèvecoeur, in his highly influential *Letters from an American Farmer*, though he lamented the depredation and disappearance of Indians, nonetheless spoke of the "improvements" and "superior genius" of the Europeans and the "new man" being born as colonists tilled the rich soil of North America.[81] In like fashion, in 1797 settler Eliphalet Stark wrote to a relative, "The Yankees have taken care of the wolves, bears and Indians . . . and we'll build the Lord's temple yet, build it out of these great trees."[82] According to Grinde and Johansen, "By the late twentieth century, humankind had fulfilled the injunction of the first chapter of Genesis so effectively that it was beginning to drown in its own effluvia."[83] This ideology of domination has been particularly troubling to Natives. Jackie Warledo (Seminole) states, "We have to deal with the notion that people have dominion over life and creation. This dominion mentality is what many people believe gives them the right to look at the environment as inferior."[84] Salvador Palomino also decries dominion theology, writing, "For us, it seems unthinkable that man—who as the 'beloved offspring,' the 'son of God,' is also divine—should be superior to other living beings and do as he pleases with the Earth, regarding Mother Nature as an object of consumption, to be conquered, suppressed, transformed, violated, poisoned to the point of destruction just to satisfy whims and not needs."[85] He states that this violation of the "mutual relationship" between humanity and the cosmos is what makes the environmental crisis "a social and historical crisis" for Native peoples. It becomes an issue of environmental justice because, "any violation of [creation's] laws and physical integrity is also an act of violence against our societies and our people themselves."[86]

In seeking a new, non-hierarchical paradigm for Christianity, Boff writes, "Above all, we should see the creation as the expression of God's joy, as the dance of God's love, as the mirror of both God and all created things. In this sense every creature is a messenger of God, and God's representative as well as sacrament. Everyone is worthy to be accepted and listened to as such."[87] He goes on to state that in this vision "the human being is not to be found at the top but behind and at the end of creation. The human being is the last to appear and is found behind, as it were, the front lines. The world is not a product of human desire or human creativity. Humanity did not see the beginning. Being antecedent to humankind, the world does not belong to humanity. It belongs to God, its creator."[88] Although there is much in such a description that Native peoples could affirm, it nevertheless falls short. It reserves for humanity a "special place." The world is, according to Boff, "assigned to humanity to till and to keep."[89] While it seeks to create for humankind an ethical responsibility, it nonetheless contains seeds of the very dominion thinking it seeks to overthrow.[90]

At first glance, the title of this volume, *Defending Mother Earth*, would seem to be so much eco-babble or enviro-gibberish. Who are humans to think that they can defend Mother Earth? Does not that set human beings in the same self-appointed, superior position that exists in Western thought? After all, the world is not going anywhere. Humanity is what may be ultimately disappearing. Viewing, however, the numerous assaults launched against creation, such a title makes sense.

Numerous Native leaders and activists, including Oren Lyons (Onondaga), Roland Crowe of the Federation of Saskatchewan Indian Nations, and Marcos Terena of Brazil, as well as official tribal statements[91] have used the language of "guardian" for the relationship to Mother Earth.[92] In an article in *Native Journal,* a Native newspaper published in Alberta, Robert Gibson writes, "Guardians are required to help nature overcome the interferences and influences brought about by the industrial age and technological changes. Caretakers of the wilds must help people and nature learn to co-exist."[93] Native peoples must be very careful in the use of guardianship language, smacking as it does of the guardian/ward relationship that has for so long oppressed Native peoples.[94] Does Mother Earth really need a guardian? Does not that once again put humanity in the same superior position as Christian dominion theology?

The terminology of defense and protection is perhaps more apt. Roland Crowe has used such language also. Similarly, Marcos Terena writes, "We don't want the march of progress and ambition to inflict further wounds. On the contrary, we want to find new allies, allies for the survival of our planet."[95] Natives long to defend Mother Earth, not because they are superior to her, but because it is the human species of which they are a part that is threatening her. Such a struggle has both practical and spiritual dimensions. Denise and John Carmody note, "To 'care' for the land has at least two connotations. A traditional native American provides for the land, tries to ensure its prosperity, avoids what we might call 'unecological' activities that seem to hurt nature. But he or she also has a tender regard for the land. The land lies on the people's heart, is a constant concern, like a much-loved child or parent, even like a lover, distant yet near, a source of joy and also a source of worry."[96] As Dale Ann Frye Sherman (Yurok/Karok/Tolowa/Hupa) says, "We are of this continent. We were not created elsewhere. We were created here. Our memories are here, and the blood of our ancestors is here. We are made of this continent."[97] In seeking to liberate the land, Natives seek not to liberate a place to build their homes but to liberate their homelands. [98]

No one can doubt any longer that the environment of the planet is indeed imperiled. The world has already lost 20 percent of its rainforests, 20 percent of its topsoil from croplands, and tens of thousands of plant and animal species through extinction. The earth has a remarkable capacity to heal itself of the damage and diseases humanity visits upon it. Yet by its constant barrage, humanity is turning Mother Earth into the ecological equivalent of an AIDS victim—a crude and offensive image for what is a crude and offensive problem. Leonardo Boff states, "Humankind does not have absolute power over God's work to the point of doing it absolute and essential harm, but it can injure it seriously."[99] This, however, is a serious misreading of the Noachic covenant, contained in Genesis 9:8-17, pursuant to which Yahweh promised never again to destroy the world by flood. Human beings may not have ultimate power to destroy the terrestrial ball of the earth itself, but they can clearly destroy themselves, take uncounted species with them, and render much of the planet lifeless in the process.

The ecologists cited by Vine Deloria in *God Is Red* may have been alarmist and ultimately wrong in their dire predictions, but evidence demonstrates that the assault on Native lands and their environment is at a crucial point. The year 2030 has been cited as a pivotal turnaround year.[100] Grinde and Johansen have warned that the current generation may be the last "to see tribal peoples living as they choose in a natural habitat."[101] Already the "last enclaves of ecologically independent Native America, notably in the Arctic . . . and the Amazon" are being threatened.[102] Felix Cohen said that Indians were the miner's canaries of American society; the multiple ills that are visited upon them are only a prelude and a harbinger of what is to be expected for society as a whole.

At the North American Native Workshop on Environmental Justice, Duane Good Striker (Blood) shared a story passed on to him by his uncle, Rufus Good Striker, about their family. His uncle told him that someday he would use the story, and that he would know when he was meant to do so. This was the time. He said:

Right at the time of Contact, there was a relative in our family named Sees-From-Afar. He and his uncle were out on a warparty against a neighboring tribe. They attacked the enemy camp, and, as the uncle attacked one of the warriors, the warrior dropped his weapon. The nephew grabbed the weapon and claimed it. The uncle protested and snatched the club from him, but the others in the party said that Sees-From-Afar had taken the weapon off the ground and therefore it was his. It was true, they said, that the uncle had knocked the warrior down, but nevertheless the weapon belonged to the nephew.

The uncle was very angry about losing his trophy and put a curse on Sees-From-Afar that never again would he get another war trophy as good. When they returned to their home, the uncle and nephew went their separate ways and were no longer close. Sees-From-Afar went down to the Yellowstone Country in Wyoming.

On his travels, he learned from the animal spirit helpers. He learned their medicine. Finally, he talked to the sandpiper, a small bird with a long beak. He learned their medicine. Then he set out for home.

About this same time, his uncle went on another warparty and got shot. He made it back to camp but was mortally wounded.

His situation was getting worse, and the medicine people couldn't get the bullet out. Just then, Sees-From-Afar returned home. His uncle knew that he possessed strong medicine and told the young man's grandmother to get him.

The old woman pleaded for him to come doctor his uncle, but Sees-From-Afar was still mad and refused to go. She went back and gave the news. The uncle then knew that he was going to die. So he started calling to him across the camp so that the whole camp could hear him. If he had to use his dying breath, at least his nephew would hear him, too.

Finally, Sees-From-Afar heard him, and his heart softened. He went over to his uncle's lodge. He told him, "I'm going to help you but only to show the people that forgiveness and compassion are stronger than all the hate I feel toward you." So he told the old woman to raise the teepee flaps all the way around so that the people could see.

He pulled out the medicine bag that he had acquired in the Yellowstone. In it were the dried skins of two sandpipers. He pulled the uncle into a sitting position and put the two sandpipers beside him. Then he began to sing. The sandpipers' heads came up, and they began to dance.

Sees-From-Afar kept singing, and the birds got up and flew. They flew around the teepee four times. Then they landed on the uncle. Going to the beat of the song, they used their long beaks and took out the bullet. They flew around four more times and then lay back down. The nephew sang the song once more to thank the sandpipers for helping his uncle. The uncle lived, and nephew and uncle forgave each other.

Good Striker suggests that the moral of the story is that perhaps Natives do not have to hear technological society crying and Native land really suffering before acting to help.[103]

In any effort to defend Indian lands, according to David Grant, director of the Pacific Institute of Native American Programs, "We have already learned that waiting for someone else to take positive action . . . is a lesson in frustration. If things are to change in line with our expectations, then the answers must ultimately come from ourselves."[104] Grinde and Johansen contend, "This recognition of the need for changes in our environmental perceptions must also encompass the realization that native peoples need once again to enforce their own environmental values, unfettered by regulations and environmental practices of the industrial state. Regaining a more harmonious environmental state means that known harmonious environmental ethics must be allowed to reemerge and become prominent as quickly as possible to facilitate the flow of ideas that will lead to a more natural relationship in all of creation."[105] Any Native defense of the environment therefore necessarily presupposes a recognition of Native sovereignty.

Put simply, sovereignty is the right to govern persons and territory.[106] Native sovereignty, the inherent right to manage their own affairs, has been recognized and guaranteed both by treaty and, in the United States, by the U.S. Constitution. Oren Lyons puts the issue succinctly: "The action of a people in a territory, the ability and willingness of a people to defend that territory, and the recognition of that ability by other nations: that's a definition of the practical application of sovereignty. It's very simple."[107] Without question, Native control over their lands and resources is a matter of sovereignty. No less so, however, is power over the environment in which Native people live–issues affecting their peoples' health, the air they breathe, the water they drink and from which they get their sustenance, the safety of the soil on which they walk and from which they derive their food. Both Lyons and Roland Crowe have linked sovereignty to environmental issues.[108] Rigoberto Queme Chay, a Mayan from Guatemala, has stated that environmental protection and sustainable development will not occur until full Native sovereignty is recognized and implemented.[109]

When Europeans came to the Western hemisphere, they deposed communal Native notions of land. Though systems varied from tribe to tribe, in general land was considered a common resource, available for all. George Barnaby (Dene) speaks of the rationale for such a system and captures the essence of many Native beliefs about the earth when he says, "Our life is part of the land. We live on the land and are satisfied with what we get from it. No one person owns the land, it belongs to all of us. We choose where we want to go and our choice is respected by others whether in the settlement or in the bush. We have no word in our language that means wilderness, as anywhere we go is our home."[110]

In place of these schemes of common use, Europeans sought to impose upon the earth their own concepts of ownership. In the United States and Canada this has generally meant British notions. Europeans reasoned that because Native tribes did not, for the most part, practice private property they therefore had no concept of ownership. Legal fictions were created which held that Natives had no title to the land but only a right to use it. Their claims to specific territory were thus inferior and subject to those of the colonizers.[111] These conceptions were written into laws, codified by Chancellor James Kent in his highly influential *Commentaries on American Law*, and recognized by courts.[112] Ideas like communal use, gathering, and hunting were replaced by foreign words like "buy," "sell," "cede," and "poach." When Natives did not understand or recognize these new beliefs and still sought to enter and use their traditional lands, they were punished and yet another term, "Indian giver," was born.[113] What was once Mother Earth was now mere property.[114]

Perez Olindo, a senior conservationist in Kenya, has noted that a word largely absent in the colonial lexicon in dealing with indigenous peoples around the globe has been "tenure."[115] Tenure is the right to hold, occupy, and use a specific thing or piece of land.[116] It "is a complicated and variable concept, implying arrangements more subtle than mere ownership. Tenure doesn't define relationships between people and resources so much as it defines relationships between people and other people. It specifies who may use, who may inhabit, who may harvest, who may inherit, who may collect, who may hunt, under what circumstances and to what extent; it also specifies, implicitly, who may not."[117] It is different from the concept of usufruct and the mere "right of occupancy" recognized for Natives by Western legal systems.[118] It is often contrary to normal Western conceptions of ownership.[119] It is the accepted "understanding of user-rights, interests and limits."[120]

All Native cultures have systems of tenure, "derive[d] from direct experience at using, maintaining and apportioning particular resources."[121] Such systems are intimately connected to a complex web of culture and spiritual practices, "and like any aspect of culture, they're constantly evolving."[122] The concept of tenure could be a powerful tool in Native claims for sovereignty and environmental justice, being, as it is, "central to the issue of who can and should conserve *what* resources for *whom*."[123] It is also an essential ingredient of those claims. As has been noted, "Without secure tenure . . . communities have no standing in the decision-making process that determines use or protection. . . . Without secure tenure . . . communities *can only* afford to consider their own short-term interests. They are compelled to exploit resources for maximum immediate gain, regardless of future consequences for themselves, for the resource base or for biological diversity."[124] For example, Cindy Kenny-Gilday (Dene), an advisor to the government of the Northwest Territories and a founder of Indigenous Survival International, asks why her own people should "maintain their own traditional strictures on salmon-harvesting along the Mackenzie River, conserving that resource for their posterity, if a new pulp mill has already begun poisoning the waters upstream?"[125]

Though land is the central focus of sovereignty and tenure, they also encompass fish, water, air, minerals, timber, game, plant life, and other resources.[126] Who, for example, has the right to use "intellectual property" derived from the traditional knowledge of indigenous peoples?[127] "Who holds the user-rights over the wet breath of the Amazon forest, exhaling oxygen and moisture back into the sky above central Brazil?"[128] As has been noted, such questions are intricately consequential. Perez Olindo states, "'Use is a necessary ingredient to the protection of biodiversity. If you outlaw use, it will be a recipe for the most rapid depletion, degradation, extinction.' And the systematic understanding that legitimizes and limits use is what's called tenure."[129] According to Winona LaDuke (Anishinaabe),

> What does this mean? Well, it starts with advocating that Indians regain jurisdiction over what the treaties define as being their land. . . . This, in turn, means that those Indian governments which would *traditionally* hold regulatory and enforcement power within these territories should have the right to do so right *now*. It means that land which is currently taxed, regulated, strip-mined, militarized, drowned by hydroelectric generation over over-irrigation, and nuked by (or with the blessing of) the U.S. and Canadian governments would not be under their control or jurisdiction any more.[130]

With secure tenure, and the sovereignty it implies, people will be able to take a longer-term view toward the environment. We will be able to see sustainable development as more than sustainable exploitation, the destruction of Native homes as more than mere profits, land as more than simple property.[131]

Carole and Jon Belhumeur (Métis) write, "Our human connection to our Mother Earth is plain to see. Her sea water is much like our own blood. Her energy meridians are like those in our own bodies. Her soil, our flesh; her stone, our bones. Hydrogen, sodium, oxygen, magnesium, carbon, and so on, all in Mother Earth, all in us. . . . If we . . . are killing the Earth, are we not committing global suicide as well?"[132] In connecting the demand for environmental justice with traditional knowledge, tenure, and sovereignty, Natives are not looking backward to some supposed pre-Contact idyll. They do not want to remain static. They do not want to stop the clock of time.[133]

There is a story that recently has been making the rounds in Indian Country, undergoing local variations as it goes. It involves the trickster figure of the particular people telling it. Though it is of modern origin, it has similarities to much older stories told in various cultures about Trickster. A version, involving Tseg'sgin', one of the Cherokee tricksters, goes simply, "Tseg'gin' tried to make love to Death. And he died. That's all."[134] In the embrace of Western thought, of Western technological society, of so much that has brought us to where we are, are we not perhaps locked in an embrace with Death as well? As Georges Erasmus, a president of the Dene Nation, says, "Our old people, when they talk about how the [traditional] ways should be kept by young people, they are not looking back, they are looking forward. They are looking as far ahead into the future as they possibly can."[135]

Allen Badger (Cree) writes:

The focus . . . is Justice. The word itself makes us think of the judicial system, prisons, and police officers. It is much more. Being fair and just must be all-encompassing. Mother Earth must be treated fairly and with respect, just as we expect to be treated. She unbiasedly provides for and loves all her children, even those that abuse her. Many of her children poison her, strip her barren and act like it is they that give her life. Many are the atrocities heaped upon our mother with just as many excuses for doing so.

She continues to be patient. She still provides shelter without rent. She provides our clothes and food. When you are bored and see no meaning to life, she whispers, "Come and sit on my lap and I will show you some of the most breathtaking wonders and mysteries ever created by our Father from the most minuscule to the majestic."[136]

What does justice mean when we abuse not only one another but Mother Earth as well? That is the question of environmental justice. The case studies that follow pose that question in ways that cannot be ignored.

Notes

1. John Joseph Mathews, *Sundown* (New York: Longman, Green, 1934), pp. 64-65. For a complete discussion of Mathews, particularly his views on Indian sovereignty, see, Robert Allen Warrior, *Tribal Secrets: Recovering American Indian Intellectual Traditions* (Minneapolis: University of Minnesota Press, 1995).

2. Famous Cheyenne peace chief killed by George Custer and his 7th Cavalry at the Washita Massacre in 1868.

3. N. Scott Momaday, "The Man Made of Words," in Rupert Costo, ed., *Indian Voices: The First Convocation of American Indian Scholars* (San Francisco: Indian Historian Press, 1970), p. 83. The essay has been much anthologized. See, e.g., Geary Hobson, ed., *The Remembered Earth* (Albuquerque: Red Earth Press, 1979).

4. Felix Cohen, quoted in Walter Echo-Hawk, "Loopholes in Religious Liberty: The Need for a Federal Law to Protect Freedom of Worship for Native People," *American Indian Religions* 1:1 (Winter 1994), p. 5.

5. Donald A. Grinde, Jr., and Bruce E. Johansen, *Ecocide of Native America: Environmental Destruction of Indian Lands and Peoples* (Santa Fe: Clear Light Publishers, 1995), p. 3.

6. Hobson, p. 3. See also, Jace Weaver, *Then to the Rock Let Me Fly: Luther Bohanon and Judicial Activism* (Norman: University of Oklahoma Press, 1993), pp. 138-145.

7. Rigoberto Queme Chay, "The Corn Men Have Not Forgotten Their Ancient Gods," in Inter Press Service, comp., *Story Earth: Native Voices on the Environment* (San Francisco: Mercury House, 1993), pp. 27-28.

8. Gabina Perez, North American Native Workshop on Environmental Justice, Iliff School of Theology, Denver, Co. (March 17, 1995); Anthony DePalma, "Racism? Mexico's in Denial," *New York Times* (June 11, 1995), p. 4E.

9. Vine Deloria, Jr., *God Is Red.* 2d ed. (Golden, Co.: Fulcrum, 1992), p. 52.

10. Ibid., pp. 52-53.

11. For a complete discussion of the fraudulent nature of the familiar speech by Seattle and various versions of that speech, see, Rudolf Kaiser, "Chief Seattle's Speech(es): American Origins and European Reception," in Brian Swann and Arnold Krupat, eds., *Recovering the Word: Essays on Native American Literature* (Berkeley: University of California Press, 1987), pp. 497-536.

12. Jay B. McDaniel, *With Roots and Wings: Christianity in an Age of Ecology and Dialogue* (Maryknoll, N.Y.: Orbis Books, 1995), p. 68.

13. Ibid., pp. 192-214. The as-told-to works cited by McDaniel are Mary Crow Dog (with Richard Erdoes), *Lakota Woman* (New York: HarperCollins, 1990) and John Fire Lame Deer (with Richard Erdoes), *Lame Deer: Seeker of Visions* (New York: Simon and Schuster, 1976). The objections to spiritual appropriation that the author cites are from Andy Smith, "For All Those Who Were Indian in a Former Life," in Carol Adams, ed., *Ecofeminism and the Sacred* (New York: Continuum, 1993), pp. 168-171. Smith was a participant at the workshop that led to the present volume and authored the piece on population herein. Finally, it must be noted that throughout this essay, although I refer to Native religions, when one speaks of religion and Native religious beliefs and practices, one is engaged in a kind of incommensurate discourse because of the all-pervasive nature of the Native beliefs and practices in their cultures.

14. Geoffrey R. Lilburne, *A Sense of Place: A Christian Theology of the Land* (Nashville: Abingdon, 1989), pp. 37, 35-44.

15. Grinde and Johansen, p. 11; see also, Jace Weaver, "Ethnic Cleansing, Homestyle," *Wicazo Sa* (Spring 1994), pp. 27-39.

16. See, Djelal Kadir, *Columbus and the Ends of the Earth: Europe's Prophetic Rhetoric as Conquering Ideology* (Berkeley: University of California Press, 1992).

17. Ward Churchill, *Fantasies of the Master Race: Literature, Cinema and the Colonization of American Indians*, M. Annette Jaimes, ed. (Monroe, Me.: Common Courage Press, 1992), pp. 195-196.

18. Ibid., p. 196.

19. Grinde and Johansen, p. 30.

20. Calvin Martin, *Keepers of the Game: Indian-Animal Relationships and the Fur Trade* (Berkeley: University of California Press, 1978), pp. 105-108. Emphasis mine. The point is that the source was not *even* an adopted *Cree.*

21. Ibid., p. 109.

22. Grinde and Johansen, p. 29.

23. See, Calvin Martin, ed., *The American Indian and the Problem of History* (New York: Oxford University Press, 1987), pp. 3-34, passim.

24. See, Weaver, "Ethnic Cleansing," p. 34.

25. See, James Mooney, *History, Myths, and Sacred Formulas of the Cherokees.* Reprint (Asheville: Historical Images, 1992), pp. 250-252.

26. Martin, *Keepers*, pp. 131-141.

27. Ibid., pp. 187-188.

28. Dennis McPherson and J. Douglas Rabb, *Indian from the Inside: A Study in Ethno-Metaphysics* (Thunder Bay, Ont.: Lakehead University, Centre for Northern Studies, 1993), p. 90. See also, Grinde and Johansen, pp. 269-270.

29. Grinde and Johansen, p. 44; but see, M. Annette Jaimes, ed., *State of Native America* (Boston: South End Press, 1992).

30. Grinde and Johansen, p. 11.

31. See, Russell Thornton, *American Indian Holocaust and Survival* (Norman: University of Oklahoma Press, 1987), pp. 15ff.; see also, McPherson and Rabb, pp. 92-93. McPherson and Rabb provide a good discussion of the debate between J. Baird Callicott and Daniel Guthrie on both this point and Native attitudes toward nature in general. See, Daniel Guthrie, "Primitive Man's Relationship to Nature," *Bioscience* 21:1971; J. Baird Callicott, "American Indian Land Wisdom? Sorting Out the Issues," in *In Defense of the Land Ethic: Essays in Environmental Philosophy* (Albany: State University of New York Press, 1989).

32. Grinde and Johansen, pp. 11-12.

33. Marcos Terena, "Sing the Song of the Voice of the Forest," in Inter Press, p. 37.

34. Dene Nation, *Denedeh: A Dene Celebration* (Toronto: McClelland and Stewart, 1984), p. 78.

35. See, Norma Kassi, "A Legacy of Maldevelopment," herein.

36. Tanien (Daniel) Ashini, "We Have Been Pushed to the Edge of a Cliff," in Inter Press, pp. 15-16.

37. Dene Nation, p. 93.

38. Joseph Epes Brown, *The Spiritual Legacy of the American Indian* (New York: Crossroad, 1982), p. 73.

39. Vine Deloria, Jr., "Sacred Lands and Religious Freedom," *American Indian Religions* 1:1 (Winter 1994), pp. 75-76.

40. Jeanne Rollins, "Liberation and the Native American," in Sergio Torres and John Eagleson, eds., *Theology in the Americas* (Maryknoll, N.Y.: Orbis Books, 1976), p. 204.

41. Perez, North American Native Workshop on Environmental Justice.

42. Dene Nation, p. 7.

43. Salvador Palomino, "Three Times, Three Spaces in Cosmos Quechua," in Inter Press, p. 46.

44. Sam D. Gill, *Mother Earth: An American Story* (Chicago: University of Chicago Press, 1987), p. 129. Emphasis mine. Even among many of the Native nations that refer to and revere Mother Earth, there is no intimation that she is a "goddess."

45. Ibid., p. 130.

46. Ibid., pp. 155-157.

47. John Bierhorst, *The Way of the Earth: Native America and the Environment* (New York: William Morrow, 1994), p. 91.

48. Ibid., pp. 89-91.

49. Churchill, p. 200.

50. Vine Deloria, Jr., "Comfortable Fictions and the Struggle for Turf: An Essay Review of James Clifton, *The Invented Indian: Cultural Fictions and Government Policies*," *American Indian Quarterly* 16:3, pp. 397-410.

51. Grinde and Johansen, p. 30.

52. Gill, p. 8; see also, Bil Gilbert, *God Gave Us This Country: Tekamthi and the First American Civil War* (New York: Macmillan, 1989), p. 257. Gilbert gives a complete account of the life of Tekamthi (also known as Tecumseh). Cf., Grinde and Johansen, p. 31, for another version of a quotation by Tekamthi concerning Mother Earth.

53. Gill attributes much of the corruption to the twentieth century to the effects of scholars and American Indian activists.

54. See, Thornton, *American Indian Holocaust and Survival*; Ward Churchill, *Struggle for the Land: Indigenous Resistance to Genocide, Ecocide, and Expropriation in Contemporary North America* (Monroe, Me.: Common Courage Press, 1993), p. 19.

55. See, Emmet Starr, *History of the Cherokee Indians.* Reprint (Muskogee, Ok.: Hoffmann Printing, 1984), p. 23. Note that Starr transliterates the name "Yehowa."

56. Ibid. The names of the three fires are U-ha-he-ta-qua, A-ta-no-ti, and U-squa-hu-la.

57. Carl N. Gorman, "Navajo Vision of Earth and Man," *Indian Historian* (Winter 1973), quoted in Brown, p. 70.

58. Chay, p. 20. In citing this example, I do not mean to deny or detract from other Native cultures that consider nature animate.

59. Howard Bad Hand, Native American Religion Forum, School of Theology at Claremont, Claremont, Ca. (August 1993). Other tribes in the Siouan language family have similar concepts of deity. See *generally*, John Joseph Mathews, *Wah'Kon-Tah* (Norman: University of Oklahoma Press, 1932).

60. Norma Kassi, North American Native Workshop on Environmental Justice, Iliff School of Theology, Denver, Co. (March 18, 1995).

61. Mooney, pp. 239-240. Once again, it needs to be pointed out that this is not universally true among Native traditions. The Cherokee are of the Iroquian language group. Their creation account is similar to that of the Iroquois. For an account of the genesis of the universe from the Mbyá of Paraguay, see, Jack D. Forbes, *Columbus and Other Cannibals* (Brooklyn: Autonomedia, 1992), pp. 15-19.

62. Jack F. Kilpatrick and Anna G. Kilpatrick, *Friends of Thunder: Folktales of the Oklahoma Cherokees* (Dallas: Southern Methodist University Press, 1964), pp. 129-134.

63. Mooney, p. 239. Cf., Dene Nation, p. 10. In the Dene creation myth, the servants of the Creator shape the earth's surface by spreading "something resembling the hide of a large moose" over the earth and lifting it. They repeated the process six times.

64. Deloria, *God Is Red*, p. 78. With regard to this Native connection to the land, Tandy Wilbur, Sr. (Swinomish) notes that even urban Indians, separated from their tribes, sometimes say of traditional homelands, "This is the place where my ancestors communed with the spiritual world. I have a relationship to it even though I DO NOT LIVE THERE" (Rollins, p. 204, caps. original).

65. See, Jimmie Durham, quoted in Ronald Wright, *Stolen Continents: The Americas through Indian Eyes Since 1492* (Boston: Houghton Mifflin, 1992), p. 311.

66. Dene Nation, p. 121.

67. Palomino, p. 58.

68. Mircea Eliade, *The Myth of the Eternal Return* (Princeton: Princeton University Press, 1971), pp. xiii-xiv. Cf., Grinde and Johansen, pp. 264-265. Grinde and Johansen draw distinctions between Native societies, which sanctify time and place, and modern society, which profanes them.

69. Leonardo Boff, *Ecology and Liberation: A New Paradigm* (Maryknoll, N.Y.: Orbis Books, 1995) pp. 45, 47; Brown, p. 71.

70. Deloria, *God Is Red*, pp. 90-91.

71. Vine Deloria, Jr., *God Is Red* (New York: Grosset & Dunlap, 1973), p. 91.

72. George Tinker, "Spirituality, Native American Personhood, Sovereignty and Solidarity," paper delivered at Ecumenical Association of Third World Theologians, Nairobi, Kenya (January 1992), p. 12; *accord*, Grinde and Johansen, p. 264.

73. See, Jace Weaver, "Only the Rocks and Mountains Last Forever," paper delivered at the Native American Religion Forum, School of Theology at Claremont, Claremont, Ca. (August 1993).

74. Eliade, p. 73.

75. William G. McLoughlin, *The Cherokees and Christianity, 1794-1870: Essays on Acculturation and Cultural Persistence* (Athens: University of Georgia Press, 1994), passim.

76. Elizabeth Cook-Lynn, "A Monograph of a Peyote Singer," *Wicazo Sa* (Spring 1991), p. 9.

77. Kassi, Workshop (March 18, 1995); Lucy Young and Edith V.A. Murphy, "Out of the Past: A True Indian Story," *California Historical Quarterly* 20:4 (December 1941); Cora DuBois, "Wintu Ethnography," *University of California Publications in American Archaeology and Ethnology*, vol. 36, pp. 75-76; Peter Nabokov, *Native American Testimony*, exp. ed. (New York: Viking, 1991), pp. 439-440. Margaret Sam-Cromarty (Cree) offers a humorous counterpoint, more in keeping with traditional beliefs in regeneration at the end of world cycles. She states, "They say the world is going to blow up, but I like to think everything will bloom again. Maybe next time, I'll come back, and I'll be Columbus." Margaret Sam-Cromarty, North American Native Workshop on Environmental Justice, Iliff School of Theology, Denver, Co. (March 18, 1995).

78. Susan Feld, *The Storytelling Stone* (New York: Dell, 1965), p. 83, quoting E. E. Clark, *Indian Legends of the Pacific Northwest* (Berkeley: University of California Press, 1933).

79. Grinde and Johansen, pp. 263-264.

80. New Revised Standard Version. The injunction is repeated with additions at Genesis 9:1-7, addressed to Noah and his sons after the Flood.

81. J. Hector St. John de Crèvecoeur, *Letters from an American Farmer*. Reprint (New York: Penguin, 1981), pp. 66-70, 120-124.

82. Hislop Codman, *The Mohawk* (New York: Rinehart and Company, 1948), pp. 219-222, quoted in Grinde and Johansen, p. 7.

83. Grinde and Johansen, p. 11.

84. Jackie Warledo, North American Native Workshop on Environmental Justice, Iliff School of Theology, Denver, Co. (March 18, 1995).

85. Palomino, p. 51.

86. Ibid., p. 46.

87. Boff, p. 46.

88. Ibid.

89. Ibid.

90. Boff attempts, unsuccessfully, to deal with this dilemma, stating, "But humankind, in tilling and keeping the earth is neither destructive nor dominant. We have a commitment that is profoundly ecological and intended to maintain the equilibrium of creation, which progresses and is transformed by virtue of human labor" (ibid., p. 47).

91. Grinde and Johansen, pp. 267-269.

92. Ibid., p. 264; "Protecting Traditional Rights and Resources," *Native Journal* (May/June 1993), p. 22; Terena, p. 43.

93. Robert Gibson, "The Environment Requires Guardians," *Native Journal* (November/December, 1994), p. 30; see also, Teri Lambert, "Northerners Give Mother Earth a Helping Hand," *Native Journal* (September/October 1993), p. 1.

94. In *Cherokee Nation v. Georgia* 5. Pet. 1 (1831), Chief Justice John Marshall established this principle, which still continues to exert an influence on federal Indian law and Native/non-Native relations. Marshall wrote, "They [Indian tribes] may . . . be denominated domestic dependent nations. They occupy a territory to which we assert a title independent of their will, which must take effect in point of possession when their right of possession ceases. Meanwhile they are in a state of pupilage. Their relation to the United States resembles that of a ward to his guardian."

95. Terena, p. 43.

96. Denise Lardner Carmody and John Tully Carmody, *Native American Religions: An Introduction* (New York: Paulist Press, 1993), p. 100.

97. Dale Ann Frye Sherman, North American Native Workshop on Environmental Justice, Iliff School of Theology, Denver, Co. (March 18, 1995).

98. Ward Churchill, "The Situation of Indigenous Populations in the United States," *Wicazo Sa* 1:1 (Spring 1985), p. 33; see also, Winona LaDuke, "Succeeding into Native North America," *Issues in Radical Therapy* 13:3-4, pp. 12-13.

99. Boff, p. 47.

100. See, Donald Fixico, "The Struggle for Our Homes: Native Lands, Native Traditions, Sovereignty, and the Environment," herein.

101. Grinde and Johansen, p. 1.

102. Ibid., p. 5.

103. Duane Good Striker, North American Native Workshop on Environmental Justice, Iliff School of Theology, Denver, Co. (March 18, 1995).

104. David Grant, "Indian Is," quoted in Rollins, p. 205.

105. Grinde and Johansen, pp. 19-20. Many tribes have established or are establishing environmental departments and programs. See, e.g., Duane Good Striker, "TEK Wars: First Nations' Struggles for Environmental Planning," herein.

106. "Sovereignty," *Black's Law Dictionary*, 5th ed. (St. Paul: West Publishing Co., 1979), p. 1252.

107. Oren Lyons, "An Iroquois Perspective," in Christopher Vecsey and Robert W. Venables, eds., *American Indian Environments: Ecological Issues in Native American History* (Syracuse: Syracuse University Press, 1980), p. 171.

108. Ibid., pp. 171-174; "Protecting Traditional Rights," p. 22.

109. Chay, pp. 28-30.

110. Dene Nation, p. 59. Other Native languages similarly lack a word for "wilderness" to describe the land or environment.

111. James Kent, *Commentaries on American Law*, vol. 1 (New York: O. Halsted, 1826), p. 242.

112. Ibid. That such views persist in the laws of North America can be seen in the 1991 court case *Delgam Uukw vs. the Queen* (Supreme Court of British Columbia, Mar. 8, 1991). Chief Justice Allan McEachern denied the land claims of the Gitksan and Wet'suwet'en people in language right out of Chancellor Kent. For the opinion and a complete discussion of the case, see, Don Monet and Skan'u (Ardythe Wilson), *Colonialism on Trial: Indigenous Land Rights and the Gitksan and Wet'suwet'en Sovereignty Case* (Philadelphia: New Society Publishers, 1992).

113. See, Grinde and Johansen, pp. 30-37.

114. Ibid.

115. "The Man with the Spear," *Nature Conservancy* (January/February 1995), p. 30.

116. "Tenure," in *Black's Law Dctionary*, p. 1317.

117. "The Man with the Spear," p. 30.

118. Kent, p. 242; *Cherokee Nation v. Georgia.*

119. Indeed, there is a maxim in the law: *Tenura est pactio contra communem feudi naturam ac rationem, in contractu interposita* ("Tenure is a compact contrary to the common nature and reason of the fee, interposed by contract").

120. "The Man with the Spear," p. 30.

121. Ibid.; cf., Grinde and Johansen, p. 36.

122. "The Man with the Spear," p. 30.

123. Ibid. Emphasis original.

124. Ibid., p. 32. Some of the decisions chronicled in the case studies herein bear evidence to this fact.

125. Ibid.

126. See, ibid., p. 30.

127. Winona LaDuke, address at Conference of Ford Foundation Fellows, Washington, D.C. (March 1994).

128. "The Man with the Spear," p. 30.

129. Ibid.

130. LaDuke, "Succeeding into Native North America," p. 12.

131. See, Grinde and Johansen, p. 2; Dene Nation, p. 119.

132. Carole and Jon Belhumeur, "Reconnecting with Mother Earth," *Native Journal* (October 1994), p. 4.

133. See, Dene Nation, p. 65.

134. Similar stories are told of Trickster in a variety of cultures. It is similar to one told about Maui, the Native Hawaiian trickster figure. It is also similar to an episode involving the Yaqui Rosario Cuamea in Miguel Méndez' novel, *Pilgrims in Aztlán.* See, e.g., Steven Goldsberry, *Maui the Demigod* (New York: Poseidon Press, 1984), pp. 391-399; Miguel Méndez, *Pilgrims in Aztlán* (Tempe: Bilingual Press, 1992), pp. 168-169.

135. Dene Nation, p. 65.

136. Allen Badger, "And Justice for All . . . ," *Native Journal* (May 1995), p. 1.

1.

The Struggle for Our Homes

Indian and White Values and Tribal Lands

DONALD L. FIXICO

EDITOR'S INTRODUCTION: Many people are familiar with Erik Erikson's work in developmental psychology, in which he contended that human development occurs in eight "psychosocial stages." If raised in a positive, healthy cultural environment, the individual learns *trust, autonomy, initiative*, and *industry*. During teen years, a sense of *identity* is developed. Finally, at various points in adulthood, the individual learns *intimacy*, broadens his or her vision to include the rest of humanity and the next generation (a process Erikson labels *generativity*), and develops *integrity*. According to David Rausch and Blair Schlepp (Standing Rock Sioux), however, far fewer know that Dr. Erikson formulated his theory based on his work among the Sioux and the Yurok of northern California, which he chose because of the widely divergent environments in which they lived.[1] Unfortunately, as both Rausch and Schlepp and Donald Fixico illustrate, the disruptions wrought upon Native cultures today too often result in the worst of Erikson's stages. Conditions breed mistrust, doubt, guilt, inferiority, and role confusion.[2]

Erikson stressed the role of environmental and cultural factors over biology in human development. In 1921, when Ruth Benedict, cited by Don Fixico in the essay that follows, began her work in anthropology, very few had even heard of the word *culture*. Today it is a part of the average person's everyday vocabulary.[3] A new academic discipline called cultural studies is emerging. Yet for all this new awareness, there is still woefully little understanding of just how radically different Native cultures are from the dominant culture that surrounds them. These differences lead to very different attitudes toward the natural environment, and it is these differences that make the work of Don Fixico important as preliminary matter in any understanding of Native perspectives on environmental justice.

Based on her analysis of the Pueblos of the Southwest and the Kwakiutl of Vancouver Island in the Pacific Northwest, Benedict concluded that culture is human "personality writ large."[4] Knowing something about Native worldviews is therefore crucial if one is to understand Native views of the environment. In the piece that follows, Don Fixico provides a glimpse of those worldviews and contrasts them with the dominant, Euro-American worldview. In doing so, he also provides an important perspective on traditional Native beliefs concerning the natural world.[5]

In his writings, Osage author John Joseph Mathews employed the term *Amer-European* to refer to White, non-Natives.[6] Though the bulk of Mathews' work was done in the thirties and forties, before the term *Euro-American* became popular, his usage reflects more than the lack of a commonly accepted vocabulary. *Euro-American* means Americans of European descent. *Amer-European* connotes something very different. They are Europeans who happen to live in America. Mathews's terminology reflects the difference in worldviews between the two peoples. Born of and shaped by a different continent, Amer-Europeans will never truly be of this continent, no matter how many generations they dwell here. It is to this distinction that Don Fixico speaks.

If asked the question What do you value in life?, you might pause for a few seconds and then three or four things would immediately come to mind. Family? Happiness? Wealth? Why do we value certain things, and what do they say about our lives? Do we value things related to family most? Or perhaps we prize those items that are strictly financial. Or perhaps we esteem our religion. What is the source of our value system? Do people of different cultures possess different values? If so, how did they develop them?

Actually, Native Americans and Anglo-Americans differ considerably in their value systems. The latter has established a system emphasizing capitalistic individual gain and individual religious inclination. By contrast, American Indian values are holistic and communally oriented. Both groups, however, have rationalized the significance of certain things they deemed germane to their lives. As the twenty-first century approaches, Indians (that is, Native Americans who remain close to their native ways) and Whites continue to diverge in what they value in life, in spite of over five hundred years of contact. But how Natives developed separate values from White Americans needs to be explored in order to understand Indian-White struggles over natural resources on tribal lands.

Basic values of Indians and Whites differ to the point of being polar opposites in intellectualization and cultural worldviews. This incongruity accounts for both their separate cultural development and their clash over natural resources. Unfortunately, this dissimilarity has led to a history of more than a thousand wars and battles between the two peoples. Such differences have caused myriad misunderstandings, and the history of relations between the two races has been one of violence.[7]

This polarization of the two races and their diverse cultural backgrounds are much of the reason Native Americans remain indifferent to the mainstream culture in America today, while other minority groups strive desperately to integrate themselves into that society. The task of the following essay involves observing Natives of the eastern woodlands, plains, and the Southwest to ascertain how they have developed their value systems as a general explanation of why Natives and Anglo-Americans are different. These three Native groups have been chosen because the majority of tribal natural resources are located on their lands. This cross-cultural examination involves an internal and external analysis of plains Indians, Southwestern pueblo communities, and eastern woodlands tribes in an effort to establish the basic differences between Indians and Whites. Exploring their origins and cultures helps to explain the sources of Indian and White values in mining natural resources on tribal lands. During the massive consumption of fossil fuels during the oil-embargoed 1970s, geologists estimated that more than half of the nation's coal fields were west of the Mississippi. Close to 40 percent of the country's uranium, one-third or more of the coal, and an estimated 15 percent of the nation's known oil and gas reserves are on Indian lands in the West.[8] By examining the Native cultures of these three geographic areas–plains, Southwest, and eastern woodlands–a comparative analysis demonstrates the fundamental differences between Native Americans and Whites in their attitudes, values, and worldviews.[9]

Both the Great Plains and the Southwest proved to be much more harsh and demanding environments than the eastern woodlands. The Great Plains became the homeland of an estimated twenty-eight Indian nations. The Blackfeet, Teton, Yankton, and Santee Sioux tribes, the Sarsi, Crow, Gros Ventre, Cheyenne, Arapaho, Arikara, Mandan, Hidatsa, Plains Cree, and Plains Ojibwa lived on the northern plains. Tribes of the central and southern plains included the Osage, Iowa, Oto, Omaha, Shoshone, Ute, Kutenai, Apache, Comanche, Kiowa, Ponca, and Wichita.[10] Overall, the Great Plains stretches from the northern Canadian plains of Saskatchewan, Alberta, and Manitoba southward to the Gulf of Mexico, bordered on the east by the Mississippi River and on the west by the Rocky Mountains. The area is immense, covering approximately 1.5 million square miles, one third of the United States.[11] Graced with vegetation ranging from short grass to tall buffalo grass, the prairie and plains suffer from limited rainfall. Rainfall ranges, on average, from less than twenty inches to only thirty inches per year.[12]

In the Southwest the pueblo communities continue to reside where they have been for well over five hundred years. In addition, the Hopi and the large Navajo Nation, with an estimated membership of over 200,000, live in the Four Corners area where Arizona, New Mexico, Utah, and Colorado intersect. The pueblos consist of Taos, Picuris, San

Juan, Santa Clara, San Ildefonso, Nambe, Pojaque, Tesuque, Tigua, Sandia, Isleta, Cochiti, San Felipe, Santa Ana, Zia, Jemez, Pecos, Laguna, Acoma, Zuni, and Santo Domingo.[13] Life in the Southwest depends heavily on sparse rain to supply corn and other crops to the people. The rain interfaces between the two fundamental elements of the sun and the earth, thereby becoming the catalyst for all life in an arid region with limited precipitation and summer temperatures frequently over 100 degrees. The outer world–or the surface of the earth–and humanity's relationship to it are a vital part of the Pueblo and the Navajo religions, economies, and worldviews. The earth is the giver of life, and the people's origin myths have evolved from their relationship to it.[14]

East of the Mississippi, the Saginaw Chippewas of Wisconsin and the Mikasuki Seminoles of Florida represent the primary tribal holdings of natural resources. Their resources face the biggest threat from state agencies and corporations wanting control and use of their lands through long-term leases. Aside from fossil fuels, stands of timber on eastern Indian lands are at risk, as are fish and wild rice among the Great Lakes tribes in Wisconsin and Michigan.[15] In addition to the various Chippewa or Ojibwa communities, the Menominee, Potawatomi, and Ottawa are caught in the struggle for natural resources. In the northeast, the Iroquois nations, and in Oklahoma, the Creeks, Cherokees, and Choctaws are discovering the potential of their resources.[16]

The differences in Indian and White values begin with different perceptions, constituting opposing worldviews. How people perceive things, other people, and the environment is relevant to understanding life and how and what one values. Historically, Indian people and White Americans have very different understandings of life, even though they have struggled for control over the same America and its natural resources. One might think that they would have more in common, but they operate from the distinct mindsets of two different races, from their own unique worldviews. Perception is a result of biological, physical function, but how one actually understands and interprets what one perceives is influenced by a delicate interplay of biology and cultural influences. Differences in perception and culture have been integral elements in Indian-White relations leading to separation and conflict, even as both sides struggled with the same decisions involving the same land.

Culture and its development have accounted for the divergent courses of Natives and White Americans of European ancestry. The two peoples developed from primal human needs, and the results became the material expressions of their societies. In this process of cultural development, how people perceived the external world and their physical surroundings helped shape both their primary and secondary values. Primary values might be considered as those essential for meeting human emotional and physical needs. Secondary values are those of the community that produce a culture. Both sets of values have been reinforced through retelling over generations through the oral tradition.[17]

In the Native oral tradition, Indian communities in the Americas told and retold legends, stories, myths, and parables describing how their peoples derived from the earth in some way. Among the Jicarilla Apache of the Southwest, the stories tell of the people coming from the underworld and relate a time when "all living things were below."[18] Among the western Pueblos, the Acoma believe that two girls emerged from Cipapu, the earth's underworld, when Tsitctinako, a spirit, guided them and permitted them to live above.[19] The Cheyenne believe that the Great Medicine created an earth where "it was always spring; wild fruits and berries grew everywhere, and great trees shaded the streams of clear water that flowed through the land."[20] The Hopi of Arizona understand that they emerged from the lower world through an opening called *sipapuni* into the fourth world on the earth's surface.[21]

Understandings of the origins of their cultures aided in determining differences between Native Americans and Anglo-Americans and their values. Cultural origin begins with how people perceive their surroundings or environment. The natural environment represented the primary sustenance of life to people, supplying them with shelter, food, and clothing. Basically, the natural world supplied the economy for people and their society. For example, the plains Indians discovered fifty-two different ways to utilize the buffalo.[22] Because Native Americans and Anglo-Americans developed on separate continents, their cultures developed differently as they perceived life in their own ways and attached special importance to different things. American Indians especially acknowledged nonmaterial items such as family relations. They understood the interactions between humans and physical surroundings to include an abstract, spiritual level. Long ago Europeans seemingly shared a similar background, but they moved to a reality of economic and class structures motivated by capitalism and mercantilism in the seventeenth century.

In the Western hemisphere American Indians learned to live in various regions, which were controlled by climate, water, earth, and the supernatural. Anthropologists A. L. Kroeber and Clark Wissler introduced and refined the idea of the "culture area" to help study and understand the various Native cultures, classifying them according to the region where they evolved. Other scholars introduced their own cultural systems to understand Native Americans, but the basic premise held that geographic environment heavily influenced the determination of culture. Basic culture areas included the eastern woodlands, plains, Southwest, plateau, prairie, and tundra. Living in these areas meant surviving under harsh conditions, testing the ability of the people to adapt to their environments.

Native Americans found themselves constantly dependent upon their natural environment. At a physical level they learned to rely on trees, grass, or buffalo hides for making lodges. Wild animals and plants became their food sources. Plants and herbs provided them with medicines. Among the Muscogee Creeks of the southeastern woodlands four herb roots—*pasaw* ("rattlesnake root"), *micoweanochaw* ("red root"), *sowatchko* (similar to wild fennel), and *eschalapootchke* ("little tobacco")—were highly prized for their curative powers.[23] Such plants and herbs had spiritual powers to help the people, and humans made certain that they respected these allies.[24]

On the plains some tribes grew small patches of tobacco for casual smoking and ceremonial purposes. Collecting roots and berries helped supplement the hunting of buffalo and antelope. The Cheyenne collected eight to ten varieties of roots for their food supply. Indian turnip (called *pomme blanche* by the French) was a favorite, and red turnip, the fruit of the prickly pear cactus, thistle stalks, and chokecherries were a part of their diet, as well.[25] The digging stick was given to the Cheyenne by the Great Medicine, and persons skilled at finding these foods achieved special recognition, especially during times when bison were scarce. In the Hopi country of Black Mesa, forests of pinon and juniper furnish some food, but corn, along with beans and melons, is the main staple in a land averaging only ten inches of annual rainfall.[26] Corn meal is also valued for use in ceremonials to heal and bring rain.

The environment provided for all aspects of people's lives such that their religions, philosophies, and economies were founded on this external dependency beyond the internal psychological self. This external dependence became a part of their perception and understanding. Furthermore, this dependence was beyond the simple control of the people. It was nontangible and a power much greater than themselves. Additionally, the people were awed by the massive forms and abundance of their physical environments—lakes, streams, rivers, mountains, deserts, meadows, and forests. Nature represented an awesome force in multiple ways, always overwhelming and powerfully intimidating. Nature provided everything needed by Natives, causing them to realize their inferiority and to acknowledge that power greater than themselves. That great power was the Creator, who had also created them and provided an environment for them in which to live. The people acknowledged the Creator as an all-powerful being, and they rationalized their relationship as a secondary one in status. They were dependent upon the Great Being for everything they needed—and for life itself. For example, the oral traditions of various Indian nations each had origin myths, sometimes more than one. In his speech for war against British settlers in Ohio in 1763, the Ottawa leader Pontiac recited a parable that proclaimed the power of the Creator and the subordinate status of the people: "I am He who made heaven and earth, the trees, lakes, rivers, all men, and all thou seest and all thou hast seen on earth. Because I love you, you must do what I say."[27]

In the parables, legends, songs, stories, and myths of the oral tradition, the people demonstrated that they valued life and the Creator who bestowed blessings upon them. According to the Cheyenne, "When the Great Mystery created the earth and all living things upon it, the people and the animals lived in peace."[28] The oral tradition was part of Cheyenne life and served as their means of recording history. These accounts also established their identity and reinforced it, with each new generation telling the same accounts passed down by their elders. In this manner the same basic values held steady in society as the people tried to understand the Great Mystery.

People hoped that blessings would also include empowerment with divine gifts. Such empowerment from the Creator was highly prized, so that people sought visions and prayed for divine assistance. A person with a special gift for foretelling the future, curing, or endowed with other supernatural powers had to follow certain cultural guidelines and continually be respectful for his or her gift. To be chosen by the Creator also meant fulfilling responsibilities in order to retain the gift. Part of these responsibilities was to serve one's people and to be a helpful member of the community.

Another value common to all Native American communities was the importance of wisdom and knowledge. Indian people learned from the herbs and plants and from their life experiences in both physical and metaphysical reality. In being aware of their surroundings, they learned and became knowledgeable. Through observation, patience, and acceptance of information, and with the interpretative assistance of an elder or medicine person, individuals obtained knowledge. Knowledgeable persons were respected and asked for advice, and they played key roles in society. Such a person among the Muscogee Creeks was called *key-tha*.

In many instances the elders were the wise and knowledgeable ones. American Indian societies valued their elders. They respected and listened to them. The elders played an important role by advising, making recommendations, and providing counsel in making difficult decisions. Their position in the community was especially noted during crises when crucial decisions had to be made, but they were recognized even on a daily basis for teaching the youth about the circular order of life.

The relationship of the people with the natural environment is the basis of Native values. Indian people did not see themselves as the focal point of existence, but rather a small part of the larger circular order of life ordained by the Creator. The earth represented the focus of life, as the provider of sustenance. In many tribal traditions the earth takes on a parental role as Mother Earth or Earth Mother. The earth physically and symbolically provided and continues to provide the essence of life for plants, animals, physical landscape, human beings, and spiritual beings.

The people's relationship with the earth is one of reverence and respect. Native Americans viewed themselves as a part of the earth, but separate from the animals, plants, and physical geography. At another level, they acknowledged spiritual beings and forces. All things had a separate identity, although they were all a part of the same totality of existence. Like atoms in a molecule, each particle representing a different element was pertinent to the entire being of existence in the circle of life.

The people see themselves as being no more important than the animals or plants; they are equal in brotherhood or sisterhood. Onondaga statesman Oren Lyons says, "In our [Iroquois] perception all life is equal, and that includes the birds, animals, things that grow, things that swim. All life is equal in our perception."[29] In this way, a natural democracy prevailed as part of nature's law. Although some animals were stronger or faster than others, they all had a philosophically equal role in life.

The various kinds of animals all have certain qualities or strengths given to them by the Creator. The people have a relationship with each species of flora and fauna based on respect for its special qualities and strengths. The perception is that human beings have a role and a place in the larger circle of life as prescribed by the Creator. Animals, in particular, have special roles as totems among eastern woodland tribes, who had clans bearing animal designations, and western tribes, who respected animals like the horse and buffalo, naming military societies after them. Each animal and plant is valued for its particular characteristics. For example, the turtle is valued by the woodlands people for its durability and longevity.

The relationship of Native people to flora and fauna has produced several universal truths about Native Americans, which have developed into different tribal philosophies. More precisely, kinship and understanding one's relationships to friends, relations, and all created things were considered important. The overall belief acknowledges the order of relationships as previously described: rather than focusing on the human self, importance is attached to relationship or kinship, by which all things are interrelated. In a myth about its culture hero Montezuma and the Great Flood, the Tohono O'odham of the Southwest describe a better time. "It was a happy time. The sun was much closer to the earth then so that it was always pleasantly warm. There was no winter and no freezing cold. Men and animals lived as brothers, speaking a common language all could understand, so that a bug or a bird could talk to a human."[30]

Friendship, kinship, and alliance connected Indian people in various social, family, and political relationships, so that any one person or species of plant or animal was part of the larger order of life. Black Elk, the Oglala holy man of the nineteenth century, described his people's happiness long ago: "Once we were happy in our own country and we were seldom hungry, for then the two-leggeds and the four-leggeds lived together like relatives, and there was plenty for them and for us."[31] But the absence of animals signified both physical and psychological destruction. Crow chief Plenty Coups described how the disappearance of the buffalo affected his people: "When the buffalo went away the hearts of my people fell to the ground, and they could not lift them up again." Similarly, the wise Hunkpapa leader Sitting Bull lamented, "A cold wind blew across the prairie when the last buffalo fell—a death-wind for my people."[32]

Such a system of relationships involving mutual respect among flora, fauna, and physical creations of the earth has been regarded as sacred by many Native American groups.[33] The earth was the principle focus of life, and sacred sites like the Black Hills, Blue Lake of the Taos, Mackinac Island, Mount Ranier, Mount Taylor, Bear Butte, and Devil's Tower were blessed with special powers. The earth is the physical substance that all of us, including the plant and animal beings, have in common. The earth as the home of all living things has earned a place of tremendous respect among Native peoples. Such sacredness has been integrated into the daily lives of Indian peoples and their cultures. The oral traditions of Indian peoples tell of the sacred importance, physically and symbolically, of the earth to the people. To this day, respect for the environment, elders, and the earth are dominant themes in Indian life. Respect as a value encompasses social, religious, and physical dimensions of life.

In the process of acknowledging the vital role of the earth as the provider of life, Native peoples have developed ceremonies signifying the importance of the earth and the sun. The ceremonies represent the value the people have placed on the earth. They verify and confirm the continuity of the people's relationship with the earth. This bond between the two has provided security, a sense of belonging, and Native identity. We are of the earth, and this is reinforced by both the oral tradition and by rituals that remind the people. Ceremonies reinforce the importance of the "way" of doing things so that the people will never forget, while at the same time confirming their identity, history, and heritage. For example, the Muscogee Creeks of the southeast woodlands hold their Green Corn dances, the Navajos of the Southwest have the Yeibichai, and Natives of the plains have the Sun Dance.

Traditional Native Americans believe that they are part of a whole. Indian people are not solitary. They historically have preferred a culture stressing community more than individuality. The tendency is to see the whole or the group and want to be part of it. The group is seen in the happiness of relatives and friends talking and laughing, the content of socialization among members, the security found among community and kinfolk. To want to be a part of the whole and to see oneself as a small part of the "one" refocuses the emphasis on group-ego rather than self-ego. In order to belong to the group and to be accepted by others, one places the needs of the group before the needs of the individual. At a still deeper level, the Zuñi of the Southwest believe in a oneness that transcends linear time, life, and death. They perceive a oneness with the entire universe.[34]

Family was the most basic element of Native American communities and highly valued, although this unit is today threatened by homicide, family violence, and suicide.[35] Within the family, prescribed interaction between family members and the completeness of the extended family of grandparents, aunts, uncles, cousins, and ceremonially adopted members ensured the family's continued functioning.[36] The "socialization of togetherness," involving talking, storytelling, laughter, learning, and the simple joy of doing things together bonded family members. Togetherness as a family also meant security, fellowship, good feeling, and a sense of belonging.

The youth played a very special role in Indian societies and were cherished. Children held families together, bonding the generations of parents and grandparents with the future. Without children, the community could not continue. Everyone had a role in raising them to adulthood—parents, aunts, uncles, adopted relatives, and grandparents. In Indian society one of the strongest bonds is that of grandchild and grandparent, and the latter would do most anything for the young. The children meant that the bloodlines would continue to flow, and the loss of any child was a great tragedy.

Indian communities understood the importance of family to the continuance of their people. They also valued the earth. Symbolically and philosophically, the earth was mother to all people, a term that included animal and plants as well as humans. Mother Earth yielded life to the plants that grow, provided nourishment for animals to live, and served as a parental figure to human beings. All things were related, because they all had their origin in the earth and were part of the extended family of Mother Earth and Father Sun.

After family—and closely related to it—community was of primary importance to the traditional existence of Native peoples. To see and to function with the whole was more important than one's own interest. Such a perception called for extended thinking in terms of the community. Lame Deer, a Lakota medicine man, spoke of the relationship of family to community: "Indian children are never alone. They are always surrounded by grandparents, uncles, cousins, relatives of all kinds, who fondle the kids, sing to them, [and] tell them stories. If the parents go someplace, the kids go along."[37]

This holistic understanding emphasized sharing rather than accumulation of material goods. Individual Native Americans wanted the community to continue in harmony. Hence, sharing was preferred over self-oriented behavior. Sharing was also understood pragmatically as a prerequisite to simple survival. Native Americans realized that survival was more easily achieved by helping one another in finding food or protecting against enemies or the physical elements than by acting alone. To be banished from one's village, band, or tribe meant almost certain death. Thus sharing was a learned value that grew into another—generosity.

Generosity is prevalent in many Native societies. Sharing or giving is a means of maintaining harmony in the community. Giving promotes positive relationships, while demonstrating to others that the giver is able to include others in his or her prosperity and good fortune; thus a successful hunter shared his food with persons in need. To give earns trust from others and shows them that the generous person values their company and friendship or kinship.

The circle has no beginning and no end. It thus is frequently used to represent life—the circle of life. The circle's perimeter defines the edge of a Native community. The people are inside the circle. The circle of life is steeped in the earth—also a circle—with its physical and symbolic offerings. Many native traditions record that the people came from the earth and that it is their mother. Native Americans close to their traditions hold these views as a part of their philosophies, religious beliefs, and fundamental values. From their perspective, we are of the earth and a part of its extended space, matter, and energy. But even the earth is a gift from the Supreme Creator, and this physical creation is the most precious gift that Creator bestowed on human beings. For Natives, bonding with the earth is part of their life, culture, and history.

In the wisdom of the Creator, each thing has been empowered with its own spirit. Upon the realization of one's own spirituality, the inner being is awakened to the reality of empowered energies in all things. To acknowledge the spirit of another is to affirm the interconnectedness of all things as part of the greater whole of existence—the circle of life. In the process of realization, one must attempt to meld the subconscious with the conscious mind and one's whole physical being. This awareness brings with it strength and spiritual energy. The spirituality inherent in seeing and understanding this metaphysical bond is the path to understanding creation and perhaps the meaning of life.

To help people learn and understand, symbols and colors have important places in Native American communities. They are signs from the other side of life to enlighten and to warn. For example, among the

Muscogee Creeks red, yellow, white, blue, and black are important because they represent the four directions: red and yellow represent north, white east, blue south, and black west. Among the Navajo, chants and prayers of the Blessing Way symbolize the omnipresent power of the supernatural, called upon to heal or act in an extraordinary manner. For them, dawn or east is white, the same color as spring and youth; blue represents south, the extreme heat of midday, corn, and other vegetation (since there is no green in Navajo); yellow is west, autumn, and evening twilight; and black signifies north, night, winter, old age, and death.[38] It is important to know these symbols, which are messages from the Creator. The song of a bird, a dropped feather, peculiar behavior by an animal–any of these might be a sign. One must be alert in order to learn and to become wise. There is no coincidence, some say.

Among Indian people, role and responsibility are essential to the survival and prosperity of the community. At a philosophical level, all of us have a role and a set of responsibilities as part of our place in the world. The role of each creation needs to be fulfilled, and the responsibilities connected to each role need to be carried out. To abuse either role or responsibility is to desecrate the order of life established by the Creator. To help meet these roles and responsibilities, the Creator has bestowed certain gifts and empowered all creation–plants, animals, mountains, rivers, all things, including human beings–with separate qualities of strength. Thus it is up to each of us to realize our roles and responsibilities and to use our strengths to participate morally in the world community.

In this effort to fulfill roles and responsibilities, the final value will be achieved–harmony and balance. Harmony in each of us occurs as an internal struggle every day. Externally, we seek harmony in our relationships with friends and relatives. Balance in life is the key for harmony as intended by the Creator, but it has also been intended that we must struggle. We must understand the need for struggle as a daily endeavor to expend energy and work for the conservation of nature. Thus we build for the future.

In order to assist us, the Creator made spiritual beings to help humans, plants, and animals in their mission to survive and prosper. The order of survival is basic, and to want or desire more than what is necessary for our normal requirements would be taking from others. Greed and lust are not meant to be a norm for human society when there is so much abundance. Hence, codes of both instinctive and learned morality are a part of life. Because of this, Native Americans have said that we should not desecrate the earth in any way. Its abundance and beauty are ours to respect and enjoy, but we must take only what is essential for life.

The values of Indian people as outlined vary in specifics across tribal traditions but are nonetheless fundamental. The universal belief in the Earth Mother and the Creator within a circular order of life in which all things are deemed equal remains prominent. These basic values, however, are incongruent with the values of Anglo-Americans, who come from a different place on the earth and who have thus developed a very different worldview. Such incongruity is reflected in the histories and beliefs of both peoples.

Unfortunately, this fundamental incongruity between Natives and Anglo-Americans has accounted for the miscommunication, misunderstandings, and conflicts between the two peoples. In order to understand these differences, one must trace the source back to the differences in perceptions, environments, and how they separately view their surroundings and rationalize their relationship with it in their cultural development. The results, since 1492, have been a struggle between the two sides for the earth and its natural resources in the Americas. After centuries of conflict at every level, one Hopi warned, "Everything, everyone, is the white man's; all he has to do is stake his claim. They claimed us. They claimed our land, our water; now they have turned to other places"[39] This exploitation in the form of American capitalism disregards the future for immediate financial gain. Far worse is desecrating the earth and destroying the spiritual and physical harmony and balance of all things.

A primary difference between the two races relates to the earth itself. Native Americans have viewed the earth as the mother of all things on this planet. By contrast, Anglo-Americans have considered the earth as a commodity, useful only for its soil and natural resources. Furthermore, Anglo-Americans have developed economic systems of ownership to possess the land, something initially inconceivable to Native Americans. As a result of the struggle over land ownership between Indians and Whites, Native Americans own only an estimated 2.3 percent of the land in the United States.

Anglo-Americans and Natives are fundamentally different. Ownership and stewardship are polar opposites. Oddly enough, as the twentieth century comes to an end, marking more than five hundred years of contact between Natives and Whites, the two races will likely enter yet another century still holding their separate mindsets and worldviews. These differences in worldview and in the values that go with them mean that there will always exist an Indian view and a White view of the earth that they share.

Exploitation of the world's resources has caused alarm among ecologists, conservationists, environmentalists, and scientists who study the planet. A Worldwatch Institute Report for 1994 warned that the planet was now beyond its capacity to supply the uncontrolled demand for resources. "But the pace and scale of degradation that started about mid-century—and continues today—is historically new. . . . As a result of our population size, consumption patterns, and technological choices, we have surpassed the planet's carrying capacity. This is plainly evident by the extent to which we are damaging and depleting natural capital. The earth's environmental assets are now insufficient to sustain both our present patterns of economic activity and the life-support systems we depend on."[40] As early as twenty years ago, environmentalists and conservationists predicted that significant changes in the world needed to occur by the year 2030 in order to sustain life in the face of rapidly decreasing natural resources, if the degradation of the earth were not to become irreversible.[41]

This alarm concerning the world's resources reminds us that indigenous communities around the globe are fighting for their own lands and resources. In the last decade of the century, indigenous communities everywhere face the same grim fate that has befallen American Indians in the exploitation of their persons and resources. Multinational corporations are exploiting indigenous communities for their resources in Brazil, Iran, Indonesia, Surinam, Costa Rica, Panama, Australia, Colombia, and the Philippines.[42] When will it end? Perhaps only when capitalist minds conclude that the greed for monetary gain and power today prevents a tomorrow. Until then, the world is at risk.

Native American prophecies tell of doom if the guidelines and values given by the Creator are not followed. For the Cheyenne, a pole holds up the world. It is similar to a Sun-Dance pole but much larger. The Great White Grandfather Beaver of the North is gnawing at the pole, as he has done for ages. He gnaws furiously at the pole when he is angry at the people, and "when the pole is gnawed all the way through, the pole will topple," and the earth "will crash into a bottomless nothing."[43] The Cheyenne must therefore live according to certain values, placing family and communal good in the forefront, lest the angry Grandfather Beaver complete his work.

The White River Sioux tell of a very old woman living in a cave with a huge black dog. When she completes her porcupine quilling on a blanket strip upon which she has been working for thousands of years, the world will end. She must, however, tend her fire in the cave in order to keep warm, and when she turns her back to do so the dog pulls quills from the strip, preventing her from finishing.[44] The message is that if we do not do what we are supposed to do—like tend the fire—then the world will end sooner than we expect. Catastrophe will result if people do not obey the natural laws.

The Tohono O'odham are reminded of Montezuma, who rebelled against the instructions given by the Creator and sought to change the world to his own liking: "Men began to hunt and kill animals. Disregarding the eternal laws by which humans had lived, they began to fight among themselves. The Great Mystery Power tried to warn Montezuma and the people by pushing the sun farther away from the earth and placing it where it is now. Winter, snow, ice, and hail appeared, but no one heeded this warning." Montezuma became angry, and the Creator sighed, "and even wept," and then he permitted the White man to invade Montezuma's land, "taking away Montezuma's power and destroying him utterly."[45]

As a final warning, the Brule Sioux describe two previous, imperfect worlds. This world is the third given a chance by the Creating Power. The Creating Power said to the people, "The first world I made was bad. So I burned it up. The second world I made was bad too, so I drowned it. This is the third world I have made. Look: I have created a rainbow for you as a sign that there will be no more Great Flood. Whenever you see a rainbow, you will know that it has stopped raining." The Creating Power continued, "Now, if you have learned how to behave like human beings and how to live in peace with each other and with the other living things—the two-legged, the four-legged, the many-legged, the fliers, the no-legs, the green plants of this universe—then all will be well. But if you make this world bad and ugly, then I will destroy this world too. It's up to you."[46]

In the final analysis, Indian and White values differ according to their differing perception and interpretation of reality based on the environmental surroundings in which they developed. Simultaneous with that development, their cultures cultivated separate mindsets. For Native Americans, perception and reality provided an integrated abstraction of life, including the metaphysical. Spirituality and the supernatural played a central part in the Native world as interpreted by each Native nation. Their intellectual and cultural understandings were heavily influenced by their acceptance of and desire for the supernatural as evinced by the world around them. As witnessed in their myths and legends, they based much of their values system on an understanding of the natural laws deemed to be from the Creator.

Ironically, the differences between Indian and White values have little effect on the final outcome, if history continues on its present trajectory. White America has ruled over Native America, and both will share a common fate during the forthcoming century. If American capitalistic greed continues at its current pace, with economic exploitation as its primary motive, then the country's natural resources are increasingly at risk. The conqueror does not always know best, and the conqueror will become the conquered through internal failings that spread like cancer. Such a disease has felled empires in the past and can do so again.[47] It can be hoped, however, that American greed will be cured before irreversible damage results. This warning implies an entire mending process, revisioning what is important to society in order to survive and guarantee a future for generations to come.

Notes

1. David A. Rausch and Blair Schlepp, *Native American Voices* (Grand Rapids: Baker Books, 1994), pp. 141-146.

2. Ibid., p. 151. See also, Robert Coles, *Eskimos, Chicanos, Indians*, vol. 4 of *Children of Crisis* (Boston: Little, Brown and Company, 1977).

3. Margaret Mead, "A New Preface," in Ruth Benedict, *Patterns of Culture*, (Boston: Houghton Mifflin Company, 1959), p. vii.

4. Ibid.

5. See also, Dennis McPherson and J. Douglas Rabb, *Indian from the Inside: A Study in Ethno-Metaphysics* (Thunder Bay, Ont.: Centre for Northern Studies, Lakehead University, 1993), pp. 1-16; Rausch and Schlepp, pp. 51-53.

6. See, e.g., John Joseph Mathews, *Talking to the Moon* (Norman: University of Oklahoma Press, 1945), p. 227.

7. For a chronological listing of major Indian wars and battles, see Clifford E. Trafzer and Duane Champagne, "Chronology of Native North American History, 1500 to 1965," in Duane Champagne, ed., *Native North American Almanac* (Detroit: Gales Publisher, 1994), pp. 17-55; Alan Axelrod, *Chronicle of the Indian Wars: From Colonial Times to Wounded Knee* (New York: Macmillan, 1990).

8. Donald L. Fixico, "Tribal Leaders and the Demand for Natural Energy Resources on Reservation Lands," in Peter Iverson, ed., *The Plains Indians of the Twentieth Century* (Norman: University of Oklahoma Press, 1985), p. 220; Donald L. Fixico, "Mining," in Mary Davis, ed., *Native America in the Twentieth Century* (New York: Garland Publishing, 1994), p. 343. The natural resources affecting tribal populations of fifteen different tribes are listed in Marjane Ambler, *Breaking the Iron Bonds: Indian Control of Energy Development* (Lawrence: University Press of Kansas, 1990), p. 4.

9. Michael Kearney argues that different cultures have separate worldviews due to different cosmologies and folk philosophies based on assumptions about nature, self, time, and causality, in addition to external causes of noncognitive environmental forces and internal causes of the logical relationship of intellectualizing assumptions. See, Michael Kearney, *Worldview* (Novato, Ca.: Chandler & Sharp Publishers, 1984), pp. 109-116.

10. Ethnologist James Mooney of the Bureau of American Ethnology provided general estimations of plains tribal populations as of 1780. See, Robert H. Lowie, *Indians of the Plains* (Garden City: Natural History Press, 1954), pp. 12-13.

11. William K. Powers, *Indians of the Northern Plains* (New York: G. P. Putnam's Sons, 1969), p. 9.

12. Lowie, p. 1.

13. A historical survey of each pueblo community is included in Alfonso Ortiz, ed., *Handbook of North American Indians: Southwest*, vol. 9 (Washington, D.C.: Smithsonian Institute, 1979).

14. For further information about the pueblos, see, Edward P. Dozier, *The Pueblo Indians of North America* (New York: Holt, Rinehart and Winston, 1970); Joe Sando, *The Pueblo Indians* (San Francisco: Indian Historical Press, 1976).

15. See, Robert Doherty, *Disputed Waters: Native Americans and the Great Lakes Fishery* (Lexington: University of Kentucky Press, 1990); Donald L. Fixico, "Chippewa Fishing and Hunting Rights and the Voigt Decision," in Donald L.

Fixico, ed., *An Anthology of Western Great Lakes History* (Milwaukee: University of Wisconsin-Milwaukee, 1987), pp. 481-520.

16. The Creek (or Muscogee), Cherokee, Choctaw, Chickasaw, and Seminoles are called the Five Civilized Tribes and are located in Oklahoma. Originally, they lived in the southeast woodlands of the country, and portions of their people still remain in the region–Mississippi Choctaw, North Carolina Cherokee, Alabama Creek, Florida Seminole (which actually is the Mikasuki Seminole, in that the Oklahoma Seminole are Muscogee-speaking).

17. The classic study of oral history and the various methods applied to it is Jan Vansina, *Oral Tradition: A Study in Historical Methodology* (Chicago: Aldine, 1965).

18. "The Jicarilla Genesis," in Richard Erdoes and Alfonso Ortiz, eds., *American Indian Myths and Legends* (New York: Pantheon Books, 1984), p. 83.

19. "Emerging into the Upper World," in ibid., pp. 97-98.

20. "Great Medicine Makes a Beautiful Country," in ibid., p. 111.

21. Harold Courlander, *The Fourth World of the Hopis: The Epic Story of the Hopi Indians as Preserved in Their Legends and Traditions* (Albuquerque: University of New Mexico Press, 1971), pp. 17-34.

22. Among the literature about the buffalo or bison in America, a thorough coverage is David A. Dary, *The Buffalo Book: The Full Saga of the American Animal* (Chicago: Swallow Press, 1974).

23. "Chekilli Origin of the Creek Confederacy 1735," in Colin G. Calloway, ed., *The World Turned Upside Down: Indian Voices from Early America* (New York: St. Martin's Press, 1994), p. 29. Originally quoted in Albert S. Gatschet, *A Migration Legend of the Creek Indians* (Philadelphia: D.G. Brinton, 1884).

24. A wide coverage of medicinal plants for eastern woodland Indians is Charlotte Erichsen-Brown, *Medicinal and Other Uses of North American Plants: A Historical Survey with Special Reference to the Eastern Indian Tribes* (New York: Dover Publications, 1979). A complete history of Native American agriculture is R. Douglas Hurt, *Indian Agriculture in America: Prehistory to the Present* (Lawrence: University Press of Kansas, 1987).

25. E. Adamson Hoebel, *The Cheyennes: Indians of the Great Plains* (Fort Worth: Holt, Rinehart and Winston, 1978), pp. 64-65.

26. Edward P. Dozier, *Hano: A Tewa Indian Community in Arizona* (Fort Worth: Harcourt Brace Jovanovich College Publishers, 1966), pp. 20-21.

27. Pontiac (April 27, 1763), *Chronicles of American Indian Protest* (New York: Council on Interracial Books for Children, 1979), p. 39 (originally recorded in *Michigan Pioneer and Historical Society*, vol. 8 [1886], pp. 270-271); "Pontiac, The Master of Life Speaks to the Wolf 1763," in Calloway, p. 138; "You Must Lift the Hatchet Against Them," in W.C. Vanderwerth, ed., *Indian Oratory: Famous Speeches by Noted Indian Chieftains* (Norman: University of Oklahoma Press, 1971), p. 27.

28. "The Great Race," in Erdoes and Ortiz, p. 390.

29. Oren Lyons, "An Iroquois Perspective," in Christopher Vecsey and Robert W. Venables, eds., *American Indian Environments: Ecological Issues in Native American History* (Syracuse: Syracuse University Press, 1980), p. 173.

30. "Montezuma and the Great Flood," in Erdoes and Ortiz, p. 487. Montezuma was the culture hero of the Tohono O'odham, not the Aztec emperor of the same name.

31. John G. Neihardt, *Black Elk Speaks*, 8th pr. (New York: Pocket Books, 1975), p. 8.

32. Plenty Coups and Sitting Bull, quoted in David D. Smits, "The Frontier Army and the Destruction of the Buffalo: 1865-1883," *Western Historical Quarterly* 25:3 (Autumn 1994), p. 338; previously quoted in Frank B. Linderman, *Plenty Coups: Chief of the Crows* (Lincoln: University of Nebraska Press, 1962), p. 311, and Norman B. Wiltsey, "The Great Buffalo Slaughter," in *The American West*, ed. and comp. Raymond Friday Locke (Los Angeles, 1971), p. 134.

33. See, Erichsen-Brown, *Medicinal and Other Uses of North American Plants*; also Virgil J. Vogel, *American Indian Medicine* (Norman: University of Oklahoma Press, 1970).

34. "They do not see the seasons, nor man's life, as a race run by life and death. Life is always present, death is always present. Death is no denial of life. The seasons unroll themselves before us, and man's life also. Their attitude involves 'no resignation, no subordination of desire to a stronger force, but the sense of man's oneness with the universe.'" Ruth Benedict, *Patterns of Culture* (Boston: Hoghton Mifflin Company, 1934), p. 128.

35. A discussion of the contemporary trend of family and self-directed violence on reservations is Ronet Bachman, *Death and Violence on the Reservation: Homicide, Family Violence, and Suicide in American Indian Populations* (New York: Auburn House, 1992).

36. Robert A. Ryan, "Strengths of the American Indian Family: State of the Art," in John Red Horse, August Shattuck, and Fred Hoffman, eds., *The American Indian Family: Strengths and Stresses*, Proceedings of the Conference on Research Issues, Phoenix, Az., April 17-19, 1980 (Isleta, NM: American Indian Social Research and Development Associates, 1981), pp. 30-31.

37. John Lame Deer and Richard Erdoes, *Lame Deer, Seeker of Visions: The Life of a Sioux Medicine Man* (New York: Touchstone, 1972), p. 11.

38. Donald Sander, *Navajo: Symbols of Healing* (New York: Harcourt Brace Jovanovich, 1979), pp. 206-207.

39. Anonymous Hopi, "Indian Children in Crisis," in Peter Nabokov, *Native American Testimony*, rev. ed. (New York: Viking, 1991), p. 403.

40. Lester Brown, et al., *State of the World 1994* (New York: W.W. Norton, 1994), pp. 3-4.

41. Mason Willrich, *Energy and World Politics* (New York: Free Press, 1975), pp. 40, 77.

42. For a comprehensive listing of nations and corporations, see, Frank Wilmer, *The Indigenous Voice in World Politics: From Time Immemorial* (Newbury Park, Ca.: Sage Publications, 1993), p. 129.

43. "The Gnawing," in Erdoes and Ortiz, pp. 484-485.

44. "The End of the World," in ibid., pp. 485-486.

45. "Montezuma," in ibid., pp. 488-489.

46. "Remaking the World," in ibid., pp. 496-499.

47. See, Paul Kennedy, *The Rise and Fall of the Great Powers: Economic Change and Military Conflict from 1500-2000* (New York: Vintage Books, 1989), pp. xvi-xvii.

2.

Our Homes Are Not Dumps

Creating Nuclear-Free Zones

GRACE THORPE

EDITOR'S INTRODUCTION: In 1898 George Bernard Shaw posited what the Egyptian deity Ra might have to say in the modern world. The Sun God observes that at one time human beings had only small places upon the earth, as befitted their small minds. Later, however, they proliferated and became powerful, and the great god Ra laughed because their minds "remained the same size whilst their dominion spread over the earth."[1] Nearly fifty years later nuclear physicist Albert Einstein sent a telegram to prominent Americans, in which he, like the Shavian Ra, declared, "The unleashed power of the atom has changed everything save our modes of thinking and we thus drift toward unparalleled catastrophe."[2] American Natives can attest to the truth of the statements of both Shaw and Einstein. In their handling of nuclear matters, the United States and Canada have continued the policies of conquest that have driven their actions for more than five hundred years. The process has been called "radioactive colonialism."[3]

Although only two-thirds of the uranium reserves in the United States are located on Indian lands, 80 to 90 percent of the mining and milling that has taken place in the last fifty years has been on or adjacent to reservations.[4] Numerous deaths and illnesses have been attributable to these operations, most of which have been on the lands of the Navajo and Laguna Pueblo in the American Southwest.[5]

The first lease approved by the Bureau of Indian Affairs on the sprawling Navajo Reservation in New Mexico, Arizona, and Utah went to Kerr-McGee Corporation in 1952. Not coincidentally, one of the founding owners of Kerr-McGee was Robert S. Kerr, the former governor and increasingly powerful United States Senator from Oklahoma.[6] The mine, located near Shiprock, New Mexico, operated until 1970. Of the approximately 150 Navajos who worked underground at the mine, 133 had either died of radiation-induced lung cancer or had contracted cancer and severe respiratory ailments such as fibrosis by 1980. Down's syndrome, previously unknown among the tribe, and other birth defects soared due to contaminated water, exposure to radon gas, and other radiation-related health risks. Another Kerr-McGee facility at Red Rock created similar hazards.[7] The Oklahoma-based concern continued with other operations in the area, and was joined by United Nuclear and Exxon. On July 16, 1979, a dam on a mill pond at United Nuclear's Church Rock, New Mexico, facility broke. Though overshadowed by the Three Mile Island disaster four months earlier, the resulting spill into the Río Puerco was the largest release of radioactive material disclosed to that time.[8]

The experience at Laguna Pueblo was not dissimilar. A 1952 lease to Anaconda Copper resulted in the largest open-pit uranium mine in the world. Covering twenty-eight hundred acres, prior to its closing in 1982, it was estimated that it would take enough earth to cover the entire District of Columbia to a depth of forty-five feet to fill it in.[9] Exploration was also undertaken on Mount Taylor, sacred to the Pueblos. By 1979 Laguna surface and groundwater both were contaminated with radium. Roads on the Laguna reservation were resurfaced with low-grade uranium ore, and similar material was used in the construction of tribal buildings and housing. As they had among the Navajo, cancer and birth defects increased.[10]

Parallels to the experience in the Southwest also can be found in other sites in the United States and Canada, including the Black Hills, the Spokane Reservation in Washington, and in Saskatchewan. Wastes in Saskatchewan, in chatpiles and discharged into the water, are 100 times stronger than those in the American Southwest. Of the thirty thousand persons who live in the mining area in the north of the Canadian province, two-thirds are Chipewyan or Métis. These Natives subsist on a more traditional diet than their American counterparts, with fish and game accounting for as much as two-thirds of their intake.[11] These sources have been severely contaminated by a variety of radioactive materials. Hospitalizations for cancer, birth defects, and circulatory and digestive disorders have ballooned as much as 600 percent in the Native population. As Ward Churchill concludes, "That they are suffering from the same signs of generalized health deterioration as U.S. Indians forced to live in constant proximity to uranium production sites is indicative of the extent to which the entire northern Saskatchewan ecology has . . . been contaminated by the uranium industry."[12]

Plans for new mining in North America dwarf past activities in scale. One of the most visible fights has been that of the Havasupai in Arizona, who have waged a thusfar losing struggle to prevent uranium mining on Red Butte on the border of their reservation. Red Butte is the most sacred site for the tribe, the "earth navel" from which their ancestors climbed into this world and where figures in their world renewal myth stage their periodic reunions. Basing their claims on freedom of religion, the tribe has recently lost in the United States Supreme Court.[13] The Havasupai suit has been handicapped by the fact that members of the tribe are forbidden by their religion from revealing its details. Drainage from development on Red Butte flows right through the center of Supai, their principal village. According to elder Lee Marshall, "They've got this uranium mine up there. It's going to wipe us all out—that's what we're afraid of. There'll be no future for anybody if they keep mining this uranium."[14]

Attempts at clean up and reclamation of production sites on and near Native territory have been sporadic and largely ineffectual. The Uranium Mill

Tailings Radiation Control Act, passed in 1978, has produced some benefits. It does nothing, however, to cover the mines themselves. As a result, tribes themselves have had to develop programs to reclaim their land.[15] With prohibition of human habitation in regions around uranium development the only sure way to prevent contamination, Natives fear forced removal. While Navajo chair, Peter MacDonald wrote, "Exile and expropriation has been our fate in the past. We know we can be rounded up again."[16]

As Grace Thorpe points out in the following essay, Natives have also suffered the effects of nuclear weapons production. Nuclear testing has produced fallout on tribal lands. Dumping of liquid and solid waste from the Los Alamos Scientific Laboratory between 1944 and 1952 led to radioactive sediment on sacred lands of San Ildefonso Pueblo, with plutonium levels ten times greater than those attributable to fallout.[17] The Hanford nuclear weapons plant, discussed by Thorpe, released more than 440 billion gallons of irradiated water thirty miles upstream from the Yakima Reservation in Washington between 1945 and 1989, with catastrophic effects on the Columbia River basin. Oysters caught at the mouth of the Columbia were so toxic that when one Hanford employee ate them and returned to work the following day, he set off the plant's radiation alarm.[18] Now these same interests ask Indian people to accept the waste from weapons and atomic power plants.

Around 1960, fifteen years after the inauguration of the nuclear era discussed by Thorpe, Hermann Hagedorn wrote:

> The bomb that fell on Hiroshima fell on America too.
> It fell on no city, no munition plants, no docks.
> It erased no church, vaporized no public buildings,
>   reduced no man to his atomic elements.
> But it fell, it fell.[19]

In that release, as Thorpe makes clear, Indian Country was ground zero.

The Great Spirit instructed us that, as Native people, we have a consecrated bond with our Mother Earth. We have a sacred obligation to our fellow creatures that live upon it. For this reason it is both painful and disturbing that the United States government and the nuclear power industry seem intent on forever ruining some of the little land we have remaining. The nuclear waste issue is causing American Indians to make serious, possibly even genocidal, decisions concerning the environment and the future of our peoples.

I was a corporal, stationed in New Guinea, at the end of World War II, when the first atomic bomb was dropped on Hiroshima. The so-called nuclear age has passed in the beat of a heart. As impossible as it seems, 1995 marked the fiftieth anniversary of that first blast. The question of what to do with the waste produced from commercial and military reactors involved in weapons manufacture and the generation of nuclear energy has stumped the minds of the most brilliant physicists and scientists since "Little Boy" was detonated above Japan on

August 6, 1945.[20] No safe method has yet been found for the disposal of such waste, the most lethal poison known in the history of humanity. It remains an orphan of the nuclear age.

In rich areas people have the leisure time to organize and easy access to media and elected representatives. For this reason the nuclear industry is talking about locating disposal sites in poor regions. Indians are being deluged by requests. Devastation due to nuclear energy, however, is nothing new to Indian peoples.

Between 1950 and 1980, approximately fifteen thousand persons worked in uranium mines. One-fourth of these were Indian. Many of these mines were located on lands belonging to the Navajos and the Pueblos. In 1993 Dr. Louise Abel of the Indian Health Service disclosed that, of the six hundred miners tested who had worked underground for more than a year, only five qualified for payments under the Radiation Exposure Compensation Act of 1990. By 1994 only 155 uranium miners and millers or their families had been awarded compensation, fewer than half of the claims filed to that time.[21] Radiation from tailings piles, the debris left after the uranium is extracted, has leached into groundwater that feeds Indian homes, farms, and ranches. High concentrations of radon gas continually seep out of the piles and are breathed by Natives in the area. Background levels of radiation are at dangerous levels. Thus Indians living near the mines face the same health risks as those working underground.[22]

In 1973 and 1974 two nuclear power reactors commenced operation at Prairie Island, Minnesota, only a few hundred yards from the homes, businesses, and childcare center of the Prairie Island Mdewankanton Sioux. The facility was on the site of an ancient Indian village and burial mound dating back at least two thousand years. On October 2, 1979, a twenty-seven-minute release of radiation from the plants forced evacuation of the facility, but the tribe was not notified until several days later. By 1989 radioactive tritium was detected in the drinking water, forcing the Mdewankanton to dig an eight-hundred-foot-deep well and construct a water tower, completed in 1993. Prairie Island residents are exposed to six times the cancer risk deemed acceptable by the Minnesota Department of Health.[23]

By 1986 the problem of nuclear waste disposal had become acute. The U.S. Department of Energy began to explore the possibility of locating a permanent nuclear repository in Minnesota's basalt and granite hardrock deposits. Among the sites considered was the White Earth Reservation in the northwestern part of the state. The Anishinaabe who live there took the government's interest seriously enough to commission a study of the potential impact. The Minnesota legislature responded by passing the Radioactive Waste Management Act, stating that no such facility could be located within the state without the express authorization of the legislature.[24]

The following year, however, Congress voted to locate the permanent repository at Yucca Mountain, about 100 miles northwest of Las Vegas, Nevada, on land belonging to the Western Shoshone. Plans called for the opening of the facility in 2010. The Nuclear Waste Policy Act set in motion a nationwide search for a community that would accept a temporary storage site until Yucca Mountain came online.[25] Indian tribes again were specifically targeted.

One by one, tribes who considered accepting the so-called Monitored Retrievable Storage (MRS) facility on tribal land decided against it. Today, of the seventeen tribes who began discussions and study, only three remain: the Mescalero Apache of New Mexico, the Skull Valley Goshutes in Utah, and the Fort McDermitt Reservation in Nevada (which houses both Paiutes and Western Shoshones). In addition, Pojoaque Pueblo in New Mexico announced in March 1995 that it was considering locating the MRS on tribal lands. This move, however, was an overt powerplay to persuade the New Mexico legislature to halt legislation that would expand gambling in the state to the detriment of the Pojoaque's own gaming interests. According to Pojoaque Governor Jacob Viarrial, "If the public does not want his tribe to store the waste, they should put pressure on the lawmakers to put a halt to the expansion of gaming off reservations."[26]

The National Environmental Coalition of Native Americans (NECONA) was formed in 1993 in Las Vegas to lobby against the MRS or any nuclear waste disposal on Indian lands and to encourage Native nations to declare themselves Nuclear Free Zones instead. As the number of tribes considering the MRS dwindled, pressure on Washington mounted. NECONA persuaded U.S. Senator Jeff Bingaman of New Mexico, who had been one of the moving forces behind the Radiation Exposure Compensation Act for uranium miners, to oppose the MRS on the energy and appropriations committees. As a result, Congress withheld funding for the program.[27]

With the federal government out of the MRS-construction business, but with the problem of waste disposal still unresolved, utilities began to get desperate. Dozens of plants would be forced to shut down or find alternative sources of fuel unless a temporary storage site was located in the near future. Thirty-three utilities, accounting for ninety four reactors, began seeking a location. Led by Northern States Power (NSP), the consortium approached Minnesota about locating a facility adjacent to the NSP plant at Prairie Island. Although the plant supplies 15 percent of the state's electricity, "not a single kilowatt reaches the Mdewankanton community it borders."[28]

The Prairie Island Sioux had applied for a Phase I MRS grant, which provided DOE funds for initial feasibility studies. According to tribal officials, however, the application was tactical. The intent was to use the government's own money to prove that neither an MRS nor a nuclear power plant should be located at Prairie Island.[29] One study showed that the cancer risk would be twenty-three times greater than the state standard. At the time of the NSP initiative, a survey showed that 91.6 percent of the tribe opposed construction of the MRS.[30] The tribe fought the NSP proposal before the legislature and won. They subsequently declared the Prairie Island Reservation a Nuclear Free Zone.

Meanwhile NSP had signed an agreement with the Mescalero Apache to move ahead with development of an MRS in New Mexico. Under the terms of the agreement, the tribe was to seek two twenty-year licenses to store up to forty thousand metric tons of spent nuclear fuel. Total revenues over the forty-year life of the facility, estimated at $2.3 billion, would bring as much as $250 million in benefits to the tribe.[31] Although the tribal council believed that it could proceed with the program by its own authority, it was confident enough of victory to put the issue to tribal members in the form of a public referendum. However, according to a Native newspaper, *The Circle*, opponents of the storage facility considered the Mescalero tribal government, headed by Chairman Wendell Chino, "'dictatorial,' and likely to conduct a campaign of intimidation and vote fraud if a referendum takes place."[32]

I used to work for the National Congress of American Indians when Wendell Chino was its chair. He's been Mescalero chairman since 1962, and he has done great things for the people there; I respected him. He is tough, however, and can be a very imposing figure. The sad thing is that the Mescalero don't need this nuclear waste. They have a five-star resort, a casino, two ski lifts, and a sawmill. They have wonderful resources for forestry. Everybody thinks, "Ah, the poor Apache, they need this development," but they don't.[33]

The referendum took place on January 31, 1995. The Mescaleros voted down the MRS by a vote of 490 to 362. Shortly after the vote, however, a petition began circulating, calling for a new election. According to Fred Peso, the vice chairman, "A group of grass-roots people presented the petition to the tribal council." Peso blamed, "outside interference from environmentalists and other anti-tribal groups" for the defeat of the proposal.[34] In reality, Wendell Chino's powerful political machine was behind the petition. The tribal government controls jobs, housing, schools, and the court system. One of the organizers of the petition drive, Fred Kaydahzinne, is director of the federally subsidized tribal housing program. As Rufina Marie Laws, one of the referendum's opponents stated, "It was real hard for people to turn him down."[35] Petition organizers gathered more than seven hundred signatures calling for a new vote. When a second ballot was held on March 9, 1995, the measure passed 593 to 372.

There is a great deal of uncertainty as to what will happen now at Mescalero. Opponents of the MRS could seek yet another referendum. They have stated that they will appeal the second vote to the tribal court, but they are not optimistic. The state of New Mexico has prohibited transport of spent nuclear fuel on state highways in an attempt to derail the proposal. Vice Chairman Peso has announced that the tribe will proceed with licensing applications and technological studies. Officials of NSP have announced that they will move ahead with plans for the project. Contracts are being finalized, and licensing is anticipated to be concluded by December 1996.[36]

If the Mescaleros withdraw, there are the Skull Valley Goshutes and the tribes at Fort McDermitt standing right behind them. Both reservations are isolated, and unemployment is a problem on both. At the moment, Fort McDermitt seems to be out of the running because it straddles the Nevada state line. The law says that the MRS and the permanent site cannot be in the same state, but that could change. The Goshutes already have waste incinerators, nerve-gas plants, and a bombing range bordering on their lands. There is a feeling of indifference about the MRS among the few people who live on the reservation. They have signed an accord with Richard Stallings, a federal negotiator charged with locating a temporary storage site, to provide a framework for further talks, and the University of Utah has agreed to undertake a feasibility study in conjunction with the utilities.[37]

We should also not believe that the problem is limited to the United States. First Nations in Canada are facing the issue. An article in the free-trade agreement between Canada and the United States prohibits Canada from preventing nuclear waste coming into the country. The Meadow Lake Cree in Saskatchewan are in discussions with Atomic Energy of Canada Ltd. (AECL), a corporation of the Canadian government, concerning becoming a permanent repository. According to recent reports, they have also held negotiations with the Mescalero to become the storage site for wastes temporarily housed at the proposed New Mexico facility. Meanwhile AECL continues to market nuclear technology throughout the Americas.[38] The situation in Mexico is terrible, too. They have very little environmental regulation. At NECOMA we hear reports of "jelly babies," babies born without any bones, due to environmental contamination.

Tribal officials at Mescalero and other reservations that have considered the MRS contend that the issue is one of sovereignty. They use the issue of sovereignty against the environment. It is a very tough tightrope to walk. How can you go say to a tribe, "Hey, you shouldn't be doing this. You should be protecting the earth." Then they would turn around and reply, "Hey, we can do as we please. This is Indian sovereignty." In one sense, they would be right. Allowing utilities to build MRS facilities on our lands, however, is not truly an expression of sovereignty. Those supporting such sites are selling our sovereignty. The utilities are using our names and our trust lands to bypass environmental regulations. The issue is not sovereignty. The issue is Mother Earth's preservation and survival. The issue is environmental racism. The purpose of NECOMA is to invite tribes to express their sovereign national rights in a more creative way in favor of our Mother, by joining the growing number of tribal governments that are choosing to declare their lands Nuclear Free Zones.[39] Fred Peso at Mescalero has declared, "It is ironic that the state continues to fight the tribe [over the MRS] when New Mexico has enjoyed the benefits of nuclear projects since 1945."[40] The real irony is that after years of trying to destroy it, the United States is promoting Indian national sovereignty–just so it can dump its waste on Native land.[41]

The DOE and the utilities have said that it is natural that we, as Native peoples, should accept radioactive waste on our lands. They have convinced some of our traditionalists that as keepers of the land we must accept it. As Russell Means has said, however, "We have always had our false prophets."[42] The government and the nuclear power industry attempt to flatter us about our abilities as "earth stewards." Yet as I declared to the National Congress of American Indians in 1993, "It is a perversion of our beliefs and an insult to our intelligence to say that we are 'natural stewards' of these wastes."[43] The real intent of the government and the utilities is to rid themselves of this extremely hazardous garbage on Indian lands so they are free to generate more of it.

Our traditional spiritual leaders have warned us for hundreds of years about taking resources from the earth. They have warned that the earth will become unbalanced and be destroyed. In one of the stories the Navajos have about their origins, they were warned about the dangers of uranium. The People "emerged from the third world into the fourth and present world and were given a choice. They were told to choose between two yellow powders. One was yellow dust from the rocks, and the other was corn pollen. The [People] chose corn pollen, and the gods nodded in assent. They also issued a warning. Having chosen the corn pollen, the Navajos were to leave the yellow dust in the ground. If it was ever removed, it would bring evil."[44]

Wherever there are uranium mines, wherever there are nuclear power plants, and wherever our people have been downwind of nuclear tests, the cancer rate goes up. As a result of atomic testing, many of the people among the Western Shoshone in Nevada now have thyroid cancer. They are dying a younger death. They have leukemia, which was unheard of in earlier times. In Minnesota archaeologists excavating Prairie Island thousands of years in the future could be exposed to levels of radiation high enough to cause cancer.[45] Pollution and toxic waste from the Hanford nuclear weapons facility threaten all Native peoples who depend on Columbia River salmon for their existence.[46] A few years ago a vial of nuclear material about the size of a human little finger was lost on the road from Los Angeles to Sacramento. An SOS went out to all the newspapers and radio and television stations about this little silver vial: "If you find it, don't pick it up. Alert us immediately. If you pick it up and put it in your pocket for two days, you'll get sick. If you keep it a week, it can kill you. If you breathe the equivalent of 100th of a grain of salt, it can cause lung cancer."

Now those whose visited all these horrors upon us want us to accept their nuclear waste, too. Darelynn Lehto, the vice president of the Prairie Island Mdewankanton, testified before the Minnesota State Senate during the fight against the MRS there, "It is the worst kind of environmental racism to force our tribe to live with the dangers of nuclear waste simply because no one else is willing to do so."[47] Why do we tolerate it? How long can we tolerate it? What kind of society permits the manufacture of products that cannot be safely disposed? NECOMA is currently lobbying Congress for a bill that will say simply, "Nothing is to be manufactured, used, or reproduced in the United States that cannot be safely disposed of." Is that too simple a thing for a legislator to understand? Probably it is, but it makes sense, doesn't it?

Spent nuclear fuel is permeated with plutonium, the principal ingredient in atomic weapons. Plutonium has a half life of 24,360 years. Significant amounts would therefore remain active for more than 50,000 years. The so-called permanent repository proposed for Yucca Mountain is designed to hold cannisters containing nuclear waste for only 10,000 years. The steel containers holding the material would disintegrate long before the radioactivity had decayed.[48]

Yucca Mountain, however, is nowhere near to becoming a permanent repository. It was originally to have begun receiving waste in 1998, but near unanimous opposition in Nevada slowed the process. In 1992 a earthquake measuring 5.6 on the Richter scale struck the area, raising additional questions as to the site's viability.[49] Most recently, scientists at the Los Alamos National Laboratory in New Mexico raised the possibility that wastes buried at the Nevada location could explode after the steel containers dissolve, setting off a nuclear chain reaction.[50]

These factors make the targeted date of 2010—when Yucca Mountain currently is estimated to be accepting shipments of waste—look improbable. Mescalero tribal officials, in obtaining their tribe's permission, emphasized that their proposed facility was strictly temporary and that "at no time would the tribe take possession of the fuel."[51] What will happen, however, if Yucca Mountain does not come online as projected? What if no permanent storage site is available at the end of the MRS's forty years of "temporary" storage? New Mexico Attorney General Tom Udall has raised similar questions. He fears that the state "may ultimately have to pick up the pieces."[52] Indians suspect we know better, however, who will be left holding the bag.

The debate over nuclear waste has already done serious damage to harmonious relationships among our people. Why must we go through this divisive agony again?[53]

As a mother and a grandmother, I am concerned about the survival of our people, just as Mother Earth is concerned about the survival of her children. There is currently a moratorium on construction of nuclear power plants in the United States. There is also current legislation, however, that would allow new building if arrangements are made for disposal of the waste. Is this the legacy that we want to leave for our children and for our Mother Earth? The Iroquois say that in making any decision one should consider the impact for seven generations to come. As Thom Fassett, who is Iroquois, reminds us, taking such a view on these issues often makes us "feel we're alone, rolling a stone up the hill. It keeps rolling back down on us."[54] That may be the only way, however, for us to live up to our sacred duty to the land and to all of creation.

Notes

1. George Bernard Shaw, "Caesar and Cleopatra," prologue (1898).

2. Albert Einstein, telegram to noted Americans, May 24, 1946 (published in the *New York Times*, May 25, 1946).

3. See, Ward Churchill, "Radioactive Colonialism: A Hidden Holocaust in Native North America," in Ward Churchill, *Struggle for the Land: Indigenous Resistance to Genocide, Ecocide, and Expropriation in Contemporary North America* (Monroe, Me.: Common Courage Press, 1993), pp. 261-328.

4. See, Peter MacDonald, "Navajo Natural Resources," in Christopher Vecsey and Robert W. Venables, eds., *American Indian Environments: Ecological Issues in Native American History* (Syracuse: Syracuse University Press, 1980), pp. 165-166; Churchill, p. 264. MacDonald is the former tribal chair of the Navajo Nation.

5. MacDonald, pp. 167-168.

6. See, Jace Weaver, *Then to the Rock Let Me Fly: Luther Bohanon and Judicial Activism* (Norman: University of Oklahoma Press, 1993), pp. 44, 140-141; see also, Anne Hodges Morgan, *Robert S. Kerr: The Senate Years* (Norman: University of Oklahoma Press, 1977).

7. Churchill, pp. 266-267.

8. Marjane Ambler, *Breaking the Iron Bonds: Indian Control of Energy Development* (Lawrence: University of Kansas Press, 1990), p. 175.

9. Churchill, p. 271. The distinction of the Jackpile-Paguate mine as the world's largest was supplanted after its closing by Namibia's Rossing Mine.

10. Ibid., pp. 273-274.

11. Ibid., pp. 276, 283, 288-299. Among the Crees in Québec, traditional food sources account for as much as 90 percent of Native diets. Boyce Richardson, *Strangers Devour the Land* (Post Mills, Vt.: Chelsea Green Publishing, 1991), p. 245.

12. Churchill, p. 297.

13. Havasupai Tribe v. United States, 752 F. Supp. 1471 (D. Ariz. 1990), *affirmed* 943 F.2d 32 (9th Cir. 1991), *cert. denied* 112 S. Ct. 1559 (1992).

14. Stephen Trimble, *The People: Indians of the American Southwest* (Santa Fe: SAR Press, 1993), pp. 223, 211; John F. Martin, "Havasupai," in Mary Davis, ed., *Native America in the Twentieth Century* (New York: Garland Publishing, 1994), p. 232.

15. Peter H. Eichstaedt, *If You Poison Us: Uranium and Native Americans* (Santa Fe: Red Crane Books, 1994), pp. 128, 149. The volume is a comprehensive discussion of the problems faced by Natives as a result of uranium mining.

16. MacDonald, p. 170.

17. Richard O. Clemmer, "The Energy Economy and Pueblo Peoples," in *Native Americans and Energy Development, II* (Boston: Anthropology Resource Center/Seventh Generation Fund, 1984), p. 103.

18. Churchill, pp. 286-287.

19. Hermann Hagedorn, "The Bomb That Fell on America," quoted in Wesley D. Camp, ed., *What a Piece of Work Is Man* (Engelwood Cliffs, N.J.: Prentice Hall, 1990), p. 16.

20. "Little Boy" was the name given to the first device, dropped on Hiroshima by the bomber Enola Gay. Three days later, on August 9, "Fat Man" was released by Bockscar and detonated above Nagasaki. See, "'Bockscar' 'ended' WWII," *Denver Post*, March 19, 1995.

21. Eichstaedt, pp. 151, 170.

22. Ibid., pp. 142-146.

23. Jeff Armstrong, "Prairie Island Confronts Nuclear Threat," *The Circle* (April, 1994), pp. 16-17.

24. Ibid., p. 16.

25. George Johnson, "Nuclear Waste Dump Gets Tribe's Approval in Revote," *New York Times* (March 11, 1995), p. 6.

26. "MRS Plans Back on Burner: Pueblo Pursues Own Nuclear Waste Plan," *Indian Country Today* (March 16, 1995), p. 2.

27. Johnson, p. 6.

28. Armstrong, p. 16.

29. Ibid., p. 17.

30. Ibid., p. 16.

31. Harlan McKosato, "Mescalero Nuclear Site Back on Track," *Indian Country Today* (March 16, 1995), p. 1.

32. Armstrong, p. 17.

33. According to a recent article by D. C. Cole, a Chiricahua Apache, despite these successful business ventures, unemployment remains a problem. Unemployment was estimated at 30 percent, with much of the rest of the work force underemployed. Health and education levels remain below the national averages. D. C. Cole, "Apache," in Davis, p. 46. The nuclear project is anticipated to produce between two hundred and three hundred jobs (McKosato, p. 1).

34. Johnson, p. 6.

35. Ibid.

36. McKosato, pp. 1-2; "Apache Continue with Nuclear Dump Plan," *Indian Country Today* (June 8, 1995), p. A2.

37. See, "Goshutes Sign Nuclear Waste Agreement," *News from Indian Country* (Mid December 1994), p. 5.

38. Joyce Nelson, "Candu Diplomacy and NAFTA's Nuclear Agenda," *Z Magazine* (June 1995), pp. 30-32.

39. See, Grace Thorpe, "Statement to the National Congress of American Indians" (Sparks, Nev., September 1, 1993). Currently fifteen tribes have passed resolutions declaring their lands to be Nuclear Free Zones. The first was the Sac and Fox Nation of Oklahoma, of which Ms. Thorpe is a member. In addition, through the efforts of Norma Kassi, the Yukon Territory in Canada has declared itself an NFZ as well.

40. Johnson, p. 6.

41. Grace Thorpe, "Radioactive Racism? Native Americans and the Nuclear Waste Legacy," *Indian Country Today* (March 16, 1995), p. A5.

42. Russell Means, comment at the North American Native Workshop on Environmental Justice, Iliff School of Theology, Denver, Co. (March 17, 1995).

43. Thorpe, "Statement" (September 1, 1993).

44. Eichstaedt, p. 47, quoting Anna Rondon, November 1992.

45. Armstrong, p. 16.

46. David Rich Lewis, "Environmental Issues," in Davis, p. 189.

47. Darelynn Lehto, testimony before Minnesota State Senate, March 29, 1994, quoted in *The Circle* (April, 1994), p. 17.

48. William J. Broad, "Scientists Fear Atomic Explosion of Buried Waste," *New York Times* (March 5, 1995), p. 18.

49. Armstrong, pp. 16-17.

50. Broad, pp. 1, 18.

51. McKosato, p. A2.

52. Johnson, p. 6.

53. Thorpe, "Radioactive Racism?," p. A5.

54. Thom White Wolf Fassett, North American Native Workshop on Environmental Justice, Iliff School of Theology, Denver, Co. (March 17, 1995).

3.

Custer Rides Again—
This Time on the Exxon *Valdez*[1]

Mining Issues in Wisconsin

JUSTINE SMITH

EDITOR'S INTRODUCTION: One of the many conflicting images Americans have of Indians is of resource-rich Natives, living like royalty off royalties. The stereotype probably survives from the 1920s when, thanks to petroleum discoveries, the Osage were the richest people per capita in the world.[2] In actuality, although vast mineral and energy resources underlie Indian lands, a minority of tribes possesses lands rich in such materials.[3]

Donald Fixico noted that it is one of the ironies of five hundred years of colonialism that the nation's poorest minority must make decisions about such tremendous resources.[4] As a result of this paradox, A.T. Anderson, an Iroquois who served as special assistant to the American Indian Policy Review Commission, argued in 1976 that Natives received too small a return on development of their resources. Because of difficulties in obtaining capital and credit, it was impossible for them to bargain effectively, forcing them to accept inequitable leasing agreements with inadequate royalty and lease rates. Pursuant to the Omnibus Mineral Leasing Act of 1938, nearly all these leases can be extended indefinitely if production occurs, exacerbating low-price problems. In addition, mineral development inevitably increases the non-Native population on reservations, creating political, cultural, and social problems for tribes. Finally, stated Anderson, "Indians are [virtually] unable to prevent environmental degradation."[5] Although the economic imbalance has been addressed somewhat in recent years–in 1991 mineral revenues exceeded $142 million[6]–the environmental damage of which Anderson spoke continues.

As the following article by Justine Smith makes clear, mining has had a devastating impact on indigenous peoples throughout the Americas for hundreds of years. From the earliest period of colonization, the Spaniards in the South placed a high priority on mineral production and enslaved thousands upon thousands of Natives for work in the mines.[7] Exploitation of both Natives and their lands for mineral wealth has continued to the present day. In ecological terms the effect has been equally severe. In Colorado, for example, once home to Cheyenne, Arapaho, and Ute peoples, there are abandoned mining sites from the nineteenth century that look as if the environmental damage could have been done yesterday.[8] Though reclamation technology unquestionably has improved since those mines were played out, Smith reminds us that reclaiming exhausted mining lands remains a difficult, if not impossible, task today. In 1974, two years before Anderson issued his assessment of mining operations on Indian lands, the National Academy of Sciences suggested that, in the interest of the nation's resource needs and economic stability, certain mining locations within the United States be considered "national sacrifice areas."[9] Such areas would, by virtue of extreme environmental degradation, become unfit for human habitation. Coincidentally, the areas suggested corresponded to the regions with the highest Native populations in the country. Russell Means has pointed out the particularly genocidal impact of such a policy on Natives. Because of their links to specific lands, they cannot simply uproot and move to other places, and yet to remain invites physical extermination. Thus to sacrifice any geographic location means sacrificing all indigenous people who dwell there.[10] All Natives thus become a national sacrifice people.

Because of the technological problems associated with mining there, Wisconsin has until recently been spared the resource wars that have afflicted much of Indian Country. Although the northern portion of the state was considered for designation as a national sacrifice area in the 1970s, such a move is not now under discussion.[11] Currently, only one mine, Kennecott's Ladysmith, is in operation. Both Natives and non-Natives are imperiled, however, by the proposed mine at Crandon, near Mole Lake. Anti-Indian groups that coalesced during the "fishing wars" are again accusing the tribes, which seek to block the mine, of using "special rights" to prevent economic development. With the support of mining interests, they have made connections to larger national right-wing organizations, including the Citizens Equal Rights Alliance.[12]

The events described by Smith have all the appearances of a major confrontation. Don Fixico states that "the last decade of the twentieth century represents a battleground for tribes to protect their natural resources."[13] If they are to win the battle, Natives "experienced with memories of victimization in the name of capitalism [must] operate with the vigorous shrewd attitudes of modern corporations" they oppose.[14] That means being as wise as serpents and considerably less gentle than doves.[15]

Saving the planet has never been an issue of money, but rather a matter of resourcefulness and motivation of individuals.

—Spencer Beebe[16]

In 1993 a Minnesota ninth grader wrote an essay for his English class in which he called Natives "beer-bellied, poaching maniacs," who "think that because they were in America before we were, they should be able to kill as many of whatever kind of animal they wish. But as I recall, we won the country from them fair and square." He continued, "We are a dying race. They are expanding like rabbits, and soon we will be the minority and live by their laws."[17] The paper refers to the assertion by Indians of rights guaranteed them by treaties made in the nineteenth century. It is difficult for those who do not live in the upper Midwest to appreciate fully the intensity of vituperation engendered by the demand for these rights and their vindication in courts of law.[18] Yet these remarks by a teenager may give a taste.

I became involved with these struggles in 1989. Federal courts in Wisconsin had, beginning in the early eighties, recognized the rights of the Chippewa[19] to hunt, fish, and gather on territory in northern Wisconsin that had been ceded by various treaties.[20] As a result of these court victories, many anti-Indian hate groups coalesced to protest exercise of Native rights. Many others, however, went to northern Wisconsin during spearfishing season to help protect Chippewa fishers from abusive and sometimes violent White mobs. "Spear an Indian; save a walleye," or "Spear a pregnant squaw; save two walleye" were common slogans in these protests. As the struggle continued, however, we recognized that the real issue related to development of energy resources. As long as the Chippewa maintained the right to hunt, fish, and gather on ceded lands, the treaties could be used to challenge the many mining companies that wanted to begin mineral extraction in the area. Because such mining would destroy the environment, the Chippewa effectively would be prevented from being able to conduct their traditional activities guaranteed by treaty.

Long ago, glaciers covered most of Wisconsin. Eventually they receded, despositing large quantities of rock as they did. As they pulled upward, certain areas, especially around Lake Superior, were left with massive amounts of rock and not much soil. This is the so-called Canadian Shield, occupying much of Wisconsin. In some areas, however, the surface of this heavy glacial rock was covered with very rich soil. Consequently, there are strong agricultural communities in many areas of the state. The area around Lake Superior is also very rich in mineral resources. Because, however, of the large amounts of rock overburdening these minerals, it was not technologically feasible to mine for many of them until recently. For this reason the resource wars in Wisconsin are more recent than in other parts of the country.

Many of the early treaties in northern Wisconsin revolved around access to mineral resources. The Fond Du Lac Treaty on August 5, 1826, ceded all mining rights to the United States government. They hung "peace medals" around the Natives' necks and took their wealth.[21] The following year a similar treaty with the Chippewa, Winnebago, Potawatomi, and Menominee dispossessed them of their lead mines.[22]

An 1842 treaty granted Keeweenaw copper mines to the United States. Finally, the 1854 treaty ceded the remainder of Chippewa iron. Thus, at a very early date American business interests knew that valuable resources were there. The fortunes of Morgan, Rockefeller, and other robber barons were built largely from the resources in the Lake Superior region.

In 1975 the Bureau of Mines, under contract with the Bureau of Indian Affairs, performed explorations on Indian lands. In Wisconsin they found large deposits of copper and zinc. Gold and uranium were discovered to a lesser extent. As a result, mining corporations began to take serious notice. One of the principal companies was Exxon. That same year Exxon Minerals Co., a subsidiary of the oil giant founded by John D. Rockefeller, located one of the largest zinc-copper sulfide deposits in the world (estimated at fifty-five million tons) near Crandon, Wisconsin, on land adjacent to the reservation of the Mole Lake Sokaogan Chippewa. Situated in Forest County at the headwaters of the Wolf River, the deposit was estimated to contain enough mineral to produce ore for up to twenty-five years.[23] British-based mining giant Rio Tinto Zinc began mining copper at Ladysmith, and Canadian concerns also staked claims on zinc and silver. All of these discoveries in the upper two-thirds of Wisconsin were made on ceded lands enjoying the treaty protection previously discussed.[24] Tribes threatened by the development include the Chippewa, Oneida, Menominee, Potawatomi, and Stockbridge-Munsee.

Phelps-Dodge approached the Lac du Flambeau Chippewa, near the Michigan-Wisconsin border, in order to obtain mineral exploration rights. In a fashion reminiscent of treaty negotiations of the last century, over the course of a single night of discussions the corporation proposed a contract, pursuant to which Phelps-Dodge would be allowed to explore Indian lands with the tribe putting up $250,000. Phelps-Dodge expected the tribal council to execute the agreement on the spot.[25] Unlike the tribes of the nineteenth century, however, Flambeau consulted an attorney. When they rejected the contract and made a counter-proposal, the corporation lost interest. In a similar situation, Exxon offered the Mole Lake Chippewa $20,000 to explore their territory. Exxon had paid another party, located just a few miles away, $200,000 to conduct exploration on forty acres. Here, however, they proposed only $20,000 in exchange for the right to explore nineteen hundred acres, with an automatic right to extract any resources found. According to Al Gedicks and Zoltan Grossman, a founder of the Midwest Treaty Network, "The Mole Lake tribal council showed by ripping up [the] $20,000 Exxon check . . . that their land is more precious than greed."[26]

Prior to 1983 there was a united effort by both Natives and non-Natives to protect northern Wisconsin. Tribes were attempting to protect their sovereignty. At the same time, the area is considered a pristine natural environment and is heavily dependent on tourism. Thus, non-Natives were equally concerned about mining operations in the region. This united front started to disintegrate in 1983, when courts began to recognize Chippewa rights to hunt, fish, and gather pursuant to treaties.[27] Mining companies, fearing that these treaty protections might halt their mining plans, began to support and foment anti-Indian sentiment, spreading misinformation that it was Native spearfishers, not mining operations, that caused environmental degradation. Consequently, non-Indians began to focus their anger on Indians rather than mining interests. Two organizations, PARR (Protect America's Rights and Resources) and STA (Stop Treaty Abuse) began to encourage racially motivated violence toward spearfishers, their families, and Indians in general. To raise money, these groups began marketing Treaty Beer with anti-Indian messages on the can.[28]

After a decade of strong opposition from tribal and environmental organizations, Exxon abandoned its plans to develop the Mole Lake site in 1986, claiming that mineral prices were too low to make production viable. It returned, however, in February 1994, announcing its intention to conduct operations through Crandon Mining Co., a newly formed joint venture between Exxon and Canadian-based Rio Algom.[29] It plans to begin construction in autumn 1996 and estimates that it stands to make $4.5 billion from the operation—despite the fact that mineral prices are largely unchanged from 1986.

The proposed mine at Mole Lake will have far-reaching environmental consequences. The Great Lakes bioregion is one of the most geologically and ecologically sensitive places in the hemisphere. Any mining in this geological formation will have devastating and long-lasting effects.[30] The mine itself would cover an area of 866 acres and produce fourteen thousand tons of ore a day. Over its lifetime, it will generate an estimated sixty million tons of acidic waste, the weight of twelve Great Pyramids in Egypt. About half of these materials will be dumped back to fill mine shafts. The remainder will be dumped into tailings ponds ninety feet deep and spreading over 365 acres.[31]

Under one version of the proposed project, the mine would contaminate the Wisconsin River, which flows into the Mississippi. The Mississippi flows through ten states before reaching the Gulf of Mexico. In addition, Crandon would discharge waste into the Wolf River. The Wolf flows into Lake Winnebago. Lake Winnebago then empties into Green Bay, which in turn empties into Lake Michigan. Proposed operations would thus pollute both the Mississippi and the Lake Michigan watersheds. Over fifteen thousand lakes, plus numerous rivers and streams, are part of the unique geology of Wisconsin. All these sources, however, comprise only 3 percent of the water supply in the state because of immense groundwater reservoirs. At Mole Lake, the twenty-five-hundred-foot shafts would drain groundwater "in much the same way that a hypodermic needle draws blood from a patient."[32] After use in the mining process, this water would then be discharged into the Wolf. Operations would cause the water table to drop by as much as seven feet over a four-square mile area. Exxon justifies this by saying that the process will create wetlands[33] and thus enhance rather than degrade the environment. In reality, the mine could destroy eighty acres of wetlands, and those that would be "created" would be merely the result of drawing down lakes to a depth at which they would qualify for wetland status. The corporation is targeting the area of waste discharge in Rice Lake, the site of the Mole Lake communities wild rice crops. Contamination would endanger both fish in the lake and the rice crop, discharging six million gallons of water over the seven-acre site.[34] Although the Chippewa complained that the mine would destroy the wild rice, critical to their way of life, a biologist for Exxon reportedly mistook the rice crop for "lake weeds" and could not understand the concern over them. When pressed, Exxon did admit that its environmental impact study reported that the mine would render the Mole Lake reservation's subsistence usages as "less than effective." Despite this, recent changes in Wisconsin's environmental regulation have removed from Exxon any responsibility to monitor groundwater within the mining boundaries, and the Wisconsin Department of Natural Resources has exempted the company from the need to obtain a permit for the Crandon mine, finding that the water would not be discharged into a wetland.[35]

The stakes at Mole Lake are raised greatly because the mine would be a sulfide mine. Sulfide wastes have a toxicity and persistence level similar to radioactive nuclear waste. There is an area in California known as Iron Mountain, which is so contaminated from sulfide mining that streams flowing through the area will never again be able to support any aquatic life or vegetation of any kind. When metals such as copper, zinc, silver, or gold are mined, metallic sulfide waste results. When this waste comes into contact with air or water, it oxidizes, forming sulfuric acid and highly poisonous heavy metals, including mercury, lead, arsenic, and cadmium. Though it is possible to extract uranium from the ore, Exxon has not acknowledged such an interest.[36] In a wet area like Wisconsin, the potential for contamination is high. In addition, there is no technology to reclaim a sulfide mine, and the Bureau of Mines admits that contamination is a virtual certainty. Finally, though the waste will remain poisonous for centuries, Exxon's responsibility for the Crandon site would continue for only ten to thirty years after the mine closes.[37] In England, there are sulfide mines nearly a thousand years old where toxic waste still persists.

The one difference between radioactive and sulfide wastes is that, over time, radioactive waste eventually degrades. Sulfide waste never degrades. Waste dumped into tailings ponds eventually will have to be treated. Much of the water will be discharged into the Wolf River. Further, these proposed ponds are just above the water table. If they leak, the surrounding communities will have nothing but contaminated water to drink. In order to control the potential for leakage, Exxon plans to line the ponds with just eight inches of clay. The Environmental Protection Agency has acknowledged that in almost any situation leaks "will inevitably occur." Even Exxon's own geologist admitted that "contamination is bound to occur no matter how wisely [the facility] is designed," and one of its engineers bluntly stated, "You couldn't think of a more difficult place to mine." The state Department of Natural Resources estimates that sulfate levels in surrounding waters would increase by five times; lead and arsenic levels would rise by three times.[38]

When the United States Congress passed the Wild and Scenic Rivers Act of 1968, the lower half of the Wolf River, flowing through the Menominee Reservation, was one of eight rivers set aside for immediate inclusion as a National Wild and Scenic River. In addition, the entire Wolf was been designated an Outstanding Water Resource (OWR) by the state of Wisconsin. It is one of the preeminent trout streams in the nation.[39] These designations mean that absolutely no environmental degradation is allowed. If any company uses the river, it must leave it as pure as it was before the usage. Exxon, although it opposed the OWR designation, contends that it can meet this standard. Environmentalists and sports enthusiasts have testified, however, that it is impossible.

The Wolf eventually joins the Fox River. The Fox is currently one of the most contaminated in Wisconsin. When discharge from the Wolf hits the chlorine pollution of the Fox, it will react, creating an entirely new set of poisons. In addition, the trout of the Wolf would be adversely affected, and when the waters empty into Green Bay, major fisheries there would be damaged as well.

Exxon currently is considering an alternate plan in case it is prohibited from dumping waste into the Wolf. In that event, it contemplates possibly constructing a bypass into the Wisconsin River. As already noted, the Wisconsin feeds the Mississippi. This demonstrates the need for a broad resistance to the proposed mine. Although many groups have organized to protect the more scenic Wolf River, this will be insufficient if waste simply can be diverted into the Wisconsin.

Unlike the current condition of the Wolf, the track records of participants in the Mole Lake/Crandon project are considerably less than pristine.

Wyoming found Exxon "unusually uncooperative" in dealing with environmental, occupational health, and other problems at its Highland mine in that state. In 1989 the company had the worst safety record among the top twenty underground mining firms in the United States.

At its El Cerrejon mine in the Guajiro Indian country of Colombia, one of the largest coal mines in the Americas, its activities resulted in its being listed as one of the ten top violators of indigenous rights around the world by Survival International. It also reportedly lobbied the Colombian government to revise its mining and tax laws to eliminate restrictions on its operations there.[40] It desecrated indigenous cultural areas and built rail lines over Native burial sites. Resulting pollution contaminated water tables. Though Exxon promised economic prosperity to the indigenous people of the South American country, only a few actually got jobs, and these were fired if they protested unsafe or abusive working conditions. Between 1986 and 1990, thirty-two mine workers died in job-related incidents. The Exxon vice president supervising operations at El Cerrejon, Jerry Goodrich, is now president of Crandon Mining.[41] Similarly, the public relations representative for the Crandon project is J. Wiley Bragg, who previously handled information flow concerning the Exxon Valdez oilspill in Prince William Sound in Alaska.[42]

Before Mole Lake, Rio Algom, Exxon's partner in the proposed mine, was best remembered in Indian Country for its Elliot Lake uranium mine near the Serpent River Reserve in Ontario in the 1950s. As with Exxon in Colombia, Rio Algom promised jobs to local Ojibways (Chippewas) on the reserve, but only six were actually hired out of the approximately four thousand jobs created. Radioactive waste was dumped into the waterways without treatment, killing all aquatic life. Later, the company introduced non-indigenous species of fish into the lake in a misguided attempt to reclaim it, but these soon died. Contamination sent rates for cancer, birth defects, and other medical conditions soaring.[43] As a result of "potential liabilities" relating to Elliot Lake, Rio Algom's parent, Rio Tinto Zinc (Rio Tinto), sought a buyer for the subsidiary, but because of the debacle no purchaser could be found. Instead, Rio Algom went public.[44]

Rio Tinto is also parent of Kennecott Copper, which opened and began operation of a mine at Ladysmith, Wisconsin, despite intense local opposition. Kennecott Copper engaged in a massive public relations effort in the area in order to get the word out that it was environmentally friendly. As with the two other firms previously discussed, it dangled the prospect of large numbers of new jobs in front of a region that was economically depressed. In reality, the unemployment rate barely has been affected since the mine opened; most workers were brought in from the outside. As for its promise not to damage the environment, Ladysmith is an open-pit mine. Such operations are difficult to backfill and reclaim and almost always involve at least some environmental degradation.[45]

Finally, Wisconsin currently has a very pro-mining administration, headed by Governor Tommy Thompson. Prior to the Thompson administration the state was noted for being an environmentally conscious state, sometimes with regulations stricter than federal standards.[46] That has changed. One of those in the administration is James Klauser, a former Exxon lobbyist. In cooperation with Kennecott and the Wisconsin Alliance of Manufacturers and Commerce, he oversaw a rewriting of Wisconsin extraction and environmental laws in favor of mining interests.[47]

Wisconsin Native nations have begun to wage a battle on many fronts to block the Mole Lake/Crandon mine and to halt environmental devastation in general in the state. Together the Sokaogan Chippewa, Potawatomi, Menominee, Stockbridge-Munsee, and Oneida have formed the Nii-Win Intertribal Council to coordinate activities.[48] The council is working with an alliance of environmental and sporting groups on a comprehensive campaign known as the Watershed Alliance Toward Environmental Responsibility (W.A.T.E.R.). Their stand against "'environmental racism' may help preserve nearby waterways for Indians and non-Indians alike."[49]

Because the mining site lies on a twelve-square mile tract promised to the Sokaogan Chippewa in 1855, the Mole Lake tribe is asserting its treaty rights over the location. As tribal judge Fred Ackley stated, "If they go ahead with their mine, our tribe is going to be devastated."[50] Meanwhile, the Menominees also are filing suit, claiming their rights to hunt, fish, and gather on ceded lands. The Menominee claim covers the whole of northeastern Wisconsin down to Milwaukee. If they are successful, this will create additional leverage to challenge all mining operations in the area. In a move reminiscent of the 1980s and early 1990s, the day the lawsuit was filed anti-Indian groups again began protesting, accusing Natives of attempting to destroy all the fish and take away all the resources. Despite such opposition, Nii-Win chair Hilary Waukau Sr. has vowed that, if Crandon receives the required permits, the tribes will sue in federal court.[51] An attempt in state court to get an injunction against preliminary work at Mole Lake failed on November 7, 1994.[52]

According to Ackley, the mine impact area is an ancient burial ground.[53] The Sokaogan could thus seek to prevent the development under the Native American Graves Protection and Repatriation Act of 1990 and other historic preservation legislation.[54] Exxon claims that, although there are graves completely surrounding the site, mysteriously there are none in the exact location. Were the assertion true, the graves would have to have been dug in a circle around the proposed mine site.

The Forest County Potawatomi have moved to have the air quality designation of their reservation upgraded pursuant to the Clean Air Act. The tribe seeks redesignation as a Class I area, allowing less air pollution than currently permitted.[55] Both Exxon and the state of Wis-

consin have gone on record as opposing the redesignation. Following
the Potawatomi lead, both the Sokaogan and the Menominee are seeking redesignation of their water quality under the Clean Water Act.
While these actions do not affect off-reservation lands like the Crandon
site, they will allow closer monitoring of pollutants not currently covered by Wisconsin environmental laws.

The Nii-Win tribes are also seeking allies who own stock in Exxon.
Already sympathetic religious organizations who are stockholders have
been attending Exxon shareholders' meetings and calling for an environmental impact study that would address the effect of the Crandon
mine on all Native communities in the area.

The tribes may get their wish for an environmental impact assessment from the federal government. At least seven endangered and
threatened species have been located within the mining impact area,
including the goblin fern, mountain cranberry, the northern blue but-
terfly, the bald eagle, the osprey, the red-shouldered hawk, and the
dwarf bilberry. Additional species could be affected by blasting, pollution, and loss of wetlands in the area. Despite the claim of the Sierra
Club that the goblin fern, in particular, will be destroyed if the mine
proceeds, Exxon spokesperson Wiley Bragg has announced that any
species on the endangered list were located in areas that would not be
affected by the proposed mining.[56] Because the mine could harm wetlands, the U.S. Army Corps of Engineers has stepped in. Col. James T.
Scott, district engineer of the Corps, states that he has "concluded that
the project has the potential to cause significant adverse impacts to
area wetlands, lakes and streams, including the Wolf River" and that it
may also have "significant cultural and socioeconomic effects on Native American communities."[57] The Corps therefore has announced
that it will require the mining company to perform an impact study
and submit it to the Corps before proceeding.

The late Glen Miller, a former Menominee tribal chair, was confident that the ordered study would "show this proposal is detrimental
to all of Wisconsin." He stated that the Corps of Engineers' action
"means the true impact of this ill-conceived project will get a fair hearing and assessment."[58] If it does, the proposed mine almost certainly
will be barred. Others, including current Menominee chair John Teller,
are less sanguine; they fear that the project will be given the go-ahead
no matter what. In the meantime, it will be necessary for the tribes
involved to continue broad, intentional, and orchestrated resistance.
Wisconsin is, after all, a pro-mining state. And if the record of indigenous peoples throughout the Americas shows us just one thing, it is
that mining projects are difficult to stop once they have gotten started.

Notes

1. The title for the piece comes from Zoltan Grossman, Al Gedick, and the Madison Treaty Rights Support Group, "Exxon Returns to Wisconsin: The Threat of the Crandon/Mole Lake Mine," *Dark Night Field Notes* 1 (Summer 1994), p. 15.

2. In reality, the oil wealth proved to be, for the Osage, at best a "mixed blessing," creating significant social dislocation and leading to the "Osage Reign of Terror," during which tribal members were cheated and murdered for their holdings by non-Natives. Terry P. Wilson, "Osage," in Mary Davis, ed., *Native America in the Twentieth Century* (New York: Garland Publishing, 1994), p. 412.

3. David. H. Getches, Charles F. Wilkinson, and Robert A. Williams, Jr., eds., *Cases and Materials in Federal Indian Law*, 3d ed. (St. Paul: West Publishing Co., 1993), pp. 22-23. As much as two-thirds of U.S. uranium, one-third of its low-sulfur coal, and one-fourth of its oil and natural gas are beneath reservation areas. In addition, significant deposits of gold, silver, copper, bauxite, and molybdenum have been found. Canadian distribution patterns are similar. Ward Churchill, *Struggle for the Land: Indigenous Resistance to Genocide, Ecocide, and Expropriation in Contemporary North America* (Monroe, Me.: Common Courage Press, 1993), p. 261. According to recent estimates, mineral resources on Indian land are as follows: Methane: 1.005 trillion MCF (million cubic feet); coal: 44.23 billion tons; phosphate: 743.2 million tons; copper: 1.25 billion tons; silver: 276,000 oz.; gold: 44,400 oz. BIA Division of Energy and Mineral Resources, *Indian Mineral Resource Horizons* (Washington: Government Printing Office, 1992).

4. Donald Fixico, "Mining," in Davis, p. 343.

5. A.T. Anderson, *Nations within a Nation: The American Indian and the Government of the United States* (Chappaqua, N.Y.: Privately printed, 1976), p. 44.

6. BIA Division of Energy and Mineral Resources. In almost all cases, royalties are collected by the Minerals Mangement Service of the U.S. Department of the Interior and then disbursed to tribes and individuals. In 1975, twenty-five tribes formed the Council of Energy Resource Tribes (CERT) to deal with matters involving natural resources. Though CERT remains a controversial organization among Indians, regarding both its ultimate effectiveness and its agenda, membership in the organization today has grown to over forty tribes. Sage Douglas Remington, North American Native Workshop on Environmental Justice, Iliff School of Theology, Denver, Co. (March 17, 1995); Duane Good Striker, ibid. The 1988 membership of CERT was as follows: Acoma, Blackfeet, Chemeheuvi, Cherokee Nation of Oklahoma, Cheyenne-Arapaho, Cheyenne River Sioux, Coeur d'Alene, Crow, Flathead, Florida Seminole, Fort Belknap, Fort Berthold, Fort Peck, Hopi, Hualapai, Jemez, Jicarilla Apache, Kalispel, Laguna, Muckleshoot, Navajo, Nez Perce, Northern Cheyenne, Pawnee, Penobscot, Pine Ridge Sioux, Ponca, Rocky Boy, Chippewa-Cree, Rosebud Sioux, Saginaw Chippewa, Santa Ana, Shoshone-Bannock, Southern Ute, Spokane, Standing Rock Sioux, Tulé River, Turtle Mountain Chippewa, Uitah and Ouray Ute, Umatilla, Ute Mountain, Walker River, and Zia.

7. Salvador Palomino, "Three Times, Three Spaces in Cosmos Quechua," in Inter Press Service, comp., *Story Earth* (San Francisco: Mercury House, 1993), p. 52.

8. Norma Kassi, North American Native Workshop on Environmental Justice, Iliff School of Theology, Denver, Co. (March 17, 1995); George Tinker, ibid. (March 18, 1995).

9. Donald A. Grinde, Jr., and Bruce E. Johansen, *Ecocide of Native America: Environmental Destruction of Indian Lands and Peoples* (Santa Fe: Clear Light, 1995), p. 125; Thadis Box, et al., *Rehabilitation Potential of Western Coal Lands* (Cambridge, Mass.: Ballinger Publishing Co., 1974), p. 85.

10. Russell Means, "The Same Old Song," in Ward Churchill, ed., *Marxism and Native Americans* (Boston: South End Press, 1983), p. 25.

11. Justine Smith, North American Native Workshop on Environmental Justice, Iliff School of Theology, Denver, Colorado (March 17, 1995).

12. Ibid.

13. Fixico, p. 344.

14. Ibid.

15. Matthew 10:16.

16. In Kevin Moore, "Forces Converging to Stop Proposed Exxon Mine Near Mole Lake," *News From Indian Country* (Late November 1994), p. 13.

17. Robert Franklin, "Student Essay against Indians Fans Racial Tension," *Minneapolis Star Tribune* (January 27, 1993), p. 5B; see, Jace Weaver, "Native Americans in U.S. Society," in Donn Downall, ed., *Challenge: Racism* (Nashville: Cokesbury, 1994), pp. 40-42.

18. Getches, Wilkinson, and Williams.

19. These people are referred to variously as Chippewa, Ojibway, or Ojibwa. Their name for themselves is Anishinaabe.

20. Getches, Wilkinson, and Williams, pp. 883-885; Ronald N. Satz, *Chippewa Treaty Rights: The Reserved Rights of Wisconsin's Chippewa Indians in Historical Perspective*, Transactions of the Wisconsin Academy of Sciences, Arts, and Letters 79:1 (Madison: Wisconsin Academy of Sciences, Arts, and Letters, 1991), pp. 187-197; Francis Paul Prucha, *American Indian Treaties: The History of a Political Anomaly* (Berkeley: University of California Press, 1994), pp. 421-422. For two Chippewa discussions of these and other treaty rights, see generally, Ron Paquin and Robert Doherty, *Not First in Nobody's Heart* (Ames: Iowa State University Press, 1992) and Wub-e-ke-niew [Francis Blake, Jr.], *We Have the Right to Exist* (New York: Black Thistle Press, 1995).

21. See, Prucha, pp. 141, 225.

22. Ibid., p. 141.

23. Al Gedicks and Zoltan Grossman, "Exxon Returns to Wisconsin: The Threat of the Crandon/Mole Lake Mine," *The Circle* (April 1994), p. 8.

24. See generally, Al Gedicks, *The New Resource Wars: Native and Environmental Struggles against Multinational Corporations* (Boston: South End Press, 1993).

25. Glenn Morris, North American Native Workshop on Environmental Justice, Iliff School of Theology, Denver, Co. (March 17, 1995).

26. Gedicks and Grossman, p. 8.

27. *Lac Courte Oreilles Band v. Voigt*, 700 F.2d 341 (7th Cir. 1983), *cert. denied*, 464 U.S. 805 (1983).

28. See, Prucha, pp. 400-422; Getches, Wilkinson, and Williams, pp. 883-885.

29. Gedicks and Grossman, p. 8.

30. Grossman, Gedicks, and MTRSG, p. 15.

31. Ibid.

32. Gedicks and Grossman, p. 8.

33. Wetlands are bodies of water less than six feet in depth.

34. Moore, p. 13; "Chippewa Lose Crandon Mine Challenge," *News from Indian Country* (Late November 1994), p. 2; Grossman, Gedicks, and MTRSG, p. 15.

35. "Chippewa Lose Crandon Mine Challenge," p. 2; Gedicks and Grossman, p. 8.

36. Gedicks and Grossman, p. 8.

37. Ibid.

38. Ibid.

39. Getches, Wilkinson, and Williams, p. 22; Gedicks and Grossman, p. 8.

40. Gedicks and Grossman, pp. 8-9.

41. Ibid.

42. Moore, p. 13; Gedicks and Grossman, p. 9.

43. See, Gedicks and Grossman, p. 9. Rio Algom has also been challenged concerning increased incidences of childhood leukemia in the area of its East Kemptville tin mine and smelter in Nova Scotia (ibid.).

44. Ibid.

45. See, Jace Weaver, "Triangulated Power and the Environment," herein.

46. Ibid.

47. Gedicks and Grossman, p. 8; Grossman, Gedicks, and MTRSG, p. 16-17.

48. Moore, p. 13.

49. Gedicks and Grossman, p. 8.

50. Ibid.

51. Moore, p. 13.

52. "Chippewa Lose Crandon Mine Challenge," p. 2.

53. Moore, p. 13.

54. U.S.C.A. §§ 3001-3013 (West. Supp. 1991); see, Rennard Strickland, "Implementing the National Policy of Understanding, Preserving, and Safeguarding the Heritage of Indian Peoples and Native Hawaiians: Human Rights, Sacred Objects, and Cultural Patrimony," 24 Ariz.S.L.J. 175 (1992); Rennard Strickland, "Back to the Future: A Proposed Model Tribal Act to Protect Native Cultural Heritage," 46 Ark.L.Rev. 161 (1993); Walter R. Echo-Hawk and Roger C. Echo-Hawk, "Repatriation, Reburial, and Religious Rights," in Christopher Vecsey, ed., *Handbook of American Indian Religious Freedom* (New York: Crossroad, 1991), p. 63.

55. See, *Nance v. EPA*, 645 F.2d 701 (9th Cir.), *cert. denied* 454 U.S. 1081 (1981).

56. Moore, p. 13.

57. Ibid.

58. Ibid.

4.

A Legacy of Maldevelopment

Environmental Devastation in the Arctic

NORMA KASSI

EDITOR'S INTRODUCTION: To anyone familiar with the Arctic only through the writings of outlanders such as Robert Service, Jack London, and Farley Mowat, the "Far North" is a virginal, hyperborean fastness. It is a land of mighty forests, vast open tundra, and crystalline glaciers and streams. Environmental disasters like the Exxon *Valdez* oil spill are aberrations despoiling an otherwise perfect wilderness.

American naturalist John Muir, remembering a trip to Alaska's Glacier Bay in 1879, described such a land of "swift-glancing streams . . . in blue shining channels . . . radiant crystals like flowers ineffably fine growing in dazzling beauty along their banks."[1] He waxed, "In the evening, after witnessing the unveiling of the majestic peaks and glaciers and their baptism in the downpouring sunbeams, it seemed inconceivable that nature could have anything finer to show us."[2] More than a century later, author Barry Lopez echoed Muir's sense of wonderment. He wrote, "I looked up at the icebergs. They so embodied the land. Austere. Implacable. Harsh but not antagonistic. Creatures of pale light. Once, camped in the Anaktiktoak Valley of the central Brooks Range in Alaska, a friend had said, gazing off across that broad glacial valley of soft greens and straw browns, with sunlight lambent on Tulugak Lake and the Anaktuvuk River in the distance, that it was so beautiful it made you cry."[3]

Today the American and Canadian Arctic is still a beautiful place. Prince William Sound, despite the damage of the Exxon disaster, remains lovely. It is still possible to find the "deep, brooding stillness"[4] that has acted as a magnet for generations of those seeking solitude. It is still the place where even I, normally garrulous, learned the trick of quiet. To the indigenous people who make their homes there, it is a sacred land where the veil between Creator and created is thin.

Yet, as Norma Kassi reminds us, it is also a place of ecocide, of open and hidden sores upon Mother Earth. A hundred years of development and resource exploitation have left a heritage of toxic waste, sickness, scarred land-scapes, and violence toward people and their animal kin.

She knows whereof she speaks. She has represented indigenous peoples in government and worked as an environmental specialist on their behalf. She is a member of the Gwich'in of the Dene Nation. The story to which she alludes in the closing of her article is that of Yamoria, a culture hero of the Dene who served as a demiurge for their Arctic home.[5]

The Dene remain passionate defenders not only of Denedeh[6] but of all of Mother Earth, still holding to the laws that Yamoria set down for them. They regard the earth not as an inert mass of rock but as a living person. Besides the six ambassadors of the Gwich'in discussed by Kassi, other Dene have taken the message of the destruction of the Arctic to the global community. Amen Tailbone of the Northwest Territories states, "The land, the water, and the animals are not here to play with. It was given to us to look after and protect. The land is the only thing that we depend on for everything, and it is not for sale."[7] Cindy Kenny-Gilday, one of the founders of Indigenous Survival International and a Dene advisor to the government of the Northwest Territories, repeats the plea voiced herein by Kassi when she declares, "The majority of aboriginal peoples . . . have never known the meaning of economic prosperity in modern times, only economic survival. Yet these same people retain ancient cultural practices that could save the Earth. By allowing or nurturing the empowerment of indigenous peoples, industrial society could empower itself to regain the balance of environment and economy—thus addressing prosperity for all peoples."[8] Not to mention simple survival.

Much of what we, as Native people, know and have to share, we learned from our elders. The elders taught us that we are all related. We are related because we all come from the same Creator and share the same planet. We also all share the same air. What I have just breathed in, you had just breathed out seconds ago. Our relationship to the environment and to each other is that complex and that intimate.

I offer greetings from the Gwich'in and other Yukon First Nations. My Indian name is Gwahtla Aaishih. I am of the Wolf Clan of the Gwich'in Nation. We were once known as the *Loucheux*, a French term meaning "skinny-eyed people." We are Athabaskans and part of the Dene Nation. We traditionally occupied an area in northeastern Alaska, the northern Yukon, and into the Northwest Territory. We are called the Caribou People of the Lakes. *Vuntut Gwich'in* means "people of the lakes."

I received a lot of my teachings from my ancestors, from my grandfather and my mother. I was a representative in government. My elders decided that I was outspoken enough to be able to work with large groups of aboriginal people, so I was elected to the Yukon Territorial Legislative Assembly representing the Gwich'in people in government. I served for eight years. I currently work as Arctic Environmental Strategy Coordinator for the Council for Yukon Indians. In 1987 I was one of six persons commissioned by the Gwich'in to tell the world of the massive environmental devastation being visited upon the Arctic region. I cannot do that, however, without first putting our current problems in the context of how we once lived, how I was raised, and the changes brought by so-called civilization.

I was raised on the land. I was taught to respect and love everything in creation as a relative. The caribou, the wolf, the insects, the plants–everything–is a relative and we are equal to them, not superior. Everything is related and interrelated. As a child I learned that if we hurt a spider that was crawling on the branches that made up our floor or our caribou skin mattress, then rain would come when we didn't need rain. I have experienced some of the consequences of such things personally. I've always believed very strongly that if we look at all things as our relatives, then all life commands great respect. I was raised that way. When we regard something only as a resource to be used and exploited, we can trash it and do all sorts of things to it. If, however, we think of ourselves as belonging to the Great Energy, the Creator, we have a sense that we are all closely related, and we have to have a greater respect for the other creatures with whom we share the planet.

From a young age my mother and grandfather taught me to respect the land. I lived on the land and trapped and hunted. We had to work with the elements in order to survive. I never had store-bought shoes. All I had were caribou skin clothes and rabbit-skin parkas. I was probably the last one in or around my village to have diapers made from moss. I had some very spiritual and very sacred teachings in those first few years of my life. It was a time when we only spoke one language, the Gwich'in language.

Everything we did from the time we woke up until the time we went to bed was in and among nature. Our existence up there around the lakes called Vuntut was about survival. We had everything we needed–the love of our family, strength from the land, nourishment from the caribou. We interacted with the animals. We asked the crows and the ravens to tell us when the caribou were coming, and they did. I remember my mother getting up early in the morning and talking to the crows. Sometimes she'd come back smiling and sometimes she'd look sad, and I would know just by watching what the crows had said. Both our men and our women hunted with great determination and skill. We had to follow the wolf. We had to be like wolves and emulate the total dedication of the wolf to the pack.

We walked on the land with great respect. We used trails that our ancestors made. Though we occupied an area of thousands of square miles, we could not simply roam anywhere over the land. We kept to a single path, a narrow footpath, alongside the well-worn track of the caribou. We used the willow to guide us to stay on the paths we were taught. We did not destroy branches or leaves in our path.

From the age of two or three I learned by watching my elders. Sometimes in the mornings I would see my grandfather over there sharpening his knife. When he finished, he would chip at pieces of branch to see if it was sharp enough. I could see his face. It would be relaxed, with a pleasant expression. I would know what he was thinking. Then I would watch my mother bring in special kinds of wood. I would understand that the season was changing and that we had to start building a cache. My aunt would bring in special willows and branches to make the freshly scented flooring of our caches and our camps. This was all done in absolute quietness. I remember as we prepared things that the silence was so strong I could hear it.

My mother would get up early. She would go outside and stand there a long time. Then she would say, "Vehsih yehno nah ha ooh." That means, "The caribou are just under the mountain over there, and they're coming." Everyone would get excited. We children would start running around. Her predictions were always proven out. My grandfather would go out and hunt, and he would not come back until he could bring home some meat. By then we'd be really hungry for meat, because often all we had during those times between caribou hunts was flour, sugar, and rice. That was all we had—nothing else. That's how I was raised. There would be feasts among all the Gwich'in when the caribou would come.

My grandfather would cut special parts of the animal that he needed to build his own strength and bond with the caribou. The end part of the velvety horns of the bull caribou in the springtime is stick-like but very soft. The old men would take that and go off by themselves to roast it. I would hear them laughing, telling jokes and stories, but I was never allowed to go around where they were. Women weren't allowed to eat that part of the caribou. Recently Asians came to my community to collect a lot of caribou horns for use as an aphrodisiac because they served as a source of strength for our men.

Children weren't allowed to eat certain parts of the caribou. For instance, if we ate the offal close to the mother's calf, then we would never be able to run fast and we'd be bad hunters in the future. There were, however, special parts that the children did eat. Women in our time were never allowed to eat fresh meat. We were too powerful, and if we ate the fresh flesh we would diminish the spiritual energies of the hunter, the powerful connection that the caribou had to the hunters. In our villages there would be great joy at the time of the caribou feasts and lots of dancing, drumming, and giggling.

This has always been the tradition of the Gwich'in. It springs from a deep respect for all creation and spiritual beliefs thousands of years

old. We believe that our spirituality is our highest form of consciousness. We worshiped the elements. We gave thanks.

We shared our lives, and we sacrificed for one another to be able to
survive and live under extreme natural conditions. My mother and I
would use our five-dog team to haul firewood in 70-degrees-below-
zero weather in order to survive. We were happy. We weren't rich in
material things. We just had the very basics, and everything we had
was made from the land. But we were happy, and we were a close
family.

We took care of the land. We worked with it and obeyed all the laws
of nature, because we had to. We never tried to control the natural
environment. Over the years I've seen some people who have tried to
control nature and its laws. They laugh at animals and scoff at the old
ways. I also have seen extreme consequences of such behavior. But I
also cherish stories such as this one about my grandmother. She took
her hide outside to dry and stretch it, and it started to rain. She offered
her thanks and communicated with the Great Energy—the Great Spirit—
and not a single drop of rain fell on her hide. It rained all around her,
but she was able to fix her hide without it getting wet.

We had our own ways of conservation. I remember times when my
grandfather would take me for a walk. He always carried me on his
back, and when he'd get tired we'd sit. Then he'd start telling me stories over tea and bannock. He'd say to me, "You know, someday your
brother is going to fly across this lake." I would think, "What does he
mean by that?" Years later, the skidoo[9] came along, and my brother
would "fly" across the lake. Grandfather talked about the laws of conservation. He told me, "You see those lakes under that mountain over
there called Shun? You young people aren't to go there. I'm not going to
be with you very much longer, but you don't trap there, you don't hunt
the beavers there, you don't fish there until your grandchildren are big
enough to do it." Now I tell my grandchildren they can go there. In all
the intervening years nobody went there. The beaver and muskrat have
rejuvenated and replenished themselves, and the fish have come back.
So, even today, we have very strict laws of conservation.

When we needed the land, she provided for us. When we had to
move with the seasons, there was no debate. We had to move because
it meant survival. As a result of all our struggles for survival, my people
had great powers, well-honed abilities to heal. We had strong medicines the land gave us. I remember times when I would get cut doing
crazy things. My mother would chew a plant and put the saliva on my
sores or plop a piece of whatever she chewed on my hand as a poul-
tice. The next morning the wound would have healed and disappeared.
We had tremendous medicinal powers.

In the old times my people experienced very little sickness. The fur
trade and the missionaries brought many diseases. My mother had

eleven brothers and sisters. She is the only one left. All my aunties and uncles died of smallpox, tuberculosis, and measles. Most of them were taken away to residential schools[10] by missionaries, Indian agents, and police. Some never came back. I remember my mother crying, trying to locate where her sister might have been buried. The Anglicans who ran the residential school had no record.

I've lived through 160 seasons, and I've seen many changes. I have experienced the terrible consequences of the vast intrusions on my people. We are very much isolated. My community is about 250 miles from the nearest town. It's only accessible by air and by the Porcupine River. Despite such seeming isolation, we've experienced the consequences of introduction of commerce, the fur trade, and money. Over time, these have created a lot of infighting over things—material things. The fur trade demanded ever-increasing amounts of furs. Finally, the animals rights movement took up the issue. They did tremendous damage to my people, since, as a result, a lot of our people don't go out to the trap lines as much as they used to. I've watched government officials come to my village with their shiny shoes and empty promises. I've also watched the missionaries attempt to sever our people from our ancient beliefs and our sacred relationship to the land and animal kingdom. Reflecting on it now, I suppose our experience is similar to that of any indigenous people anywhere on the planet.

Yet despite this brutal and sustained assault on our people and on our families and our cultures, we have refused to vanish. Much to the chagrin of those who tried to destroy us, we are still here, and we still have a voice. We have refused to assimilate or abandon our culture or our language. Some of us were lost along the way, though a lot of us still survive. Our ceremonies and our healers are beginning to re-emerge in my nation now. Our drum was safely kept by the Nestyh Gwich'in. The caribou songs are coming back. These elements of our culture are coming back very strongly. Our young people are reclaiming our sacred ways, and those ways are a vital force in their lives.

Our elders are very strong. Some of our young people say that we can no longer remain passive. They say that we have to get militant, to fight back. Our elders, however, always say no. They advise us that the longer one walks with respect, revering one's ancestors and the teachings of Mother Earth, doing things in the kindest ways possible, then the better the ultimate outcome. As a result, all across Canada today there is a tremendous resurgence of First Nation peoples, living out their traditional ways and demanding redress and accountability from the government and the churches.

Today, pursuant to the Umbrella Final Agreement with the Canadian federal government, First Nation peoples are in the process of selecting lands in settlement of their territorial claims. In this process the issue of environmental contamination is of prime importance. Everyone thinks of the North as an undefiled wilderness, but it is far from pristine.

The Arctic seems to be a pocket for tremendous amounts of contaminants from industrialized areas in the United States, Russia, and Europe. Long-range pollutants arrive from as far away as South Africa. These toxic chemicals all flow toward the north, where they settle. Some scientists are still convinced that eventually they will go away, but they are showing up in very high concentrations in our food chain now. Large amounts of chemicals are being discovered in our snow and ice, where they just stay. We are finding high levels of PCBs, DDT, and mercury. We are also detecting radioactive waste from nuclear submarines that have sunk in the Arctic Ocean.

Much of the Yukon has been a toxic dump since the Gold Rush of 1898. There are hundreds of abandoned mine sites where rusting equipment and dilapidated structures litter the landscape. There are tailings piles where arsenic used in the gold extraction process is seeping into the water table. In addition, there is a variety of toxins resulting from military activity in the area. We recently conducted an inventory of all the dump sites in the territory. The whole Yukon is covered with them.[11]

All along the North Slope the United States has built forty-two DEW Line bases in the name of its national security. Thus far twenty-one of those sites have been tested by scientists pursuant to the Arctic Environmental Strategy, and they found very high levels of PCBs within 20 kilometer radius of each site. One can assume that the same holds true for the remaining locations as well. Much of this pollution runs off into our rivers and into the ocean. It is showing up in our food. It is showing up in the breast milk of Inuit and Native women.

As far back as 1992 soil tests disclosed concentrations of esteron, fenuron, and tordon 101. This finding led to a suspicion that Agent Orange had been employed in the area as part of the chemical spraying done in connection with the construction of roads and oil pipelines. Agent Orange is one of the most toxic known substances. It was used during the Vietnam War as a defoliant. The U.S. Army totally disregarded the First Nations people when it needed a road for national defense. It used toxic chemicals to clear the brush for hundreds of miles of pipeline routes and roads. Today nothing grows along those stretches where the chemical spraying was done.

Because of the soil test results, the Council for Yukon Indians began to seek out elders from the area. We also sought military personnel who had served in the area between 1942 and 1965.[12] One member of the Champagne-Aishihik First Nation in the southern part of the Yukon Territory told us that he remembered as a small boy hunting with his grandfather and his father. He recalled looking up and seeing a plane was flying overhead. He then felt a light rain falling and covering him.

Recently he told us that he found out that what fell on him as a misty precipitation was Agent Orange.

The corridors cleared out by defoliation were used as easy access for hunting and picking berries by our people. Because the plants would die instantly, by the next year the wood would be dry and brittle. The women picked the wood and used it to smoke their fish and meat. That concentrated the toxicity. Our people also picked berries and gathered medicine in the area. Animals grazed on the foliage and consumed toxins, which were passed on when they were hunted.

In September 1994 United States personnel that served in the Yukon during and subsequent to World War II came forward with information concerning buried contaminants on the border between the Yukon and British Columbia. As a result, forty barrels of DDT were recovered from an abandoned U.S. Army pumping station at Rainy Hollow, British Columbia, immediately south of the Yukon border. Rainy Hollow is the traditional territory of the Champagne-Aishihiks. It is in close proximity to the Chilkat Eagle Preserve, home to the largest bald eagle population in the world. In addition, the decaying containers were buried near the Klehini River, which in turn flows into the Chilkat River, raising concerns that the contamination may have spread to waterways.[13]

There are five similar military installations in the Yukon along the Haines Fairbanks Pipeline route. There is evidence that army personnel may have buried toxic waste at them as well. It will take years to search and test these sites for contaminants.[14]

Other contaminants are gradually being identified in oil barrels. PCBs, DDT-toxaphine, and other chemicals were dumped in our major lakes in the Yukon during the construction of the Alaska Highway. PCBs are known to cause diabetes. Very high levels of the chemical are showing up in northern Inuit and indigenous women. The Ta-an Kwach'an of the southern Yukon Territory, near Lake Labarge, can't eat their fish anymore because of the high concentration of toxaphene, a chlorinated camphene insecticide.

We are having a hard time getting the government to acknowledge the contamination. Letters to the Canadian federal government and to the United States military have gone unanswered. We know now, however, that the contamination is coming from a local source, and we are trying to get these governments to be responsible and clean it up. We are concerned that we will be transferred land pursuant to the Umbrella Final Agreement that has been poisoned, and we want our land back clean. According to Judy Gingell, president of the Council for Yukon Indians, "It would add insult to injury if any First Nation were to obtain lands that have been contaminated from past military or mining activities."[15]

Now these chemicals are showing up in the food chain, and as indigenous people we really rely on the land. Almost all that we eat—all our fish and game, everything—comes from the land. Often my people eat meat and fish three and four times a day. They are the primary components of our diet. Scientists are now telling us that we cannot eat the internal organs of animals and fish, which have served as medicines for our people for thousands of years. It is just one more example of the slow erosion of our traditional lifestyle, our health, and our culture. We strongly believe now that these pollutants are the reason for exceedingly high rates of cancer, diabetes, and gallbladder problems among our people. We cannot, however, simply change our diet. If we were to change suddenly and start eating store-bought foods more, then disease would increase and our rate of death would be higher, because it would be too rapid a change, too much of a shock to our systems. We also know that the caribou are tainted by toxins. We depend upon the caribou and must continue to eat them to survive in the Arctic. We are part of the land from which we come. We live off the animals that are there. The proportion of our diet made up by caribou is still very high. Thus far, we are told, our caribou are still safe to eat, even though traces of cadmium and cesium have been discovered. In some areas we can't eat the fish.

Our cultural connections to our traditional foods have to continue. Otherwise our culture is irrevocably damaged. In the southern Yukon the indigenous people at the turn of the century had a caribou herd that numbered in the hundreds of thousands. With the Gold Rush, non-Natives came and indiscriminately slaughtered them. Developments reduced the herd's habitat. In less than seventy-five years, there were fewer than five hundred caribou left. Now, the Natives are desperately trying to bring them back. They send hunters as far away as the Dempster Highway in Gwich'in country in search of caribou. More often than not they get caribou at the trading post. There is no cultural connection to that caribou; it's only a package in their freezer. The women no longer take care of the caribou. The men no longer hunt it in a spiritual manner. Much of their culture is being lost.

Other issues currently facing Yukon First Nation peoples relate to exploitation of natural resources. Clear-cut logging has become a major problem. Japanese timber concerns have begun to move into the southern area. We are trying to organize a coalition of First Nation and non-Native people against it. These sub-Arctic forests are as important to the earth's ecosystems as the rainforests of the Amazon basin.[16] Once they are cleared, because the growing season at that latitude is so short, they will be gone forever. The Dene people have a saying, "Trees are born, trees die, the forest lives."[17] That will no longer be true if these old-growth forests are destroyed.

There also are huge mineral developments. A new government in the Yukon has opened up vast areas to mining. There are currently seventy thousand active leases in our small territory. These mines are turning to heap leaching to remove the metals and are transporting arsenic-cyanide to use in the process. We do not know a great deal about these new operations yet, but we are investigating. It is a situation that needs careful monitoring.

Our foremost immediate concern, and a subject very close and dear to my own heart, is the proposed oil and gas development on the calving grounds of the Porcupine Caribou Herd, currently estimated at 170,000. The caribou is the very essence of the livelihood of the Gwich'in people and the Inuvialuit of the western Arctic. Located in northeastern Alaska, the Arctic National Wildlife Refuge is a very special part of Mother Earth. If you walk across the tundra, your footprints will be there for a long, long time. That is how sensitive the earth is there. It is a place where many species of birds lay their eggs. Many of the geese that come through the United States lay their eggs there. It's a birthplace for numerous animal species. Even in times of extreme starvation the Gwich'in never went over the mountains to hunt caribou there, because it was a time to leave them alone so they could bear their young. The area is very, very sacred. The caribou calve there, and it would be detrimental to my people if oil and gas were to be developed in that area.

The U.S. Congress first proposed exploration in the refuge in 1987. When they heard of the plan, our elders told all our chiefs in the Gwich'in Nation to gather. It was the first time in a hundred years that our people had gathered. For four days we met in Arctic Village, Alaska. We invited every press outlet that we could think of. We lobbied *National Geographic, People, Glamour*–any magazine that we could–to cover our story. We went on the radio. The elders told us stories of the caribou and our people. Then they gave us their counsel. They chose six people from the Gwich'in Nation: Sarah James, Kate Wallace, Gladys Netro, Johnny Charlie, Alicetine Andre, and me. They sent us out to begin to speak about the issue.

Our people traditionally have been very quiet. Until this threat arose, there was not much known about the Gwich'in people, and we wanted it to stay that way. The elders then gave us permission to start sharing our stories with the world. Recently, with a tremendous amount of effort on the part of many people, we managed to hold off a bill in the United States Senate that would have authorized exploration in the refuge. The issue, however, is far from settled.

The Canadian Porcupine Caribou Management Board, an ad hoc group of indigenous people committed to preservation of the herd, recently issued the following statement:

The American Congress is considering oil exploration and development in the "1002" section of Alaska's Arctic Wildlife Refuge.
. . . There's a 20% chance that enough oil will be found there to
supply the United States for 200 days at projected demands for
the year 2005. The "1002" lands cover the core calving grounds
of the Porcupine Caribou Herd and experts both in the U.S. and
Canada believe that industrial disturbance of this critical habitat
could have drastic impacts on the herd which now numbers
170,000 animals.

A decline in the Porcupine Caribou population would be devastating to our native communities of the north Yukon and lower
Mackenzie River in Canada. Our aboriginal people have a 20,000
year bond with the Porcupine Caribou Herd which continues to
be the mainstay of our culture, economies and fundamental identity with the land. We view the proposed "1002" development as
a no-win situation for both the Porcupine Caribou Herd and the
people who depend on it. At the very least there will be some
negative impact and at the most, a virtual extinction of the caribou and our way of life.

Porcupine Caribou are a wildlife resource shared by Canada
and the United States. By international agreement these two nations have pledged to conserve the Porcupine Caribou Herd for
future generations. We believe that the majority of Americans
would not wish to sacrifice this herd and its habitat from America's
dwindling wilderness assets for the sake of fuel that could be saved
by any number of simple economy measures. And above all, we
realize that while the final decision will be made by United States
Congressmen, the deciding opinion will come from their con-
stituents–the American people. We therefore ask you to urge your
elected representatives to support protection of the "1002" section of the Arctic National Wildlife Refuge with permanent
wilderness designation. This is the only sure way of guaranteeing
the future of the Porcupine Caribou Herd for both of our countries.[18]

Our people are now getting together to lobby both countries to desig-
nate the refuge a World Heritage Park with significant participation
and control by the Gwich'in in the area.

Our elders are powerful. They can see things that others do not see.
I'm getting older, too. I'm beginning to see a lot farther. My vision is
getting stronger. In the Arctic, we have twenty-four hours of sunlight,
beginning in April. The sun used to go behind the mountains and set
for a few minutes at about one o'clock in the morning. We wouldn't see
it for a while, and then it would come back out. Now it doesn't go
behind those mountains anymore. Because of the increased intensity

of the sunshine, our land is drying up. The permafrost is melting, and the rivers are getting wider. Our elders tell us that the earth tilted not long ago. They tell us that the salmon are acting strangely; they go up the stream a little way and then turn back. Salmon never turn back. Our birds are acting peculiarly, too. The elders say that the salmon and the birds are trying to warn us. They say that a great cleansing is coming. The ones who are most closely connected to the land are the ones who will survive. Perhaps, then, we will have learned our lesson.

Some of our people fell away for a while. They took the abundance of nature for granted. Now, however, the old spiritual ways are returning, and there is more respect for the environment. Our community is eliminating styrofoam and plastics. We are reducing paper usage. We have to be strong in our spiritual connections if we are to be in partnership with Mother Earth and truly walk with her and help her. If, however, we are to help and heal the earth, we need non-Native people to join with us. We need allies to assist us by recognizing our history and our traditional knowledge. They must regard us as partners at every level in developing strategies to save our Mother.

My people believe that long before the Europeans came and invaded our land, the Great Energy sent an emissary to us. He set everything in its proper place and established laws of relationship among all the elements of creation, promising that if we followed those laws we would survive as a people. He eliminated whatever was harmful to human beings. After a century of maldevelopment, we must all ask ourselves how long we will continue to put back those evils the Creator took away. *Mahsi-cho.*

Notes

1. John Muir, *Travels in Alaska* (Boston: Houghton Mifflin, 1915), p. 265.

2. Ibid., p. 152.

3. Barry Lopez, *Arctic Dreams* (New York: Charles Scribner's Sons, 1986), pp. 224-225. Lopez does indicate some familiarity with environmental problems in an endnote. He writes of pollution, toxic dumping, and the "reluctance of the Canadian government to protect critical wildlife habitat in the high Arctic from natural resource exploitation" (ibid., pp. 373-374).

4. Muir, p. 152.

5. For a more fulsome telling of the exploits of Yamoria, as well as a discussion of the development issues in Norma Kassi's paper, see, Dene Nation, *Denedeh: A Dene Celebration* (Toronto: McClelland and Stewart, 1984), p. 135.

6. *Denedeh* is the term for the traditional territory of the Dene in Alaska and Canada. It means "land of the People."

7. Dene Nation, p. 3.

8. Cindy Kenny-Gilday, quoted in, "The Question of Sustainable Development," *Nature Conservancy* (January/February, 1995), p. 12.

9. *Skidoo* is a northern term for a variety of snowmobile.

10. Boarding schools run by Christian missionaries. The experience of many Indians in the United States in boarding schools is very similar to that of Canadian Natives with residential schools.

11. For a discussion of environmental threats facing the Yukon Territory, see, Teri Desjarlais, "Agent Orange Suspected in Yukon," *Native Journal* (October 1994), p. 1.

12. "Put Mother Earth First," advertisement in *Native Journal* (October 1994), p. 24.

13. Desjarlais, p. 1.

14. Ibid.

15. Ibid.

16. See, Ward Churchill, *Struggle for the Land: Indigenous Resistance to Genocide, Ecocide, and Expropriation in Contemporary North America* (Monroe, Me.: Common Courage Press, 1993), p. 363, for a discussion of the importance of the Northern forests.

17. The Dene Nation, *Denedeh: A Dene Celebration* (Toronto: McClelland and Stewart, 1984), p. 118.

18. Statement of the Canadian Porcupine Caribou Management Board, Whitehorse, Yukon Territory.

5.

Beyond the Water Line

PHYLLIS YOUNG

EDITOR'S INTRODUCTION: As the century turned, W. E. B. Du Bois told the first Pan-African Congress convened in London that the problem of the twentieth century was to be "the problem of the color line."[1] While one cannot minimize the role race has played in global affairs this century, the problem of the western United States, as Phyllis Young illustrates in the following essay, has been the problem of the water line.

The hundredth meridian is the water line in the United States. This longitudinal marker is more than an imaginary demarcation. It sheers off the panhandles of Oklahoma and Texas like a knife cutting a cake. Imagine driving from the body of western Oklahoma into the Panhandle. On one side is red, bauxite-rich soil. On the other the earth is thin and yellow as if any nutrition had long ago been leached out of it. You have just crossed 100° of longitude west. With rare exception, everything ahead of you beyond that line is desert.

This harsh, dry environment has led to a water law unlike anything else in the country. In the East, water law is borrowed from England. The governing principle is one of riparian rights. Simply stated, whoever owns land adjacent to a stream or lake is entitled to the reasonable use of water from it as long as it does not interfere with the rights of other riparian users.[2] The right runs with the land and may not be sold separate from it. A rule made for the green meadows of Devonshire and the fertile fields of Ohio was wholly unsuited, however, for application to the Dakota badlands or the arid mesas of Arizona.

In the West, water law is essentially that of Morocco.[3] Brought to the Iberian Peninsula by the Moors, it was carried to the American Southwest by Spanish conquistadors and colonists. The basic rule of western water rights is the doctrine of prior appropriation. This principle creates a hierarchy of users based upon the date each first began to withdraw water from a given source. Those first in time are first in right. The amount of water that may be used is limited to a specific amount dedicated to approved beneficial uses. Disuse results in a forfeiture of rights to other appropriators in the use chain. Finally, in times of shortage, allocations are honored in the order of their original appropriation.[4] In addition, unlike their riparian cousins, these rights can be sold separately from land.

Necessity ensured that this peculiar vestige of Spanish law would survive while other tenets, more in keeping with traditional Native concepts of communal ownership, would wither. For example, in the days of Spanish colonialism in New Mexico, each village was granted an *ejido*, communal lands reserved for hunting, grazing, and wood gathering. Following the so-called Mexican-American War of 1848, the Treaty of Guadalupe Hidalgo required the United States to recognize these grants. The concept of the *ejido*, however, did not mesh well with American doctrines of private property. The communal lands were "lost, sometimes stolen, many of them absorbed years later into the public domain as [U.S.] Forest Service property."[5] Moorish notions of water rights survived.

In 1906 the United States government brought suit against farmers in Montana, claiming that the latter were diverting excessive amounts of water from the Milk River to the detriment of the Fort Belknap Reservation downstream. A federal district court judge agreed and issued an injunction against the farmers, finding that "when the Indians made the treaty granting rights to the United States, they reserved the right to use the waters of the Milk River, at least to the extent reasonably necessary to irrigate their lands."[6] In January 1908, in *Winters v. United States*, the Supreme Court upheld the decision. The *Winters* doctrine, and its concept of reserved water rights, became the keystone of Native water rights in the West. The High Court found that when tribes entered into treaties for the creation of reservations, they implicitly reserved to themselves enough water to fulfill the purposes for which the reservation was created. For purposes of the prior appropriation doctrine the priority date assigned to the tribe was the date on which the reservation came into being, thus effectively ranking Natives first in the hierarchy of appropriators. Indians could use the water for any purpose that fulfilled the reservation's purpose. Most important, the tribes' rights could not be extinguished or diminished through disuse.[7]

The doctrine of prior appropriation often has produced disastrous results. In times of shortage, allocations are honored according to the original date of their appropriation. Thus during droughts those highest up the appropriation chain receive their full allotment, while those at the bottom receive none. Further, the "use-it-or-lose" provision of the doctrine encourages wasteful consumption because, if one's full allocation is not used, it is lost. There are thus persons engaged in rice farming in the deserts of California in order to preserve their appropriation priority. Though the *Winters* doctrine is often the target of non-Indians who criticize the system of appropriation, neither the doctrine itself nor the Natives who demand adherence to its principles are responsible for these problems.

Although the basic doctrine was articulated by the Supreme Court in 1908, it left several significant issues unresolved. For precisely what purposes were reservations established? How was one to quantify exactly how much water Natives were entitled to according to their priority? Indians lacked the resources for development of their lands. Indian reserved water rights thus "lay substantially dormant" for over half a century.[8] During the intervening years the United States government pursued a policy of aggressively encouraging settlement in the West and establishment of small family-based agriculture on its dry, unsuitable soil. To further that policy, massive irrigation projects were constructed, diverting water that flowed on or near Indian lands. As the following article points out, Indian lands were often drowned in the process. According to a report of the U.S. National Water Commission in 1973, "With few exceptions the projects were planned and built by the Federal Government without any attempt to define, let alone protect, prior rights that Indians might have had in the waters used for the projects. . . . In the history of the United States Government's treatment of Indian tribes, its failure to protect Indian water rights for use of the Reservations it set aside for them is one of the sorrier chapters."[9]

As a result, since the late 1950s, reserved water rights have become a major topic of controversy and litigation. Court cases have sought to define the purpose of reservations as providing homelands for the tribes who settled there.[10] A principle for the quantification of reserved rights, based on the number of practicably irrigable acres to produce a marketable crop, has evolved.[11] Congress has considered several proposals to legislatively quantify Native reserved rights but has thus far taken no action.[12] Still unresolved is the issue of whether tribes are entitled to a specific quality of water under the *Winters* doctrine. The principle itself and subsequent judicial decisions would seem to answer the question in the affirmative. The United States, in arguing *Winters* before the Supreme Court, contended that it was necessary to fulfill reservation purposes that water flow be "undeteriorated in quality," but the Court remained silent on the point, as have subsequent tribunals.[13]

Despite its clear language, the *Winters* doctrine has not proved an absolute guarantee that tribal water rights will be protected.[14] Tribes are facing increased pressure from non-Indians who want to use water that originates on or passes through reservations.[15] As Phyllis Young points out, since the Reagan administration the policy of the federal government has been one which seeks to force negotiation of limitations on Indian reserved water rights. A more conservative federal judiciary has been increasingly resistant to Indian claims. In the 1980s, of the six major water-rights cases to come before the Supreme Court, tribal interests lost five. Further recent federal rulings have allowed water-rights claims to be adjudicated in state courts, traditionally much more hostile to Indian claims than their federal counterparts. As a result of these forces, tribes are inevitably turning to negotiation rather than litigation to settle disputes. They do so in return for what have proven to be largely illusory federal promises for water developments to deliver water to tribal lands.[16]

All of this occurs against a broader backdrop of growing awareness of water scarcity globally. "Exhausted rivers, falling water tables, and shrinking lakes testify to extensive human abuse of the world's water resources," one report concluded.[17] Around the planet, societies that once took water for granted and failed to treat it as the scarce commodity it is are experiencing its limits. The Worldwatch Institute, an organization dedicated to research into environmentally sustainable economies, has recommended a market system for the world's water, based on the Moroccan system in effect in the western United States and Spain, as a possible remedy for increasing global shortages.[18] If Du Bois was correct that the defining problem of the twentieth century was the problem of the color line, that of the next is quite likely to be the problem of the water line.

*M*ni *wiconi* means "water is life" in Lakota. Water has been my life struggle. The power of water comes from the seven stars. Since birth and life itself begin in water, the power of women comes from water. That's a traditional perspective on water. Water is our future as well. The fight for water rights is an ongoing struggle for Indian people all over the Americas. It represents the last asset that Indian people have in terms of property.

My home is on the Standing Rock Reservation, which straddles the border of the states of North and South Dakota. The Lakota people on Standing Rock live along a hundred miles of the Missouri River. There are at least twenty-six Indian nations or tribes who reside along the Missouri, the last virgin river in the country.[19] There are three major water systems in the western United States—the Columbia, the Colorado, and the Missouri. The water in the other systems has been totally adjudicated and overallocated. The only water that has not been allocated or adjudicated is water in the Missouri River. There are approximately twenty-six million acre feet of water in the Missouri. This water belongs to the many people who live along the entire river basin. Although it has never been acquired, it has been overcommitted by the federal government.

When I was ten years old my family was removed from its lands so that the Oahe Dam could be built. We lived right in the cradle of the Missouri River basin. It was referred to as the most valuable land in the entire world next to the basin of the Nile, and acknowledged by the Congress as such during hearings on the project. There was more land taken from Lakota people by building dams than for any other public project in America—all the way down from the Fort Peck Reservation in Montana to Standing Rock, Cheyenne River, Crow Creek, Lower Brule, and Yankton reservations. Out of those dams came the largest generation of hydroelectric power in America. More hydroelectric power is generated from the Missouri than from the Colorado and Columbia combined. Operations return a surplus to the United States Treasury every year of not less than $100 million.

Before I get into the economics of the development, I would like to explain a little bit about how it affected me. When I was ten years old, I was sent away from home to a boarding school. I had never known alcoholism. I had never known welfare. I had never known any other life. My family was removed from our lands. My people were removed from their lands to build hydroelectric dams. The results were devastating. At the time of the projects there were no requirements to meet the demands of the National Environmental Policy Act or to produce an environmental impact statement.[20] The environmental damage was immense. But the cultural depredation that occurred to the people was worse. It was the degradation of Indian culture. A self-sufficient society was replaced by a welfare system that stripped Lakota people of what traditional pride and dignity was left after being confined to a reservation.

Standing Rock was the last reservation established by the United States government. It was established specifically for Sitting Bull, and he didn't want it. During the 1950s a number of projects of the U.S. Army Corps of Engineers and the Bureau of Reclamation, the agency of the Department of the Interior in charge of irrigation projects on Indian lands, threatened to drown Indian Country. In North and South Dakota, the Pick-Sloan Plan led to the construction of a series of dams on the Missouri. These were intended to control flooding, provide irrigation for both Indians and Whites, and generate hydroelectric power.[21] The Lakota people negotiated for almost ten years under Pick-Sloan. The Standing Rock Sioux held out the longest. In the end, however, the plan proved disastrous for the Standing Rock, Cheyenne River, Crow Creek, and Fort Berthold reservations. The Indians there could only watch as water flooded their farmlands, villages, and sacred sites.[22] Old men sang their death songs when they heard the rushing waters coming in on a cold January night. They didn't wait for the spring thaw or the June rise. In fact, they destroyed the June rise, a term that my grandmother used to describe the beauty of the river rising in the springtime. At the June rise you heard the birds sing and all the sounds of nature, and you could smell, feel, and hear the water. Sometimes I go back just to sit on the bank of the river to try to hear what we used to hear when we were small, but I can't hear it anymore. So I can feel some of the pain our grandfathers must have felt when those waters cascaded down over our land.

There was an old man named Red Tomahawk who was blind. He sat on the highest hill, and he wondered what was happening because he could not see. All he could hear was the rushing water. He sang his death song because he heard. It was the coldest night of the coldest month in the winter of 1959. This was a typical happening up and down the Missouri River during those years, as the government built six multipurpose dams in Montana, North and South Dakota, and Nebraska.

As I said, this all took more of our land and devastated our people. It took place at a time when the country was being swept with a wave of patriotism and national pride. Indeed, the building of these dams was one symbol of national pride and national accomplishment. President John Kennedy signed Public Law 85-915, which authorized construction of many of these dams, into law. Although he was our president too, he thereby took more land from Indians than any modern president. Since that time, self-determination and sovereignty have supposedly been the cornerstones of federal Indian policy. In practice, however, things have changed little. President Carter's water policy was practically an open declaration of war against Indian people in America, nationalizing all water rights and thereby federalizing the reserved water rights and treaty rights of Indians. President Reagan's policy initiated a process at the Department of Interior that was designed to extinguish Indian water rights and foster states' rights by forcing Natives to negotiate the end to their rights. He also created the Presidential Commission on Indian Reservation Economics, which called for the quantification of Indian water and for the development of a water trust corporation. The primary objective was to quantify the water. The secondary objective was to manipulate the regulations controlling the quantification process in order to limit Indian interests, so that there would be more water for others.

During the Reagan years major legislation was introduced calling for a massive diversion of water in the western United States, first proposed decades earlier. Once again the priority was on a supposed national interest and use by non-Indians. Once again, Indians were to be the ones to suffer. In 1984, during the Congressional hearings on this diversion, known as the Garrison Diversion Project, Indian people mobilized. They went to every hearing held in the states of Montana, North Dakota, and South Dakota, forming a network of persons to address different aspects of the environmental and cultural impact of the Garrison Diversion. They worked in cooperation with the National Audubon Society, which had successfully fought the project for twenty-four years.

Through our struggles against the water plot, we learned how to organize and mobilize and grew in awareness of who we were. As a result, we screamed genocide in the congressional hearing. Something that you do not do in congressional hearings is accuse Congress of genocide. We felt, however, that it was important and, in fact, necessary—even critical—for us to do so, because to strip us of our land, to build dams and dam the water for public purposes, and now to divert that water for the use of others definitely was genocidal. Senators got on the telephone immediately and told our elders and tribal officials to talk to their young people, claiming that we could not use that kind of terminology in the Congress of the United States. We initially refused to retract our statements in the congressional record. After protracted negotiation, however, we agreed to change the record, but only if we could have a commission for ourselves. Ann Zorn, a member of the presidential commission, had been appalled when she heard our testimony, appalled not at our conduct but at the fact that Indian land was being taken by the project. She went to the press. She questioned why the figures on acres of land lost presented by the state of North Dakota differed from those provided by Lakota people. She raised other crucial questions as well, and with her help, we got our commission, known as the Joint Tribal Advisory Committee (JTAC). We were allowed to name one person to represent us on the commission, and we chose Dr. Brent Blackwelder, then president of the Environmental Policy Institute in Washington.

At that time I was the director of reservation resources for the Standing Rock Sioux. We prepared a claim detailing our economic loss based on the loss of land. If one went down the river one could see the absurd approach the government took toward compensation. Fort Berthold lost 156 thousand acres, for which they were paid $12 million. Standing Rock lost 56 thousand acres and was paid $12 million. There was 105 thousand acres lost at Cheyenne River, and they were paid $12 million as well. Of that $12 million, $8 million was a government grant, which other tribes not involved also received. Thus it really wasn't compensation. In making our case, we knew that we had to be dramatic in our illustrations. Examining a variety of economic factors, including the billions of dollars in value of the hydroelectric power that would be generated and the percentage Standing Rock's loss was in relation to total lands lost as a result of the project, we claimed $356 million in additional compensation. That claim covered only our economic compensation for the land. We did not negotiate, and we have never to this day negotiated, for our water rights. By 1987 JTAC legislation covering only Fort Berthold and Standing Rock had been drafted. In 1992 President Bush signed the bill into law, providing for $90 million. This legislation also included a provision for the return to the tribes of seventeen thousand acres of land that was not to be used for the public project. In the interim, however, some of this land was sold to private individuals or to the state of South Dakota for recreational purposes. It was deemed to be economically infeasible for Congress or the BIA to facilitate the land return, however, so this provision was repealed quietly in 1994 in a rider to appropriations legislation for the relief of victims of that year's earthquake in California.

President Clinton's plan is virtually the same as President Carter's policy in terms of the priority given to water resources. The purpose is to sell hydroelectric power to the private sector. It continues to ignore Indian peoples' rights in the name of some broader national interest. President Clinton is now proposing to privatize the Western Area Power Administration, which accounts for much of the energy in the West. No mention is made of what belongs to Indian people. As I said, water is the last asset that Indian people have—especially Lakota people.

At the end of the twentieth century Indian people still have to contend with the sick perversions of the frontier mentality. When one colonel in the Army Corps of Engineers was reprimanded by his superiors in Washington for his bad faith actions in negotiating with Indians, his response was, "Well, it was those people from the Standing Rock Reservation that killed Custer, and I'm not going to forget it." So that mentality actually carries on to this very day.

We Indians will carry on as well, though, and that frontier mentality will carry on into the twenty-first century with us. We've had a long struggle, and I believe that there has been a little bit of progress. But we cannot afford to forget the planning that continues behind our backs in the "national interest." One of the major objectives for President Reagan was quantification of water resources, preparatory to appropriation of those resources. We were very fortunate in that we grasped what was happening in terms of water. Now, however, we need to develop our economies and promote our own methodologies, because the problem is ongoing—and for Indian peoples it does not matter whether Democrats or Republicans are in power.

I think that if Russell Means taught me one thing, it was to be Indian, to *speak* Indian, to be Lakota. To be Democrat, to be Republican, to be a Marxist, to be a leftist, to be whatever is only a label. It doesn't describe me. Being a Lakota is the only thing that fits me. That has to be my perspective, and that is the only way that we can move forward in our development. To grasp the non-Indian way of thinking and scientific methods has been a struggle up until now. We didn't understand what "diversion" meant when the Garrison Diversion Project came up. Then we started reading, and we understood that they were taking our water. They were taking it!

We started to look at why they were taking it. Historically non-Indian development has been on the east side of the river where all the money interests were. Japanese concerns were coming in to North Dakota farms. All the small family farms were disappearing and being replaced by large corporate farms. That had a lot to do with why they wanted the diversion on the east side of the river.

It really was a local issue for me—*my* tribe, *my* reservation, *my* homeland where I came from, where *I* lived. I lived right on the shore of the Missouri River. As I stated earlier, when I was ten years old I was sent away to boarding school. I didn't understand why. By the time I was twelve years old, I began to see my relatives pick up alcohol, which I had never seen in the first ten years of my life. I didn't understand why. I didn't know why. I didn't understand it. Now I understand very clearly what was happening to all of us with each new development, with each new presidential policy, with each new Congress. I understand clearly now the colonialism that we have endured and that we continue to endure, and I understand the devastating effects that colonialism has had on our people, our land, and our culture.

Twenty-five years ago we had to stand against the ETSI pipeline.[23] Corporations negotiated with South Dakota to sell fifty thousand acre feet of water for a proposed coal-slurry pipeline and a water line—a dual-purpose, dual-system line from the Dakotas to the states of Louisiana and Arkansas. It would have crossed thirty waterways on its way across Indian Country. When they were discussing this in the South

Dakota state legislature, a group of women attempted to get an amendment to Senate Bill 1002 to include the Sioux Nation as a beneficiary of the water sale. In 1977 and 1978 it was very radical to suggest that we be included in some kind of development or some kind of settlement. It was an immensely difficult time. The state observed the absolute minimum requirements of public notice in announcing hearings on the matter, so there were times when we loaded up cars and trucks at 4:00 in the morning to try to make it to hearings in Pierce or Philip– little towns in the middle of nowhere that I had never seen. The hearings in those towns and in those times were very scary, but we went and we testified. We took our elders. We didn't have any money, but we made it, and I think that the long-term benefits for us in South Dakota were the friendships and the partnerships that we created with non-Indian people.

Real people, a common struggle, and strange bedfellows. I made friends with a redneck cowboy. He and I were the last to just hang in there and attend those ETSI hearings. He did not want the ETSI pipeline for his own reasons, as a rancher. I was there for my own patriotic reasons, for my people. I did not want the ETSI pipeline either. But we were there together. We would just smile at each other and think, "Here we go again!" For me, it was a beginning of an understanding that people must stand together. Without partnerships we could not be where we are today. Over the twenty-five years that I've been involved in work among Indian people, we have formed many partnerships and alignments with a variety of groups, including the Sierra Club, which was our staunch ally in defeating ETSI. The Sierra Club, the farmers, the ranchers, and the Indians eventually won; we defeated the ETSI pipeline. But we were not successful in getting ourselves included. The governor at that time vetoed that legislation.

It is now twenty-five years later, and we are still fighting the same issues. The current governor of South Dakota, William Janklow, probably has even greater plans for development of water in the state.

Nineteen eighty-five was the National Year of Water in the United States. It was part of a larger International Decade of Water (1980-1990). During that decade we worked with indigenous and third-world peoples from around the globe to coordinate our concerns and to integrate some of the goals and objectives of the international community into Lakota Country. One of our major accomplishments was the *Mni Wiconi* project on Pine Ridge Reservation, which is the largest water development project in Indian Country. Unfortunately, it was politically safe for members of Congress to support because it was a water project. It will probably eventually be the largest water system in the hemisphere. It did, however, meet our main objective for the Decade of Water–clean, safe drinking water for Lakota people.

Because of the overall scarcity of water in the western United States, Indian water rights have been a matter of great controversy. In 1908 the United States Supreme Court declared that Indian rights to water on Indian lands were not grants of rights from the federal government pursuant to treaty but were rather "reserved" rights. Whatever rights were not explicitly granted by treaty were reserved to the tribes.[24] The Court ruled that Indians had reserved enough water to fulfill the purposes of their reservations, to provide a homeland.[25] Later court rulings have sought to quantify the amount of water covered by these reserved rights. A complicated process has been mandated by the courts. According to the formula that has evolved, Indian tribes are entitled to water based on the "practicably irrigable acreage" (PIA) on the reservations multiplied by the amount of water necessary to irrigate each acre. In order to determine the PIA, one must ascertain the total of potentially irrigable acres and then look at the economic feasibility of irrigating them.[26] Although enough water is supposed to be reserved to meet future as well as present needs on the reservations, the concept of PIA and the economic feasibility criterion act to diminish Indian water rights. We are effectively prohibited from using our land as a base for economic development. If we were permitted, we could have economically viable projects based on our water, but the economic feasibility criterion and the PIA prohibit this development. Thus we have institutional barriers that automatically go up when we accept any program. These requirements should not apply to Indian Country. New methods need to be developed when we look to the scientific community. What we Indian people need to do is promote our traditional technologies, which have existed for thousands of years. And we need to develop new technologies based on scientific knowledge in addition to out traditional programs or methodologies based on the productivity of the land. Our traditional relationship to the land needs to be taken into account. The concept of sacredness must be incorporated into the legal principles of Western law.[27]

The state legislature of South Dakota, like many state legislatures currently, is debating legislation on "takings." The takings concept is designed to provide compensation for a financial loss incurred due to regulations that restrict the uses to which land can be put. Homestake Mining Company, as well as other industrial and mining interests, supports the initiative. The measure would require a "takings assessment," a cost/benefit analysis that would value property rights taken or restricted by regulation. This is directly related to quantification of water. It is all tied into industrial use of water. Homestake has the largest gold mine in the Western hemisphere in the Black Hills. It has been engaged in mining operations there since the last century. Now Homestake is actively insisting that it has the water rights in the Black Hills. It has conducted a very technical survey of all the creeks and other water, breaking down precisely how many acre feet it is claiming. We Indians are trying to force a hearing process in which we could press our claim that we have a prior right to the water based on reserved and treaty rights.

Lakota people have signed thirty-three treaties. We have more treaties with the United States than any other people, stretching from 1805 until 1868. Almost every provision you can think of is in those treaties, but there are very specific conditions attached to them as well. The Fort Laramie Treaty of 1851 sets the boundary of our land and establishes our ownership of the Missouri River and its water as well. According to the 1851 treaty, we own the water of the river to the eastern bank—which means the entire river. Subsequent agreements cut this back to the middle line of the river. Even under these terms, however, we still own half the river. So we still hold legal title to the water of the Missouri River based on the treaties; we have a reserved right pursuant to treaty. Our position at Standing Rock, therefore, differs somewhat from other tribes in the West. Unlike other tribes, it is our position that we have riparian rights based on treaty and reserved rights. We thus reject the doctrine of prior appropriation that governs much of water law in the West.

Homestake Mining, however, is attempting to claim water rights in the Black Hills. Non-Indian environmental groups in South Dakota are calling upon the Lakota people to intervene because of our treaty rights from 1851 and 1868. Our claims are thus prior to those of Homestake, who claimed a priority date of 1918. We are therefore attempting to mobilize the Lakota people in South Dakota so that we can influence hearings before the state water board. Standing Rock, Cheyenne River, and Pine Ridge reservations are all intervening to claim our right to the water in the Black Hills. Based on research and work I did during the time I spent with the Environmental Protection Agency, dealing specifically with water issues, I can attest that Homestake devastated many of the creeks and the waterbeds in the Black Hills. White Wood Creek in Spearfish Canyon is totally dead. The environmental damage to that stream was almost complete. The EPA has allowed Homestake, which pledged $18 million, to attempt to reclaim it. That damage to White Wood Creek can never be repaired. It is so contaminated that it can never be fully reclaimed. In addition, there is also extensive environmental damage from mining operations of companies other than Homestake.

Today, if you stand on Bear Butte, one of our most sacred sites, you can see the destruction. It is not going underground anymore. The whole earth is going to open up right there. I tell my children that I am terribly afraid that they are not going to be able to come there to pray much longer. I try to take my children there every fall and spring. We have had some good visits there and some good times. But that pristine beauty will not be there for very much longer if this mining is not stopped. The water table is being destroyed as well. If the South Dakota state legislature is successful in passing takings legislation, then non-Indians will be allowed to be compensated for the lands on which they have lived illegally for generations. Because that will justify their existence there over the last fifty to one-hundred years, they will have to be compensated. Native claims will continue sitting on the "back burner," waiting for compensation for their taking it from us to begin with.

Attempts to diminish or extinguish our water rights are just one manifestation of many attempts to cut back or eliminate our treaty rights. Our treaty rights are under attack across the board. Right now we have a Congress that is attempting to wipe out numerous programs and services in the name of fiscal responsibility. Included in that diminishment is going to be the diminishment of Indian programs. Indian programs, however, are based on treaty rights. Consider, as only one example, the food stamp program. Our treaty rights include provision of food rations and other commodities.[28] Thus, when the food stamp program gets wiped out, our treaty right is also being abolished. I think that maybe the new Republican Congress may be the best thing to happen to us in Indian Country, because if we get slapped around enough we're going to stand up and demand our rightful place again. That's my opinion.

Because of the Supreme Court's 1908 decision, we have a law that upholds the water rights of Indian people. Even so, our reserved rights are constantly attacked. There have been more than fifty lawsuits on different aspects of Indian water rights. As I said, it was President Reagan's policy to try to force negotiations for the relinquishment of Native water rights. Those who didn't want to negotiate were out. The Standing Rock Sioux did not want to negotiate. We said, "Why should we negotiate?" In any negotiation the federal government would simply sit us down and say, "Here's the Indian here, here's the state governor here." To negotiate meant to negotiate with the state. We said that Indian nations have a status higher than states. In fact, in 1964 South Dakota became the only state in the entire United States to vote by referendum not to interfere in the jurisdiction of Lakota people. I feel that that is a tool that we need to continue to use, because the people voted for it–non-Indian people. My ancestors from Standing Rock told people night and day to participate in that election. We were not a wealthy tribe–we were still a very poor tribe–but because we got a payment for our loss as the result of the Oahe dam, we were able pay for gas and food to get people to the polls and make a difference.

We have been successful in fighting many battles on the issue of our water rights, but private and governmental interests continue to attempt to seize our property. The treaty rights that we declared include our claim that the boundaries established by the Fort Laramie Treaty of 1851 set the boundaries of the Lakota Nation. That includes the Missouri River to the east bank. We hold that as the most sacred and important of our rights.

We, as Indian peoples, need to reorganize, get our energies back, and begin to address our common issues. I want to recommend a proposal I began to advocate ten years ago, for an International Water Tribunal. This would call for the opinions and recommendations of qualified scholars and eminent jurists to create new procedural mechanisms to meet circumstances of indigenous peoples. Such a tribunal would review the water rights of indigenous peoples around the world and publicize violations of those rights. It would draft the instruments necessary to gain access to international organizations and tribunals such as the International Court of Justice in The Hague. It would foster by its research and findings understanding of the factors that create group tensions and thus help to promote the growth of a consciousness regarding Indian water rights. This is a forum that indigenous peoples could create for themselves.

I think that the challenge now is to take the dialogue further. Our greatest challenge is for us, as indigenous people, to be accountable to ourselves as we plan and prepare for the future of our children in order to allow them to enjoy the benefits—financial and otherwise—derived from an intact land base. We must prepare for the settlement of the issue of ownership of water. We must restore the faith of Indian people in America. We must help afford our own people the dignity and pride of representing and governing themselves. We must restore economic justice to the Native people of the Americas, because without economic justice we cannot have environmental justice.

Notes

1. W. E. B. Du Bois, speech before the first Pan-African Congress, London, England (January 1900).

2. See, John R. Wunder, *"Retained by the People": A History of Indians and the Bill of Rights* (New York: Oxford University Press, 1994), p. 51.

3. For an excellent general discussion of Moroccan law, see, Lawrence Rosen, *The Anthropology of Justice: Law as Culture in Islamic Society* (Cambridge: Cambridge University Press, 1989). See also, David H. Getches, Charles F. Wilkinson, and Robert A. Williams, Jr., *Cases and Materials on Federal Indian Law*, 3d ed. (St. Paul: West Publishing, 1991), p. 789.

4. See, Lloyd Burton, *American Indian Water Rights and the Limits of Law* (Lawrence: University Press of Kansas, 1991), pp. 19-20.

5. George Johnson, "In Northern New Mexico, Some Seek the End of the Rainbow Gathering," *New York Times* (July 2, 1995), p. 16.

6. Burton, p. 20.

7. *Winters v. United States*, 207 U.S. 564 (1908).

8. Getches, Wilkinson, and Williams, p. 782.

9. United States National Water Commission, *Water Policies for the Future—Final Report to the President and to the Congress of the United States* (1973), pp. 474-475.

10. Often the underlying purpose has been viewed as agricultural. See, e.g., *In re Rights to Use Water in the Big Horn River System*, 753 P.2d 76 (Wyo. 1988), *affirmed sub nom, Wyoming v, United States*, 492 U.S. 406 (1989).

11. *Arizona v. California*, 273 U.S. 546 (1963).

12. Getches, Wilkinson, and Williams, p. 832.

13. *Winters*, 207 U.S. at 567.

14. Mark Mathews, "Water Rights: Are Montana Tribes Getting Their Fair Share?," *Indian Country Today*, Northern Plains ed. (June 29, 1995), p. B7.

15. "Tribal Water Rights Said at Risk," *Indian Country Today*, Northern Plains ed. (June 29, 1995), p. B6.

16. Ibid.; Lloyd Burton, "Water Rights," in Mary Davis, ed., *Native America in the Twentieth Century* (New York: Garland Publishing, 1994), pp. 691-692.

17. Sandra Postel, "Emerging Water Scarcities," in Lester R. Brown, ed., *The World Watch Report on Global Environmental Issues* (New York: W. W. Norton, 1991), p. 127.

18. Ibid., p. 138.

19. As will become obvious, by "virgin" the author does not mean unspoiled or undammed. The author uses the term to refer to the unallocated status of the river system.

20. NEPA, as it is known, establishes a comprehensive policy for government land-use planning. It requires federal agencies to consider environmental, historical, and cultural values whenever the federal government modifies federal land or uses federal funds to modify private lands. It also requires environmental impact studies and statements.

21. See, Paul H. Stuart, "Government Agencies," in Davis, p. 212.

22. David Rich Lewis, "Environmental Issues," in Davis, p. 189.

23. ETSI is the acronym for Energy Transportation Systems, Inc.

24. *Winters v. United States*, 207 U.S. 564 (1908).

25. *United States v. Adair*, 723 F.2d 1394, 1409 (9th Cir. 1983), *cert. denied sub nom. Oregon v. United States*, 467 U.S. 1252 (1984).

26. *Arizona v. California*, 460 U.S. 605 (1983)

27. See, Jace Weaver, "In the Absence of the Holy: Native Land and Religious Freedom Claims and American Jurisprudence," Fourth International Native American Studies Conference, Lake Superior State University, Sault Ste. Marie, Mi. (October 1993).

28. See, Francis Paul Prucha, *American Indian Treaties* (Berkeley: University of California Press, 1994), pp. 10-11.

6.

Family Closeness

Will James Bay Be Only a Memory for My Grandchildren?

MARGARET SAM-CROMARTY

EDITOR'S INTRODUCTION: In northern Québec the Cree still live primarily by the traditional methods of hunting, fishing, and trapping. They follow a spiritual way of life designed to balance their own needs with those of the animals on which they depend. In such a system human beings are not dominant. They are merely fellow creatures, predators like the wolf, who must kill in order to survive. According to Boyce Richardson, all animals, plants, and natural forces "are personalized in the Cree mind and are spoken of in the Cree language in the personal form."[1] Cree hunters and fishers develop *metew*, power derived from special relationships with natural forces and the animals they hunt. They understand that nature operates in a complex scheme of reciprocities.[2] In the last quarter-century, this ancient lifeway has come under increasing attack from hydroelectric development.

In 1970 Québec Premier Robert Bourassa, faced with the need to live up to a campaign promise to create 100,000 new jobs, announced plans to dam three major rivers (the Nottaway, Broadback, and Rupert) that drained into James Bay, an adjunct to Hudson Bay at its southernmost end. The following year the Société d'Energie de la Baie James (SEBJ) was established to shepherd the development. The project subsequently was expanded to include dams on the La Grande River, the third largest in the province.[3]

Construction began on Phase I, two dams on the La Grande, in 1972. At the height of activity in 1978-1979, twenty-two thousand workers labored nearly round the clock on four dams on the river. The first two dams were completed in 1984, having moved enough earth to build the Great Pyramid of Cheops eighty times over at a cost of $20 billion.[4] As they neared completion, the Bourassa government began negotiating a series of ambitious agreements with utilities in the United States to supply them with energy. In order to achieve the necessary generation capacity, it proposed Phase II of the project. This included completion of the two remaining facilities on the La Grande, five dams on the Great Whale River, and massive diversion of the Nottaway and Rupert into the Broadback via no fewer than eleven new dams. The Great Whale Project alone was projected to flood at least forty-four hundred square kilometers of land at a cost of $12.6 billion. The Broadback diversion had an estimated construction cost of an additional $44 billion.[5]

The Cree immediately organized to oppose James Bay II. They had fought Phase I in the courts with the partial support of the Canadian Department of Indian Affairs and Northern Development.[6] Now they returned to the judicial system. They refused to negotiate with Hydro-Québec and began to lobby for non-Native support in both Canada and the United States. As a result of their efforts, contracts for power in the United States were delayed, modified, and rescinded.

Finally, after the defeat of Bourassa's Liberal Party, the new Québec premier, Jacques Parizeau, canceled James Bay II in late 1994. In making the announcement, he declared, "The obsession Coon-Come [Matthew Coon-Come, Grand Chief of the Cree] has about the consequences of the Great Whale project was possibly quite understandable when the liberals were in power. That was their project, but it isn't ours."[7] By the time of the cancellation, however, much of the damage, which in a 1972 scientific report had been characterized as "culturally genocidal" for the Cree and neighboring indigenous peoples, had already been done. The Native inhabitants had been turned into "national sacrifice peoples" to be destroyed for the Canadian national good.[8]

James Bay I had rendered the La Grande River and its tributaries a series of stagnant lakes incapable of supporting most life.[9] Whitefish from first rapids of the river provided 20 percent of the diet of the Fort George Cree. This place of immense spiritual and practical importance was destroyed.[10] Concentrations of methyl mercury in the new reservoirs soared, poisoning fish and the animals and Cree who depended upon them. Cree suffer permanent neurological damage from eating the contaminated fish and game. Erosion increased dramatically, and the increased flow of fresh water into James Bay damaged delicate coastal ecosystems.[11] Animal and bird migration patterns were disturbed. In September 1984, ten thousand caribou drowned in an attempt to cross the flooded Caniapiscau River, a tributary of the La Grande.

In 1980 Fort George, a village on Governor's Island at the mouth of the La Grande, was evacuated because of the dangers of erosion. The SEBJ financed the construction of a new town, Chisasibi, on the mainland for relocation of the Fort George Cree. In Chisasibi, traditional life disintegrated. Diabetes, coronary disease, and obesity, previously unknown among the Cree, became common. Alcoholism, substance abuse, domestic violence, crime, and suicide became endemic. Like the fragile ecosystem of James Bay, Cree society was dying.[12] By 1990 few people remained in the new town, having instead spread out into the countryside.[13] In 1992 several families, disgusted with their altered lifestyle, returned to the largely abandoned and decaying Fort George.[14]

Margaret Sam-Cromarty has been among those Cree who have worked tirelessly to block the James Bay project, writing and lecturing throughout Canada and the United States. She goes far toward dispelling the image propa-

gated by Robert Bourassa of the Cree as "squalid savages" or that of Robert
Boyd, chief executive of the SEBJ, as "lazy" and indolent.[15] In her book *James
Bay Memoirs*, she writes, "In my memory stands a Cree village of Fort George
not flooded or abandoned but full of happy Crees. It's the way I would like to
remember Fort George Island—my people living together, happy and free."[16]
Shortly after writing those words, she and her family joined those who moved
back to Fort George.

In the following piece, Sam-Cromarty speaks in the fierce and lyrical language of the poet that she is. She vividly depicts traditional Cree ways, the
ravages upon them brought by the development, and the degraded life in
Chisasibi. She ends on a triumphant note with her return to Fort George. She
has announced that she will entitle her next book *They Dance with Joy*.[17] The
political situation in Québec, however, makes a change in government inevi-
table, and with that change may come a resumption of dam construction. Her
poignant question remains: "Will James Bay be only a memory for my grandchildren?"

Know When the Loons Cry Out

Crees know their country well.
They understand every stick and stone—
know when the loons cry out,
know the ground under their feet.

This is Cree country.
On their way
they will pass dangerous rivers,
misty lakes.

They are not expected,
when they wish.
The Crees will make camp,
wait for better weather.

Some will ride
the rapids.
They are masters.
They are brave.

Questions are not asked:
Who will lead?
They are bush men
with keen eyes and brown skin.

In the space of a second,
up ahead,
like demons between trees,
a waterless forest in flames.

This is Cree country.
They wait
at the edge of a river.
They know when the loons cry out.

I talked to a young Cree mother one day. She had young Cree teen-agers, and she wanted to protect them. In normal times she wouldn't worry, but twentieth century humanity is abusing the environment. And she and her children are caught in it. Will her Cree children be driven off the land, away from family hunting territories, or will her children be the ones who will stand up to protect Cree rights?

I smiled as I glimpsed the promise of a future in this young Cree mother. She will fight for things that count more than money. There is a reason why Mother Earth is called a female. There's a special power in a woman and a mother.

Far to the North (in James Bay, Québec), the Crees have lived for six thousand years. Europeans first came to our land only three hundred years ago, in the seventeenth century. They established a thriving fur trade and brought many changes. We still managed to keep our way of life. Very little did we adapt to many of the foreigners' changes—until now. Today development of hydroelectric projects threatens the Crees. We want new houses, new cars, new boats. We can't keep up the payments. We lose our new houses, our new cars, our new boats. We lose our families. This is change—so different from the traditional times of my father and mother. We have new problems today. I am sad, and I am angry sometimes.

Long ago we Crees followed the good whitefish. In August they used to fish at the first rapids. It was a good time, a fun time. I remember playing along the rocky shores. At the first rapids, the fresh smell of cooked fish filled the air. The smell always made me hungry. My mother used to smoke and dry fish. After it was thoroughly smoked and dried, it would be put away for the winter.

The memories of my childhood are gone. A few years ago a dam was built at the first rapids. Today fish are no longer fit to eat. The White man is there now at the first rapids.

We Crees still have the old ways in us. We still do things the way our ancestors did. So we Crees of today really aren't too much different from those of before. We are supposed to be more "civilized" and "educated," but weren't we so before the White man came? Maybe not in his ways but in ours.

Hydro-Québec said, "There's a shortage of jobs. These projects are good for the economy. The alternative is that the people go on welfare." Sure, if these dams are built, it will give White people jobs for a few years. Then what? James Bay I went ahead because there were many unemployed White people. Today, however, more attention is paid to protecting the environment and respecting Native rights.

Not long ago we Crees of James Bay were unknown. We were not important to anyone until Hydro-Québec wanted our rivers. Then the twentieth century came to our backward villages. No longer could I feel the closeness and safety I experienced when my village was small. Then, although we were poor, we had peace and love–and comfort that money can't buy. We spent our whole lives among our families, generations living under one teepee. No one was left alone or unattended, from the very young to the very old. Cree women worked just as hard as men. They worked close to home, raising their children. Manufactured toys were never seen. Wooden toys were made for boys in order to teach them practical things. Little girls carried around their baby sisters or brothers instead of dolls. Even now, I can hear the laughter and the sounds of delight.

In the old days Crees used to walk great distances to visit each other. Today no one wants to go visiting. There used to be a closeness at Fort George before we were forced to move to the mainland. There is no closeness at Chisasibi, the new town built by Hydro-Québec. There is no visiting back and forth, even though many Crees now have cars. In the new town it is hard to make ends meet. People break into your home when you're away. We have to pay for heat. We have to pay for our telephones. We have to pay for everything.

Of course, the Band Council or the Cree Nation have to make difficult decisions. When they do, they are accused of lining their own pockets. At least in the old days, Crees blamed the Indian Affairs agents. Today they blame each other. This new money–this new power–sets one Cree against another.

Despite all the changes, however, James Bay is still a beautiful place, because beauty lasts. Perhaps nature poses a threat to the material-minded. In nature there is balance. Everything has a meaningful purpose. Tribal communities enjoyed a balance akin to nature. They shared everything, and everyone was respected equally. Nature's balance makes everyone equal. North Americans have been persuaded by material wealth and power to renounce the spiritual and emotional side of nature.

When I was small my people taught their children to honor one another, not to steal, borrow, or beg. I was taught traditional manners. In turn, I cherished my father, mother, and grandparents. Today Cree women work to earn wages. They are no longer the healers of their people. There is violence against Cree women. We were once good parents. We were good neighbors. We were good people. We, who once followed the laws of the seasons, now must follow the laws of a foreign people.

Try to imagine what it means for the Cree to have their traditional homes flooded and destroyed by the dams of James Bay. What if the oceans swallowed up the entire United States? No longer could anyone live as he or she had. If you can imagine that, perhaps you might feel the pain of the Cree. Why do we have to pay for your electrical conveniences? Just beyond your doorstep, the Northern Continent drowns. Everything we have and are is stolen from us. This process of theft began with Christopher Columbus's men, who chopped off the hands of Natives who could not meet their daily quota panning for gold.

Understand the wisdom of our people. They belonged to the earth. They believed that the earth was something to care for and not simply something to be subdued or ravaged for its wealth. How would you feel seeing a member of your own family brutalized repeatedly for another's gain? The earth is our mother. Our connection to the land is as to a beloved person. It is our land, our earth, and we love it. Now it is wounded by huge hydroelectric dams, and behind them by great manmade lakes.

I spent some years at Chisasibi, the new town built with Hydro-Québec money. It is linked to the outside world by a paved road. In 1992 I got so disgusted with Chisasibi—with its materialism, alcohol, and other depredations—that I moved back to Fort George, my old home where I grew up. I found peace there. I am back in the bush, eating bannock and goose roasted over an open fire. It's a good life.

We do not understand the sickness called AIDS. I've heard about it. Some would rather turn away and not know or hear about it. Others say it's God's punishment. What if it's God's way of testing our compassion? The ravages of AIDS on the human body are a mirror of what we're doing to our Mother Earth.

In the future humanity will fight over water, food, and even pure air. Some would rather not hear about this either. Others are too busy fighting for material riches. We must have compassion for our earth. Life around us is so busy that we no longer take time to say thank you. We have drifted away from that. Yet the beautiful world and all its magnificent creations are still there. The world is a spiritual creation.

Burbot of the La Grande River

Burbot is a freshwater fish,
        my mother told me.
It's very good,
        this river cod.

The river cod,
    so excellent in taste.
This rich fish is my fondest memory
    of my tradition.

They call it progress.
At the same time,
We voice our concern
    about the river cod.

It's full of mercury,
    they said.
I try not to cry.

Notes

1. Boyce Richardson, *Strangers Devour the Land* (Post Mills, Vt.: Chelsea Green Publishing, 1991), p. 7; cf., Winona LaDuke, "Cultural and Biological Diversity: An Indigenous Perspective," *Common Future* (Spring 1995), pp. 8-9.

2. Ibid., pp. 7-10.

3. Ward Churchill, "The Water Plot: Hydrological Rape in Northern Canada," in Ward Churchill, *Struggle for the Land: Indigenous Resistance to Genocide, Ecocide, and Expropriation in Contemporary North America* (Monroe, Me.: Common Courage Press, 1993), p. 336. For a complete history and discussion of the James Bay hydroelectric plan, see, Richardson, *Strangers Devour the Land*, and Sean McCutcheon, *Electric Rivers: The Story of the James Bay Project* (Montreal: Black Rose Books, 1991).

4. Churchill, pp. 336-341.

5. Ibid., pp. 344-345.

6. Jean Chrétien, *Straight from the Heart*, rev. ed. (Toronto: Key Porter Books, 1994), pp. 64-65.

7. "Great Whale Hydro Project on Cree Land Collapses," *News from Indian Country* (Mid-December, 1994), p. 1. Parizeau's statement was somewhat disingenuous. Bourassa had been defeated by Parizeau's Parti Québecois (then led by René Lévesque) in 1976. During the period of PQ rule from 1976 to 1983, construction of James Bay I continued. For firsthand accounts of the PQ government, see, René Lévesque, *Attendez que Je Me Rappelle. . .* (Montreal: Éditions Québec/Amérique, 1986); Claude Morin, *L'art de l'Impossible: La Diplomatie Québecoise depuis 1960* (Montreal: Boréal, 1987); and Claude Morin, *Lendemains Piégés* (Montreal: Boréal, 1988).

8. Churchill, pp. 333, 337.

9. Ibid., p. 341.

10. Richardson, p. 341.

11. Ibid., pp. 344-347.

12. Ibid., pp. 249-250, 342; Churchill, p. 347.

13. Richardson, pp. 339-340.

14. William Cromarty, North American Native Workshop on Environmental Justice, Iliff School of Theology, Denver, Co. (March 17, 1995).

15. See, Robert Bourassa, *James Bay* (Montreal: Harvest House Publishers, 1973); Churchill, pp. 337, 367-368.

16. Margaret Sam-Cromarty, *James Bay Memoirs: A Cree Woman's Ode to Her Homeland* (Lakefield, Ont.: Waapoone Publishing, 1992), p. 64.

17. Margaret Sam-Cromarty, North American Native Workshop on Environmental Justice, Iliff School of Theology, Denver, Co. (March 18, 1995).

7.

Triangulated Power and the Environment

Tribes, the Federal Government, and the States

JACE WEAVER

Editor's Introduction: At environmental conferences I have attended, I often have heard non-Natives refer to ecological devastation as the worst crisis in human history. While not minimizing the situation confronting humanity today, I believe that many Natives would disagree with that statement. The problem is essentially perspectival in character. If one were to ask a Bosnian Moslem to name his or her greatest problem, I doubt the response would be global warming.[1] Invaded, nearly exterminated, and today often marginalized by the dominant culture, the leading item on the Native agenda is one of sovereignty, the right to make the decisions that affect their lives. In 1942 Felix Cohen wrote, "The most basic of all Indian rights, the right of self-government, is the Indian's last defense against administrative oppression."[2] It is also the best defense against forced assimilation and extinction.

This is not to deny that Native peoples are suffering from multiple environmental crises. The present volume demonstrates that fact. Donald A. Grinde, Jr., and Bruce Johansen correctly have referred to the "ecocide of Native America."[3] The two issues, however, are inextricably linked.[4] Natives view the environmental depredations being visited upon them as merely one more manifestation of the colonialism that has attacked their lives for over five hundred years. Ecojustice, therefore, if it is to be meaningful, cannot be discussed apart from that racism and colonialism.[5]

In 1994 the World Conservation Union task force for indigenous peoples, chaired by Dene activist Cindy Kenny-Gilday, stated that conservation "cannot be separated out from the integrated claims of indigenous peoples relating to self-determination, rights to lands, the right to control land and manage resource use and wildlife."[6] Norma Kassi puts it succinctly when she declares that if we don't "confront the abuse that's happening in our communities and if we don't look at the oppressive history and begin to heal that, all we are doing is setting up self-administration, not self-government."[7] Thus, discussion of environmental justice from a Native perspective requires an analysis of sovereignty and the legal framework that governs environmental matters in Indian Country.

I first examined these issues nearly fifteen years ago in the *Columbia Journal of Environmental Law.*[8] That article was written before a series of amendments in the 1980s that changed existing federal legislation to permit Indian tribes to formulate and enforce environmental regulations on their lands. It also was written before the controversial Supreme Court decision in *Brendale v. Confederated Tribes & Bands of Yakima* in 1989, which calls into question that right. At the time, during the Reagan administration and at the height of the energy crisis, the issue was primarily state governments attempting to enforce within their boundaries more stringent environmental policies than those of the federal government, which was bent on rapid development regardless of the impact. Today the issues are more complex, and the complicated interplay among tribes and federal and state governments deserves reexamination.

In 1631 John Winthrop, the recently arrived governor of Massachusetts, wrote concerning the indigenous inhabitants of the "new England": "This savage people ruleth over many lands without title or property; for they inclose no ground, neither have they cattel to maintayne it, but remove their dwellings as they have occasion, or as they can prevail against their neighbors. And why may not Christians have liberty to go and dwell amongst them in their waste lands and woods (leaving such places as they have manured for their corne) as lawfully as Abraham did among the Sodomites?"[9] He went on to justify the conquest with a detailed exegesis of the Hebrew scriptures, envisioning the Europeans as the ancient Israelites and the Natives as the Canaanites driven from the Promised Land.[10] What makes this bit of articulated conquering ideology noteworthy is that Winthrop preached it almost verbatim in 1629 in England, before he ever set eyes upon the North American continent, and later repeated it aboard the *Arbella*, the ship bringing him to his new appointment.[11]

In 1823 Chief Justice John Marshall incorporated the doctrines of discovery and conquest into the law of the youthful United States. In *Johnson v. McIntosh* he wrote: "We will not enter into the controversy, whether agriculturists, merchants, and manufacturers, have a right, on abstract principles, to expel hunters from territory they possess, or to contract their limits. Conquest gives a title which the Courts of the conqueror cannot deny, whatever the private and speculative opinions of individuals may be, respecting the original justice of the claim which has been successfully asserted."[12] Five years later, however, Chancellor James Kent, often called the father of American jurisprudence, codified the principle that Marshall refused to entertain. Citing the work of Swiss jurist Emerich Vattel, he pronounced that "cultivators of the soil" had priority over hunters in terms of rights to property. He adopted fully Winthrop's vision of the continent as "a wilderness, sparsely inhabited" by Indians who merely roamed over the land with "no fixed abode."[13]

Kent's view, and not that of Marshall, ultimately was to prevail. In 1985, in one of the leading cases in environmental law, the Ninth Circuit Court of Appeals observed, "Indian reservations may be considered as potential locations for hazardous waste disposal sites . . . because they are often remote from heavily populated areas."[14] To those in the dominant culture, Indian Country is still sparsely inhabited by rude hunters. The environment of Native lands can be sacrificed to the greater good of society because both they and those who inhabit them are of lesser value than more densely "settled" areas.

Indian lands have suffered from the polluting effects of heavy industry, toxic dumping, contamination of air and drinking water from off-reservation sources, and from fallout from nuclear testing and arms production. Most particularly, they have been damaged by the impact of mining operations on reservations or adjacent to them.[15] To some extent, all mining degrades the environment. *In situ* mining (traditional deep mining) is the least harmful in this respect, but traditionally it has the potential for considerable damage due to mine waste and geological subsidence.[16] New techniques of exploitation, however, can reduce this risk.[17]

By contrast, surface mining, a common technique of coal exploitation on western reservations, has a severe environmental impact because a great deal of earth must be moved in order to extract resources. Surface mining takes one of three basic forms: strip mining, open-pit mining, or terrace mining. Although these techniques are safer and easier than *in situ* mining, "gas, dust and noxious odors can be expected near the mines. Both the overburden and the tailings from the processing plant . . . present substantial disposal problems."[18] Strip mining is capable of extracting minerals to a depth of approximately 180 feet in relatively flat terrain. Reclamation normally consists of flattening the piles of overburden, replacing topsoil, and replanting. Open-pit mining is feasible for deeper deposits and irregular terrain. Overburden and minerals are removed together and carted out of the pit by means of a series of haulage roads or conveyor belts. The minerals are taken to processing plants, while the overburden normally is dumped distant from the pit. It is generally considered impractical to backfill the pit with overburden. Terrace mining is a variant of open-pit mining employed when deposits cover an extended area but are relatively shallow. Overburden is trucked away and stored, at least temporarily, rather than being dumped directly back into the pit. The process results in a very large worked-out area, which must be reclaimed.[19]

The impact of mining in western states has placed a severe burden on the environment. The associated problems, perceived need for development and resources, and a myriad of other environmental issues have created tensions among Native nations and the federal and state governments. Historically, western states have pressured the federal government and the tribes to permit a sharing of responsibility with regard to Indian lands. They have done so under the banner of proper balance between environmental protection and development. With the onset of the energy crisis in the 1970s, states became determined "to acquire additional control over developmental activities within their borders regardless of whether such development occurs on private, state [tribal], or federal lands."[20] In the absence of federal or tribal authorization to regulate Indian lands within their borders, states unilaterally sought jurisdiction over such lands.[21]

Dialogue among the three levels of government (tribal, federal, state) has revolved principally around three interrelated issues. The first is the question of federal plenary power over, and trust responsibility to, Indians. The second is the question of federal preemption and the right of states to pass reasonable regulations relating to lands within their borders pursuant to their police power when such regulations do not conflict with federal legislation. Third is the inherent sovereign power of tribes recognized by treaty and the United States Constitution. Each of these strands must be kept in mind when discussing environmental regulation on Indian lands.

The Articles of Confederation gave Congress "sole and exclusive power of . . . managing all affairs with the Indians, not in any of the states, provided that the legislative right of any state within its own limits be not infringed or violated."[22] Article I, section 8 of the Constitution dropped the states' rights proviso, granting to the Congress exclusive authority "to regulate commerce . . . with the Indian tribes."[23] With this power came a concomitant responsibility. In *Cherokee Nation v. Georgia*, Chief Justice Marshall determined that Indian tribes were "domestic dependent nations."[24] The federal government stood in a protective relationship toward the tribes, similar to a "guardian" over a "ward." From this grew the trust relationship between the federal government and Natives. "Later courts stretched the notion of a protective duty to tribal governments into almost unbridled power over them."[25] The doctrine of Congress's "plenary" power over Indians evolved.[26]

Such plenary power has been interpreted as giving the federal government authority concerning Indian lands equal to that exercised by it over federally owned lands in the public domain pursuant to the Property Clause.[27] The United States Court of Appeals for the Eighth Circuit declared in *Griffin v. United States:* "The power of Congress over the lands of the United States wherever situated is exclusive. When that power has been exercised with reference to land within the borders of a state neither the state nor any of its agencies has the power to interfere."[28] While the power of the federal government may not be

restricted by state regulation, the states may prescribe reasonable police regulations insofar as those regulations do not conflict with
congressional action and are thus preempted.[29] Once Congress has
acted, however, such action overrides conflicting state laws. As the
Supreme Court noted, "A different rule would place the public domain
of the United States completely at the mercy of state regulation."[30]

The third leg in this triangle of relationships is that of the sovereignty of the tribes themselves. According to Felix Cohen, "Perhaps
the most basic principle of all Indian law, supported by a host of decisions . . . , is the principle that *those powers which are lawfully vested in an
Indian tribe are not, in general, delegated powers granted by express acts of
Congress, but rather inherent powers of a limited sovereignty which has never
been extinguished.*"[31] For Cohen, treaties and legislation were not grants
of power to tribes but to the federal government. "What is not ex-
pressly limited remains within the domain of tribal sovereignty."[32] Tribal
governments thus exercise over Indian lands what is commonly referred to in the law as a "clipped sovereignty."[33] The precise extent of
such inherent sovereignty is a much debated point. According to
Getches, Wilkinson, and Williams, "In challenges to state assertions of
authority over Indians, however, the existence of congressional plenary power has proved to be a formidable shield guarding the
reservations as enclaves for the exercise of tribal governing authority.
A tension persists between the federal trusteeship obligation, with its
preemptive exclusions of state intrusions that impede tribal sovereignty,
and exercises of congressional powers that often remove or denigrate
Indian rights and tribal sovereignty."[34]

For many years states largely acquiesced in the exercise of federal
and tribal power over Indian lands within their borders; when conflicts did arise, they were resolved by cooperation rather than conflict.[35]
Beginning in the 1920s, however, energy-producing states enacted
measures for the conservation and orderly production of petroleum
and natural gas.[36] These enactments provided for prorationing,[37] spacing of wells, and the pooling and unitization of land overlaying a single
reservoir.[38] Conflict arose when a common source of supply underlay
both private or state land and federal or Indian lands.[39] States felt that
the conservation laws of the state in which the wells lay should govern,
particularly in cases where state lands lay over the same pool.[40] Otherwise state attempts at regulation largely would be rendered ineffective.
The situation was resolved by federal and tribal deference to the states.

During the early days of drastic prorationing in Oklahoma, the Osage, the richest energy-producing tribe in the state, frequently appeared
before hearings of the Oklahoma Corporation Commission concerning allowable production on controlled lands.[41] Although they
steadfastly maintained their jurisdictional immunity, the Osage always
abided by the orders of the commission in the interest of conserva-

tion.[42] Similarly, the federal government acquiesced in the conduct of lengthy spacing hearings, under the laws of Utah, concerning the Aneth Field, which underlay controlled lands in that state.[43]

In the early 1970s, with a growing awareness of degradation of the environment and the end to inexpensive, seemingly limitless resources, good will and cooperation among the three levels of government disintegrated. In response to increasing pressure for both land and natural resource development, western states began to enact comprehensive land-use legislation.[44] Contending that any effective land-use system must include federal and Indian lands within their borders, the states undertook to legislate controls for such lands, drawing little or no distinction between them and private or state-held property. The question quickly became whether state governments would be permitted to effectuate their plans and impose environmental requirements on controlled lands.[45]

The answer was a series of court challenges in Idaho, Oregon, and California.[46] In *Andrus v. Click*, involving state regulation in a national forest, the Idaho Supreme Court ruled that standards more stringent than those set by the federal government were not preempted. It stated that "the mere fact that federal legislation sets low standards of compliance does not imply that the federal legislation grants a right to an absence of further regulation."[47] Facing a nearly identical issue, the Oregon Court of Appeals, following the logic of *Click*, found "the preservation of the environmental quality of its lands is a subject particularly suited to administration by the states."[48] When a federal court finally addressed the issue, however, it found the broader view of federal power over controlled lands to be dispositive.[49] Since that time, western states have continued to assert aggressively the right of states to regulate the environment on Indian lands.[50] The result has been ever-increasing conflict between the states, on one hand, and the federal government and tribes, on the other.

There is little dispute that tribes have the authority to regulate conduct affecting the environment when it occurs on trust lands within the boundary of a reservation, subject to the plenary power of the federal government. Such conduct can be regulated even when it involves nonmembers of the tribe in question. States sometimes have attempted, however, to assert jurisdiction over conduct of both Indians and non-Indians on trust lands. When such an assertion takes place, courts are called upon to undertake a careful balancing of tribal, state, and federal interests in order to determine the appropriate regulatory power.[51]

Because of the General Allotment Act of 1887[52] and similar laws, which allocated reservations into individual parcels and opened "surplus" lands for settlement, significant portions of land within the exterior boundaries of many reservations are held by non-Indians. The result is a "checkerboard," in which adjacent parcels may be owned by Indians and non-Indians. Controversies arise as to which level of government has the power to impose environmental regulation upon these fee lands in non-Native hands. The issue is especially critical because of the migratory nature of resources such as air, water, and wildlife. Activities on non-Native property can have substantial effects on Indian lands.

Recognizing the potential for environmental damage to tribal trust lands from activities on adjacent lands held by non-Indians on reservations, the United States Supreme Court found that tribes had the right to regulate such conduct under certain circumstances. While the high Court overturned a ruling by the Ninth Circuit Court of Appeals that took a broad, traditional view of tribal sovereignty, it nonetheless recognized the inherent sovereign power retained by tribes. In delivering the opinion of the Court, Justice Potter Stewart stated that a "tribe may . . . retain inherent power to exercise civil authority over the conduct of non-Indians on fee lands within its reservation when that conduct threatens or has some direct effect on the political integrity, the economic security, or the health and welfare of the tribe."[53] In the ensuing years, lower courts have utilized this "*Montana* exception" to recognize tribal regulatory authority over non-Indian conduct affecting natural resources within reservations because of potential effects on "the health and welfare of the tribe."[54]

In 1989, however, the Supreme Court's decision in *Brendale v. Confederated Tribes & Bands of Yakima* created a controversy concerning the continued vitality of the exception. *Brendale* involved the attempt of the Yakima Nation to impose zoning restrictions on two parcels of land owned by nonmembers on its reservation. The first property was located in a part of the reservation that was 97 percent tribal land. The other was in a heavily checkerboarded area. While the Court ultimately decided that the tribe could regulate the first lot but not the second, it was badly divided, with none of three separate opinions speaking for a majority. In his opinion, speaking for four Justices, Byron White raised questions about the *Montana* exception permitting tribal exercise of authority over non-Indians.[55]

Most commentators agree that "considerable care is necessary to divine rules" from *Brendale.* Lower courts have struggled as to its meaning.[56] The Environmental Protection Agency (EPA) does not recognize it as controlling authority, instead continuing to rely on the clearer *Montana* decision, with which it finds the *Brendale* "fully consistent."[57] Western states, however, have been quick to seize upon the latter case as a means to attempt to gain control over reservation lands. The Conference of Western Attorneys General points to Justice White's opinion and repeatedly overstates the scope and reach of the case, writing "*Brendale* effectively replaced the *Montana* criteria and limited tribal jurisdiction over nonmember fee lands to circumstances where such lands constitute a small percentage of distinct reservation units maintained in a natural state."[58] The attorneys general contend that the EPA's stance with regard to the decision "diverges from Supreme Court requirements and raises questions whether determinations controlled by [its] regulations will accurately reflect the relative limits of state and tribal authority within Indian reservations."[59] Such a disingenuous reading of *Brendale* only serves to confirm Joseph Singer's statements concerning the assumptions underlying power and property in America. In analyzing *Brendale* and other recent cases, Singer writes:

> The Supreme Court has assumed in recent years that although non-Indians have the right to be free from political control by Indian nations, American Indians can and should be subject to the political sovereignty of non-Indians. This disparate treatment of both property and political rights is not the result of neutral rules being applied in a manner that has a disparate impact. Rather, it is the result of *formally unequal* rules. Moreover, it can be explained only by reference to perhaps unconscious assumptions about the nature and distribution of both property and power. This fact implies an uncomfortable truth: both property rights and political power in the United States are associated with a system of racial caste.[60]

The EPA refusal to recognize *Brendale* is, in fact, totally consistent with its longstanding policy of encouraging tribes to assume regulatory and management responsibilities for environmental programs.[61] In the absence of such assumption, EPA will tend to assume direct implementation and enforcement within reservation boundaries. State regulation is strongly disfavored. Though the EPA gained considerable support for its position in the mid-1980s, when amendments to various federal environmental protection laws were enacted, its position took shape as early as 1982 when the EPA Administrator commissioned a study of environmental programs on reservations that would take into consideration "the unique political status of Indian tribes."[62] Six months later President Reagan issued an "American Indian Policy Statement," which reaffirmed that "tribal governments had the primary responsibility for meeting the needs of tribal members," and the agency responded with its own policy, declaring that tribes were "the primary parties for setting standards, making environmental policy decisions and managing programs for reservations."[63] With its policy in place, the EPA began to limit state authority over reservations and act on the opinion that "tribal governments retain civil-regulatory authority over all reservation lands, regardless of ownership."[64] Pursuant to standards of federal regulatory law, courts have been willing to give extreme deference to EPA determinations denying state jurisdiction within reservations.[65]

The federal leg of the triangle of power is clearly implicated in decisions involving Indian lands. They have responsibility for controlled lands. Beyond this, however, the U.S. Supreme Court in *New Mexico v. Mescalero Apache Tribe* stated that the federal policy of promoting tribal sovereignty includes fostering economic development.[66] According to the Conference of Western Attorneys General, "Thus, federal interests are implicated where a tribe attracts an industry onto its reservation to broaden the tribe's economic base, and may be recognized as a factor against allowing states to impose strict regulations that would restrict or prohibit the industry's operations."[67]

Since 1963 with the passage of the Clean Air Act, Congress has enacted a series of laws that evidence a broad public commitment "favoring preservation of resources and protection of fragile and life-supporting ecosystems."[68] In general, these laws permit the EPA or, in the case of the Surface Mining Control and Reclamation Act, the Office of Surface Mining to delegate to states the authority to enforce minimum federal standards or, in some cases, stricter state requirements. As these enactments came up for renewal in the 1980s and early 1990s, they were usually amended to permit tribes to assume jurisdiction as "states" in lieu of direct federal administration.

Such a delegation, however, is probably unnecessary. Inherent tribal sovereignty should be sufficient to support tribal authority over both trust and fee lands within the confines of a reservation.[69] For instance, in *Nance v. EPA*, the Supreme Court let stand a determination by the Ninth Circuit Court of Appeals that the Northern Cheyenne had sufficient independent authority to regulate its reservation in order to prevent significant deterioration of its air quality.[70] Likewise the Resources Conservation and Recovery Act (RCRA) contains no provisions permitting tribal assumption in lieu of the federal government. Yet the Ninth Circuit affirmed the EPA's decision allowing tribes in Washington state to administer hazardous-waste programs despite the absence of specific legislative grants.[71] Further, the EPA itself does not view environmental legislation as delegating federal power to the tribes. As recently as July 1991 it affirmed its position that tribal governments are "the appropriate non-federal parties for making decisions and carrying out environmental program responsibilities" on reservations.[72]

The Clean Water Act (CWA) has been a particular point of contention in the struggles among federal, state, and tribal governments. Section 518 of the CWA provides for tribal assumption of responsibility for protection of water resources held by the tribe, held by the United States in trust for them, held by a tribal member if it would be subject to trust restrictions upon a change in ownership, "or otherwise within the borders of an Indian reservation."[73] Tribes and the EPA have interpreted the section as permitting tribal exercise of power within the entirety of the exterior bounds of reservations.[74] States, however, argue that the statute cannot be read in such a manner. To do so, they contend, renders the first three clauses of the sentence, which apparently set limits on tribal authority, meaningless.[75]

In the debate, the EPA and the tribes clearly have the better case. Other federal environmental statutes have similar language and have been interpreted in like fashion. The agency maintains that Congress made a legislative determination that conduct affecting water quality would have a serious and detrimental impact on tribes with the meaning of the *Montana* exception. Therefore, it concludes that "any impairment [of water quality] that occurs on, or as a result of, activities on non-Indian fee lands are [sic] very likely to impair the water and actual habitat quality of the tribal lands."[76]

The migratory nature of water makes it imperative that tribes be permitted to regulate its quality throughout the borders of reservations. Any other rule would have the potential to frustrate their regulatory schemes entirely. Checkerboarded authority over migratory resources (air, water, wildlife), mirroring the checkerboard ownership patterns, is a recipe for disaster. In making such an argument, one must be aware that it is a double-edged sword. It could easily be used to justify state regulation over reservations within their borders. Such a rule, however, would be contrary to the inherent sovereignty of the Native nations and must therefore be dismissed. "Spillover" effects from activities on reservation have been used by states to argue for on-reservation regulation by them. Those who advance this argument must be equally aware that "spillovers spill over both ways." Thus off-reservation pollution affecting the health and welfare on reservations should provide a basis for assertion of tribal jurisdiction beyond the boundaries of their territory. The Conference of Western Attorneys General contends, however, "Tribal sovereignty . . . is more limited [than that of states], and the mere allegation of on-reservation effects would not be sufficient to restore authority divested from the tribe as a matter of federal law."[77] In early 1993 Isleta Pueblo in New Mexico set water quality standards for the Rio Grande, requiring that the water be clean enough for ceremonial and recreational purposes, and the EPA approved such standards. The city of Albuquerque, located five miles upstream of Isleta, routinely discharges sewage into the river and in order to meet the tribally determined standards will have to spend an estimated $250 million over the next decade. Consequently, the city has sued to overturn the EPA action.[78]

Other aspects of EPA policy have been equally contentious. The western attorneys general argue that the administrative agency errs when it labels all property within reservations as "Indian lands," thus permitting tribal jurisdiction. The EPA definition is, they aver, in actuality that used for "Indian country," a term which includes fee lands. Federal courts have tended to define "Indian lands" as those in which

Indians have a property interest.[79] In the *Washington* case, however, the Ninth Circuit accepted the EPA's synonymous definitions as "a reasonable marker of the geographic boundary between state authority and federal authority."[80] Similarly, the attorneys general question whether the EPA can act as a neutral mediator in disputes over the proper reach of tribal jurisdiction because of federal trust responsibilities to tribes. They fear that the agency "may be pressured to err in favor of tribes."[81] Judicial review, however, should provide an adequate check upon erroneous or capricious exercises of administrative power as a result of such "pressure."

The triangulation of powers over Indian lands is virtually certain to become increasingly conflictual. No federal or state program is likely to take adequate account of Native cultural and spiritual considerations. Meanwhile, states will continue to grasp for regulatory control over Indian lands contrary to inherent tribal sovereignty.[82] According to a study commissioned in 1986 as part of amendments to Superfund legislation, there were twelve hundred hazardous waste sites located on or near twenty-five reservations studied.[83] Natives continue to fear that reservations will become "dumping grounds" for off-reservation wastes if states are permitted to control land use and environmental regulation on reservations—thus evoking the specter of disparate treatment spoken of by Singer and perpetuated by the attitude, evinced by Winthrop and Kent, that Indians sparsely inhabit the land and have no real sense of modern concepts of land use or tenure.[84]

Currently, the entire system of environmental protection in the United States is under assault at both the federal and state levels. Despite the fact that polls show that Americans want more—not less—environmental legislation if it will lead to a cleaner environment, the newly empowered Congress stands poised to roll back protections provided by a number of laws, including the Endangered Species Act,[85] the Clean Air Act, the CWA, the Safe Drinking Water Act, and Superfund.[86] Also in the works is a "takings bill," which would require compensation to landholders for any loss in value as a result of environmental controls. Known as the Private Property Protection Act, the bill would have a chilling effect on any future regulations as the "cost" required to be paid by the federal government becomes prohibitive.[87] A similar provision has already passed the Washington state legislature. Montana and Idaho have enacted legislation that will permit higher levels of pollution in the watersheds of streams and lakes. Wyoming recently placed a bounty on wolves reintroduced into Yellowstone National Park.[88]

Both federal and state governments appear intent on abandoning any pretense of national stewardship over natural resources.[89] It seems that the only ones who will speak out for the earth in Indian Country are the Indians themselves.

Notes

1. See, Tim Hilchey, "Global Warming Study Shows Sagebrush as King of Hills," *New York Times* (February 21, 1995), p. C4; William K. Stevens, "Nations to Consider Toughening Curbs on Global Warming," *New York Times* (February 21, 1995), p. C4.

2. Felix Cohen, *Handbook of Federal Indian Law* (Washington: Government Printing Office), p. 122.

3. Donald A. Grinde, Jr., and Bruce Johansen, *Ecocide of Native America: Environmental Destruction of Indian Lands and Peoples* (Santa Fe: Clear Light, 1995).

4. See, Donald Fixico, "The Struggle for Our Homes: Native Lands, Native Traditions, Sovereignty, and the Environment," herein.

5. Jackie Warledo, North American Native Workshop on Environmental Justice, Iliff School of Theology, Denver, Co. (March 18, 1995).

6. "The Question of Sustainable Development," *Nature Conservancy* (January/February 1995), p. 12.

7. Norma Kassi, North American Native Workshop on Environmental Justice, Iliff School of Theology, Denver, Co. (March 18, 1995).

8. Jace G. Weaver, "Federal Lands: Energy, Environment and the States," *Columbia Journal of Environmental Law* (7:2, 1982), pp. 213-226.

9. John Winthrop, "General Considerations for the Plantation in New England, with an Answer to Several Objections" (c. 1631); see also, Jennings C. Wise, *The Red Man in the New World Drama*, rev. and ed. Vine Deloria, Jr. (New York: Macmillan, 1971), pp. 78-79.

10. For a complete discussion of this motif in colonial rhetoric, see, Alfred A. Cave, "Canaanites in a Promised Land: The American Indian and the Providential Theory of Empire," *American Indian Quarterly* (Fall 1988); Djelal Kadir, *Columbus and the Ends of the Earth: Europe's Prophetic Rhetoric as Conquering Ideology* (Berkeley: University of California Press, 1992); Robert Allen Warrior, "Canaanites, Cowboys, and Indians," *Christianity and Crisis* (September 11, 1989).

11. John Winthrop, *Winthrop Papers*, vol. 2 (Boston: Massachusetts Historical Society, 1931), p. 141; Robert F. Berkhofer, *The White Man's Indian* (New York: Alfred A. Knopf, 1978), pp. 120-121; Neal Salisbury, *Manitou and Providence: Indians, Europeans, and the Making of New England 1500-1643* (New York: Oxford University Press, 1982), p. 183; Ronald Takaki, *A Different Mirror: A History of Multicultural America* (Boston: Little, Brown, 1993), p. 42.

12. *Johnson v. McIntosh*, 8 Wheat. 543 (1823). Marshall later backtracked on this notion in *Worcester v. Georgia*, 6 Pet. 515 (1832), calling it an "extravagant and absurd idea, that the feeble settlements made on the sea coast . . . acquired legitimate power by them to govern the people."

13. James Kent, *Commentaries on American Law*, vol. 3 (New York: O. Halsted, 1828), p. 312; vol. 1 (New York: O. Halsted, 1826), p. 243.

14. *Washington Department of Ecology v. United States Environmental Protection Agency*, 752 F.2d 1465 (9th Cir., 1985).

15. See, e.g., Grace Thorpe, "Our Homes Are Not Dumps: Creating Nuclear Free Zones," and Justine Smith, "Custer Rides Again–This Time on the Exxon *Valdez*," herein.

16. Dick and Wimpfen, "Oil Mining," *Scientific American* (October 1980), p. 185A; see, *Pennsylvania Coal Co. v. Mahon*, 260 U.S. 393 (1922).

17. For instance, in oil mining, which exploits petroleum by excavating a series of tunnels either above or below deposits and then draining or pumping oil into the tunnels rather than by surface drilling, the amount of excavated material brought to the surface and later disposed of is small compared with that brought up by conventional mineral extraction. The prospect of subsidence is slight. Further, water can be injected into the oil reservoir, thus reducing the risk further (Dick and Wimpfen, pp. 183-185).

18. Ibid., p. 188.

19. Ibid., p. 187.

20. Shapiro, "Energy Development on the Public Domain: Federal/State Cooperation and Conflict Regarding Environmental Land Use Control," 9 *Nat. Resources Law.* 397, 398 (1976).

21. Ibid.

22. Articles of Confederation, art. 9.

23. U.S. Const., art. I, § 8, cl. 3.

24. *Cherokee Nation v. Georgia*, 5 Pet. 1 (1831).

25. David H. Getches, Charles F. Wilkinson, and Robert F. Williams, *Cases and Materials on Federal Indian Law*, 3d ed. (St. Paul: West Publishing, 1993), p. 325.

26. *United States v. Kagama*, 118 U.S. 375 (1886); *Lone Wolf v. Hitchcock*, 187 U.S. 553 (1903).

27. U.S. Const., art. IV, § 3, cl. 2.

28. *Griffin v. United States*, 168 F.2d 457, 460 (8th Cir. 1948).

29. 73 C.J.S. "Public Lands" §3 (1967); see also, *Kleppe v. New Mexico*, 426 U.S. 529, 543 (1976).

30. *Camfield v. United States*, 167 U.S. 518, 526 (1897).

31. Felix Cohen, *Handbook of Federal Indian Law* (Washington: Government Printing Office, 1942), p. 122, quoted in Getches, Wilkinson, and Williams, p. 227.

32. Cohen, p. 122; *United States v. Winans*, 198 U.S. 371 (1905); see also, Lloyd Burton, *American Indian Water Rights and the Limits of the Law* (Lawrence: University of Kansas Press, 1991), p. 21.

33. See, "Clipped Sovereignty," *Black's Law Dictionary*, 5th ed. (St. Paul: West Publishing, 1979), p. 231.

34. Getches, Wilkinson, and Williams, p. 325.

35. For a discussion of the situation on the federal public domain, see, *Utah Power & Light Co. v. United States*, 243 U.S. 389, 404-05 (1917).

36. E.g., Okla. Stat. Ann. tit 52, §87.1 (West 1969 & Supp. 1980); Wyo. Stat. §30-5-109 (1977).

37. The limitation of production of crude oil or gas to some fraction of total productive capacity.

38. See, Richard W. Hemingway, *The Law of Oil and Gas* (St. Paul: West Publishing, 1971), pp. 421, 423.

39. R. M. Williams, "Relationship between State and Federal Government with Respect to Oil and Gas Matters," 19 Oil & Gas Inst. 239, 253-54 (1968); see also, I. R. Myers, *The Law of Pooling and Unitization* 390-91 (2d ed. 1967).

40. Myers, p. 389.

41. Controlled lands are federally-owned lands in the public domain and other lands controlled or supervised by the federal government, including the trust lands of Indian tribes.

42. Williams, p. 254; see also, Terry P. Wilson, *The Underground Reservation: Osage Oil* (Lincoln: University of Nebraska Press, 1985).

43. Williams, p. 255.

44. Shapiro, pp. 418-422.

45. Ibid.

46. For a complete discussion of these challenges, see, Weaver, pp. 213-226.

47. *Andrus v. Click*, 97 Idaho 791, 796, 554 P. 2d 969, 974 (1976).

48. *Cox v. Hibbard*, 31 Or. App. 269, 274, 570 P. 2d 1190, 1193 (1977).

49. *Ventura County v. Gulf Oil Corp.*, 601 F.2d 1080, 1083 (9th Cir. 1979), *aff'd mem.*, 100 S. Ct. 1593 (1980).

50. Nicholas J. Spaeth, Julie Wrend, and Clay Smith, eds., *American Indian Law Deskbook: Conference of Western Attorneys General* (Niwot: University Press of Colorado, 1993), pp. 263-300.

51. Ibid., p. 269.

52. Act of Feb. 8, 1887, ch. 119, 24 Stat. 388.

53. *Montana v. United States*, 450 U.S. 544, 567 (1981).

54. Spaeth, Wrend, and Smith, p. 265; see, e.g., *Cardin v. De La Cruz*, 671 F.2d 363 (9th cir. 1982), *cert. denied*, 459 U.S. 967 (1982); *Confederated Salish & Kootenai Tribes v. Namen*, 665 F.2d F.2d 951 (9th Cir. 1982), *cert. denied*, 459 U.S. 977 (1982); *Knight v. Shoshone and Arapahoe Indian Tribes*, 670 F.2d 900 (10th Cir. 1982) .

55. *Brendale v. Confederated Tribes & Bands of Yakima*, 492 U.S. 408 (1989).

56. Getches, Wilkinson, and Williams, pp. 713-714.

57. Spaeth, Wrend, and Smith, pp. 289-290.

58. Ibid., p. 289; see also, ibid., pp. 265-266, 291.

59. Ibid., p. 291.

60. Joseph Singer, "Sovereignty and Property," 86 *Nw.U.L.Rev.* 1, 4-5 (1991). Emphasis original.

61. Getches, Wilkinson, and Williams, p. 731.

62. Spaeth, Wrend, and Smith, pp. 286-287.

63. Ibid., p. 287.

64. Ibid., p. 288.

65. *Washington*, 752 F.2d at 1469.

66. *New Mexico v. Mescalero Apache Tribe*, 462 U.S. 324, 334-35 (1983).

67. Spaeth, Wrend, and Smith, p. 274.

68. Getches, Wilkinson, and Williams, p. 730. These laws include the Federal Water Pollution Control Act (commonly called the Clean Water Act); the Clean Air Act; the Safe Drinking Water Act; the Endangered Species Act; the Resources Conservation and Recovery Act; the Comprehensive Environmental Response, Compensation and Liability Act (commonly referred to as Superfund); the Surface Mining Control and Reclamation Act; and the Federal Insecticide, Fungicide and Rodenticide Act.

69. Judith Royster and Rory Fausett, "Control of the Reservation Environment: Tribal Primacy, Federal Delegation, and the Limits of State Intrusion," 64 *Wash.L.Rev.* 581, 583-96 (1989).

70. *Nance v. EPA*, 645 F.2d 701, 714-15 (9th Cir.), *cert. denied*, 454 U.S. 1081 (1981).

71. *Washington*, 752 F.2d at 1469. States' rights advocates point to the fact that the Washington case was decided prior to *Brendale* and that a different outcome would probably appertain today. Such an expansive reading of *Brendale* is, however, unwarranted, and given traditional judicial deference to administrative determinations, a different decision seems unlikely.

72. Getches, Wilkinson, and Williams, p. 731.

73. 33 U.S.C. §1377(e)(2).

74. "Indian Tribes: Water Quality Planning and Management, Interim Final Rule," 54 Fed Reg. 14,354, 14,355 (1989); Spaeth, Wrend, and Smith, p. 282.

75. Spaeth, Wrend, and Smith, p. 282.

76. Ibid., p. 290.

77. Royster and Fausett, p. 635; Spaeth, Wrend, and Smith, p. 270.

78. Getches, Wilkinson, and Williams, pp. 732-733.

79. Spaeth, Wrend, and Smith, pp. 291-292; *Solem v. Bartlett*, 465 U.S. 463, 468 (1984).

80. *Washington*, quoted by Getches, Wilkinson, and Williams, p. 728 n. 1.

81. Spaeth, Wrend, and Smith, p. 292.

82. See, "The Endangered West," *New York Times* (June 18, 1995), p. 14.

83. Getches, Wrend, and Smith, pp. 731-732; see also, Teresa A. Williams, "Pollution and Hazardous Waste on Indian Lands: Do Federal Laws Apply and Who May Enforce Them?" 17 *Am.Ind.L.Rev.* 269 (1992); Richard A. Du Bey, et al., "Protection of the Reservation Environment: Hazardous Waste Management on Indian Lands," 18 *Envtl.L.* 449 (1988).

84. See, *Washington*, quoted in Getches, Wilkinson, and Williams, p. 729.

85. "Endangered West," p. 14; Timothy J. McNulty, "Endangered Species Act in GOP's Cross Hairs," *Denver Post* (March 19, 1995), p. 13A; William K. Stevens, "Future of Endangered Species Act in Doubt as Law Is Debated," *New York Times* (May 16, 1995), p. C4.

86. John H. Cushman, Jr., "Congressional Republicans Take Aim at an Extensive List of Environmental Statutes," *New York Times* (February 22, 1995), p. A14; John H. Cushman, Jr., "Republicans Clear-Cut Regulatory Timberland," *New York Times* (March 16, 1995), p. E16.

87. John H. Cushman, Jr., "House Clears More Limits on Environmental Rules," *New York Times* (March 3, 1995), p. A19; Dan Gordon, "The Environment vs. Property Rights," *New York Times* (March 15, 1995), p. A25; Charles C. Mann and Mark L. Plummer, "Environmental Law Is Wrecking the Environment," *New York Times* (March 2, 1995), p. A23; James V. DeLong, "It's My Land, Isn't It?" *New York Times* (March 15, 1995), p. A25.

88. "Endangered West," p. 14.

89. Ibid.

8.

Malthusian Orthodoxy and the Myth of ZPG

Population Control as Racism

ANDREA SMITH

EDITOR'S INTRODUCTION: Just as the invisible hand of Adam Smith lies heavy on modern economics, the views of his fellow economist Thomas Robert Malthus continue to dominate debates on development and population. In *An Essay on the Principle of Population as It Affects the Future Improvement of Society*, published anonymously in 1798, Malthus theorized that population would always outstrip food production. If unchecked, population grows in geometric progression, while agriculture increases only arithmetically. Thus population would expand to the limits of subsistence and be held there by war, disease, and famine. Never did Malthus clearly set forth his premises for this pessimistic theory or test their logical foundations. He was equally lax in his treatment of factual and statistical data. Despite this, his theory of population became firmly entrenched in economics and still figures prominently in demographic discourse today.

Andy Smith demonstrates the destructive effects Malthusian analysis has had on indigenous people and those in the Third World and argues forcefully for its abandonment in current discussions of population. Like the views of the environmental crisis discussed in the previous chapter, differing perspectives on the necessity of population control reflect the divergent social conditions of those engaged in the dialogue. For those in the dominant culture in industrialized nations, control of population growth has been called the most critical issue in preserving the health of the planet. Because, as Smith points out, populations in developed countries are either stable or in retrograde, the focus of population policies is most often third-world nations or communities of color. From an indigenous point of view, to accept population-control policies commonly advanced will only perpetuate genocide against indigenous peoples already decimated by more than five hundred years of conquest and colonialism. Control of populations in the developing world is often little more than a veiled way of preserving the massive overconsumption of resources by the wealthy. While few can argue with the force of this analysis, the issue of population itself remains contentious, even among some of those who participated in the North American Native Workshop on Environmental Justice. Glenn Morris argues that the current population of North America exceeds its carrying capacity by a factor of ten.[1] Others contend that the continent outstripped its carrying capacity as early as 1840, despite massive reductions in the indigenous population.[2] They would nonetheless agree with Smith that current patterns of production and consumption must be radically altered in order to avert calamity.

Stabilizing, or even decreasing, global population will have little effect while current consumption patterns continue. By the same token, simply "reducing consumption and changing production patterns will be of little effect if we continue to add 95 million people a year to the earth's lifespace."[3] Most crucial, as Doug Hunt, a U.C.C. clergyperson from Maryland, points out, "The evidence of the last three decades is that neither of these critical factors can or will change until the economic, political, and social system are restructured on the basis of equity, justice, mutuality, and compassion."[4] This is the essence of Smith's argument.

Glenn Morris argues that attempting to deal with population and environmental problems by placing one's faith in science and technology will only result in some form of "fascism."[5] While Hunt optimistically contends that few of those with political and economic power continue struthiously to deny "the ever-more unpleasant impacts of the dominant economic and social models on an increasing proportion of the world's people," he nonetheless admits that people in power suffer from an addiction-based response to these problems, "trying to correct growing inequities, disturbances and imbalances by doing more and more of what created the situation in the first place."[6] He writes, "This resembles nothing so much as a clown staggering across the stage, trying to balance a plate on the end of a stick. The harder existing institutions struggle to get under the problem by producing 'better' technology, more goods, more food, more 'consumables,' the more out of balance the system becomes."[7]

Projecting an increase of just 1.1 percent per year, the population of the United States will double by 2050. At a meeting of the American Association for the Advancement of Science in February 1995, scientists noted that before that date, domestic oil reserves will be exhausted, water for irrigation will become scarce, and the land will be exhausted from current agricultural practices and consumption patterns. The United States could cease to be an exporter of food by 2025.[8] A positive outcome of this imbalance will be a simpler U.S. diet. Potatoes, grains, and legumes will compose a greater portion of American diets, and reliance on animal products will decrease from 31 percent to 15 percent. As Smith points out, this is actually a healthier diet and one that taxes the earth less than current production.[9]

Balance and harmony are important traditional Native values. Native communities "never entered a trajectory of excessive growth, and even today many Native American societies practice a self-regulation of population size that allows the substance of their traditional world view with its interactive environmental relationship to remain viable."[10] The Hopi have long warned that the earth is slipping into *koyaanisquatsi*, "life out of balance." In a 1970 letter to President Richard Nixon, they stated that Whites had, through "insensitivity to the way of Nature . . . desecrated the face of Mother Earth." They wrote, "This must not be allowed to continue, for if it does, Mother Nature will react in such a way that almost all men will suffer the end of life as they know it."[11] Traditional Zuñi prophecy points to one of the signs of collapse as population increasing "until the land can hold no more" and possessions turning into beasts to "devour us whole." They counsel, however, that "the people themselves will bring upon themselves what they receive."[12] In the following piece Smith asks whether we must suffer the fate envisioned by the Hopi and Zuñi or whether we can break the patterns of production and consumption that are destroying us while there is still time.

Zero population growth may be all right for the white man, because he's crowding the continent. . . . But for the Indian, it's genocidal. Let's control our own reproduction, instead of meeting the demands of the white economic-social values.

–Dr. Connie Uri[13]

[Population control proponents] begin with the fact *of exploding fertility rates. . . . The fact becomes, for them, the* cause *of the problem and they are unwilling to examine the real, hard-to-change economic and social causes of increased fertility . . . the destruction of family-based, subsistence agriculture by export farming and resource extraction. Once they've named the effect the "cause," they treat as secondary the real cause of population growth, global migration and environmental degradation.*

–Hannah Creighton[14]

Population control is nothing new to America. Since the beginning of the European conquest, colonizers have focused their destructive energies upon indigenous women. As historian David Stannard points out, "The European habit of indiscriminately killing women and children when engaged in hostilities with the natives of the Americas was more than an atrocity. It was flatly and intentionally genocidal. For no population can survive if its women and children are destroyed."[15] Because the destruction of women's capacity to reproduce is essential to destroying a people, the killing of women has long been a preferred tactic of would-be perpetrators of genocide. "It is because of a Native woman's sex that she is hunted down and slaughtered," argues Inés Hernández-Avila. "In fact, [she has been] singled out, because she has the potential through childbirth to assure the continuance of the people."[16]

These policies continue into the present in a subtler form. During the 1970s the Indian Health Service (IHS) sterilized over 25 percent of Indian women without their informed consent. Sterilization rates ran as high as 80 percent among some tribes.[17] Other women of color faced similar situations. In 1979, it was revealed that seven in ten U.S. hospitals that performed voluntary sterilizations for Medicaid recipients violated H.E.W. guidelines by disregarding consent procedures and by performing sterilizations through "elective" hysterectomies.[18] Patricia Hill Collins notes that the state's interest in limiting the growth of the Black population coincided with the expansion of post–World War II welfare provisions that allowed many African-Americans to leave exploitative jobs. As a result, the growing unemployment rate among people of color has meant that non-White America is no longer simply a reservoir of cheap labor but is now considered "surplus" population.[19] Growth in the nation's non-White population has even been called a threat to national security.[20] The link to the environment was made by one physician in *Contemporary Ob/Gyn*: "People pollute, and too many people crowded too close together cause many of our social and economic problems. These in turn are aggravated by involuntary and irresponsible parenthood. . . . We also have obligations to the society of which we are a part. The welfare mess, as it has been called, cries out for solutions, one of which is fertility control."[21]

While sterilization abuse has ebbed since the 1970s, state control over reproductive freedom continues through the promotion of unsafe, long-acting hormonal contraceptives such as Depo-Provera and Norplant for women of color. Depo-Provera, an alleged carcinogen condemned as an inappropriate form of birth control by several women's health organizations, was routinely employed on Native women by the IHS before it was approved by the Food and Drug Administration in 1992.[22] While there are to date no studies on the long-term effects of Norplant, which is designed to remain in the arm for five years, known side-effects—constant bleeding as long as ninety days in duration, tumors, kidney problems, heart attacks, strokes, sterility—lead 30 percent of all women implanted to request removal within one year. The figure increases to over 50 percent within two years. Over twenty-five hundred women, suffering from over 125 Norplant-related side-effects, have joined in a class action lawsuit against its manufacturer, Wyeth-Ayerst.[23]

As the population scare and accompanying demonization of the poor have moved into the mainstream of the dominant culture in the United States, Norplant and Depo-Provera have become front-line weapons. The Native American Women's Health Education Resource Center conducted a survey of IHS Norplant and Depo-Provera policies in 1993 and found that Native women were not given adequate counseling regarding their side effects and contraindications.[24] Meanwhile, state legislatures have considered bills that would pay women on public assistance bonuses if they accepted Norplant implantation, and the *Philadelphia Inquirer* ran an editorial suggesting that the hormone treatment could be a useful tool in "reducing the underclass."[25]

The population scare at home has its counterpart in American and European policies abroad. During the colonial period the United States and Europe depleted their third-world colonies of natural resources while systematically destroying any local industry that might compete with European and North American manufactured goods. As a consequence, since World War II third-world countries have been plunged into debt.[26] In the early 1980s the World Bank and the International Monetary Fund (IMF) began to address the debt crises of these countries by imposing "structural adjustment" programs, requiring them to reduce tariff protection for local industry, devalue currency, cut social services, and develop cash crop export economies. But as products from the Third World flooded the world market, prices dropped dramatically, preventing third-world nations from obtaining the hard currency necessary to repay their loans. Despite the fact that the six years between 1984 and 1990 saw the net transfer of $178 billion in financial resources from the Third World to its industrialized creditor nations, total indebtedness nearly doubled.[27] In vain attempts to service this debt, third-world countries increasingly diverted land and resources from meeting local needs to production of export crops and manufactured goods, in turn forcing them to spend more on costly imports. As Brazilian Marcos Arruda sums up, "The more we pay, the more we owe."[28]

Not surprisingly, as many debtor nations have bridled at the austerity policies imposed by the World Bank and IMF, the United States government and business interests have begun to blame the unrest on the Third World's "population problem." In 1977 R. T. Ravenholt of the United States Agency for International Development (AID) announced a plan to sterilize up to a quarter of the world's women, saying, "Population control is necessary to maintain the normal operation of U.S. commercial interests around the world. Without our trying to help these countries with their economic and social development, the world would rebel against the strong U.S. commercial presence."[29] In a startling analysis, one national group, the Population Institute, even went so far as to blame the Persian Gulf War on overpopulation.[30]

Relying on Malthusian logic, population alarmists have begun to espouse overpopulation as the primary cause of poverty in the world: population grows geometrically, while food production grows arithmetically. Because human fertility is assumed to go naturally unchecked, eventually the number of people on earth must outstrip the earth's "carrying capacity." Conveniently, since reproductive rates of the industrialized countries are stable at replacement levels, populationists are free to direct their time and energy to burgeoning growth rates in the Third World and to immigration rates in the United States.

The problem with such a Malthusian argument is that it assumes that "natural fertility rates" are always high and checked only by the vicissitudes of famine, war, and disease; women, however, have always had means of controlling reproduction.[31] It is commonly known among Native women, for instance, that prior to colonization women controlled their births through herbs and other methods. This knowledge, however, was destroyed in the assault on indigenous cultures. Ironically, colonial powers often deliberately tried to suppress traditional means of birth control in order to ensure a large supply of cheap labor and a market for their finished goods.[32] In recent years Nestle has discouraged breast feeding, a natural birth spacer, in order to increase sales of its infant formula among third-world women. Feminist author and theologian Rosemary Radford Ruether and others argue, erroneously, that the increase in third-world population stems from improved healthcare and declining mortality rates, without explaining why these trends have not produced a leveling of birth rates, as they have in the industrialized world.[33] By contrast, Vandana Shiva notes that the population of India was *already* stable until the advent of British colonialism in South Asia.[34] It must also be questioned whether Western medicine has actually significantly improved the health of third-world and indigenous peoples. Bernadine Atcheson (Dena'ina) and Mary Ann Mills (Dena'ina) note that the health of Alaska Natives has deteriorated because of the imposition of Western diets, Western pharmaceuticals, and environmental degradation as a result of industrialization. Mills states, "Today we rely on our elders and our traditional healers. We have asked them if they were ever as sick as their grandchildren or great-grandchildren are today. Their reply was no; they [were] much healthier than their grandchildren today."[35] Life expectancy for Natives today is approximately forty-seven years.

In addition, many proponents of family planning argue for the importance of raising women's status in order to increase the use of contraceptives. According to Zero Population Growth, "In cultures where a woman's value often depends on her fertility, she is subject to violence and abandonment if she does not 'produce' the expected number of children. . . . Often times, without her husband's approval, she cannot use contraceptives without fear for her safety."[36] Putting aside the fact that violence against women does not occur only in "those" cultures, what populationists generally refuse to acknowledge is the role of imperialism in perpetuating sexism in the Third World and among people of color. As Paula Gunn Allen (Laguna Pueblo) notes, violence against women was almost unheard of in most indigenous nations prior to colonization. She writes, "The assault on the system of woman power requires the replacing of a peaceful, nonpunitive, nonauthoritarian social system wherein women wield power by making social life easy and gentle with one based on child terrorization, male dominance, and submission of women to male authority."[37] Colonial policies of overturning communal systems of land tenure in order to vest private ownership with the male "head of household" only served to exacerbate sexism in indigenous societies.[38] Further, Gita Sen notes that Western domination can breed conservatism, particularly regarding women's status, as colonized societies attempt to resist assimilation and cultural erosion. Women, who are seen as the bearers of culture, are often blamed for cultural breakdown: "Historically, in unsettled economic and political times, attacks on women go hand in hand with reactionary tendencies and impulses."[39] Ending neo-colonial practices would significantly improve the status of women.

Nevertheless, Malthusians see third-world and indigenous women as wombs run amok. The "population establishment" spends billions of dollars each year on population programs, policy setting, and (mis)education.[40] Certainly, third-world women and women of color want family-planning services, but many programs have been forced upon them and implemented without concern for their health.[41]

Poverty, starvation, and overpopulation are the direct result of colonial practices. When colonization forced women into cash economies, it became incumbent upon them to have more children to help raise cash crops. In addition, increased mortality rates motivate women to have more children in the hope that at least some may survive. With cuts in social services as a result of structural adjustment programs, children also become necessary for old-age security.[42]

Contrary to the dire pronouncements of the populationists, there is actually enough food produced in the world to sustain every person at a three thousand calorie-per-day diet.[43] Land, however, is used inefficiently in order to support livestock for the environmentally unsustainable Western meat-based diet.[44] In addition, food produced in the Third World is often exported to pay off international debt rather than to feed local populations. Consequently, even countries stricken by famine often export food.[45]

Some populationists do contend that poverty causes overpopulation, but they add that rapid population then leads to greater poverty, creating a vicious circle. This, however, is not necessarily the case. Increased population can lead to increased food production. Conversely, some of the most poverty-ridden areas do not experience mass population growth. For example, Bangladeshi population policies are designed to "prove that population growth can be reduced without any change in health conditions, poverty, or social justice."[46] Brazil, too, is experiencing an increase in environmental destruction in *inverse* relation to a declining population. The cutting of trees in the Amazon is not related to an excess of peasants and indigenous people cutting trees for survival but to government policy supporting commercial ranching for the benefit of the United States.[47] This is not to say, however, that population growth never causes problems for communities. The fundamental problem causing poverty among third-world and indigenous peoples, however, is the extraction of resources for consumption by the developed world. Without restructuring the global economy, rates of poverty ultimately cannot be reduced.

In addition to causing poverty and starvation, overpopulation, many populationists argue, is the primary cause of environmental degradation. Environmental organizations have been aggressive in "educating" the public about environmental devastation caused by overpopulation. According to much of the literature, overpopulation is "the single greatest threat to the health of the planet."[48] In actuality, environmental damage is caused by environmentally destructive projects such as hydroelectric dams, mining, nuclear energy development, livestock production, and militarism. Such projects ultimately benefit those in industrialized countries, who are responsible for over 75 percent of the world's environmental pollution.[49] Any damage done by peasants and indigenous peoples cannot compare to that done by Western development projects and by multinational corporations, and what damage they do cause is generally a result of being driven off their lands. If the poorest 75 percent of the world's population were to disappear completely, the reduction in pollution would be only 10 percent.[50]

Neo-colonialist policies in the Third World result in increased immigration into the United States. Immigration, in turn, has led environmental organizations to complain that the United States is now "overpopulated" by immigrants. These immigrants, they claim, cause "global warming, species extinction, acid rain, deforestation. . . . Immigration . . . is threatening the carrying capacity limits of the natural environment." Because of "their excessive reproductive rates," immigrants cause massive environmental damage, "compete with our poor for jobs," and burden taxpayers through "increased funding obligations in AFDC, Medicare, Food Stamps, School Lunch, Unemployment Compensation, [etc.]."[51] Logic dictates that if these people are "burdening the taxpayer" through federal assistance programs, they are probably not the ones causing the majority of environmental degradation in this country. Environmental organizations ignore consumption patterns of those in the dominant culture, as well as the role of U.S. business, in causing ecological damage. Such groups also overlook that immigrants contribute far more in taxes than they receive in public services.[52]

Despite these facts, environmental organizations, such as Carrying Capacity Network (CCN), Population-Environmental Balance, and Negative Population Growth, increasingly are urging the closing of borders in order to "save the environment." Even more mainstream organizations are being drawn into the debate. Sierra Club members who are also members of the Federation of American Immigration Reform (FAIR) founded by John Tanton (formerly of Zero Population Growth), have pressured–thus far unsuccessfully–the Sierra Club to adopt an anti-immigration platform. A $275,000,000 gift in 1990 from one FAIR member made the population program the best-funded of any Sierra Club project.[53] Not surprisingly, many far-right groups are finding the xenophobic and racist policies of these organizations attractive. For example, Tom Metzger, founder of White Aryan Resistance, has declared support for Earth First! because of its stand on overpopulation. He states, "Don't you think, my Aryan comrades, that it's time to start using any and every means to put a stop to the . . . scum who are raping our mother earth to the point of her extinction?"[54] Similar statements have been made by the Aryan Women's League.

Women of color and third-world women, as well as concerned Europeans and Euro-Americans, have been active in combating the racism, sexism, and imperialism implicit in the population paradigm. Women of All Red Nations fought sterilization abuse in the 1970s. The Native American Women's Health Education Resource Center has organized around the issue of contraceptive abuse. The women of color delegation to the United Nations International Conference on Population and Development, held in Cairo in 1994, issued a communiqué calling for "a change of the present global development model that is built around wasteful consumption [and] economic growth pitted against social progress."[55] Opposition also formed to the draft document for the United Nations' conference on women, held in Beijing, because the document "seems to want to impose on women of the entire world a particular social philosophy, belonging to certain sectors within Western countries."[56]

A broad-based coalition of international women's organizations signed a statement calling for a "new approach" to the population paradigm and has strongly condemned population control.[57] Ananilea Nkya of the Tanzania Media Women's Association recently summarized, "We question the views of population controllers who perpetuate the notion that rapid population growth is the major cause of poverty and environmental degradation in developing countries and that provision of family planning in those countries is the solution."[58] At the historic People of Color Environmental Leadership Summit, held in Washington, D.C., in 1991, one woman echoed the concerns of many participants when she declared to leaders of mainstream environmental organizations who were in attendance, "We are not interested in controlling *our* population for the sake of *your* population."[59]

POPULATION AND CHRISTIAN CHURCHES

Liberal Protestant organizations have been largely supportive of population control. In 1969 Reinhold Niebuhr, Harry Emerson Fosdick, and Henry Knox Sherrill of the World Council of Churches signed a full-page ad in the *New York Times* calling for mass population control efforts in Latin America.[60] Most mainline denominations have issued statements supporting population control, and the writings of liberal European and Euro-American Christians concerned with environmental issues tend to accept the population paradigm.[61]

Euro-American Christian feminists, such as Sallie McFague, Rosemary Radford Ruether, Catherine Keller, and Christine Gudorf, devote much of their work on population to analyzing the relationships among overconsumption, socioeconomic injustice, and population growth. They do not, however, challenge the population paradigm. One reason may be that they do not base their analyses on work done by third-world or indigenous women. In recent writings by all these scholars, they do not reference a single work by any person of color on this issue. It is ironical that, given their feminist commitments, they do not take the communities whose populations they advocate reducing as the starting point of their discussion. Instead, they quote approvingly individuals who have supported racist population programs.[62] This gives the impression—hopefully mistaken—that they consider such persons to be more expert on the situations facing third-world and indigenous women than the women themselves. Keller, in particular, most puzzlingly states that there is a "conspiracy of silence" on the population issue, despite the work done by women of color to address it.[63]

One reason for these omissions may be that these authors inadequately understand "overpopulation" as a racialized issue. Ruether, for instance, states, "The challenge that humans face . . . is whether they will be able to visualize and organize their own reproduction, production, and consumption in such a way as to stabilize their relationship to the rest of the ecosphere and so avert massive social and planetary ecocide."[64] She seems to assume that all humans contribute equally to ecological disaster, that they are equally affected by population policies, and that all humans have the same access to power to organize their production and consumption. This is not to say that these authors completely ignore the differing positions of Western and third-world and indigenous women. McFague, for example, does acknowledge in her discussion of environmental degradation that "we are not all equally responsible, nor does deterioration affect us equally."[65] She goes on to state, however, that ecology is a "people" issue in relation to nonhuman creatures. The problem, therefore, is "human" overpopulation. In fact, since most industrialized nations have replacement-level reproduction, with some even experiencing declining populations, it is clear that these citizens are not those who are considered to be "overpopulating" the earth or who are recipients of most population programs.[66]

Keller and Gudorf state that all women should make the commitment to have no more than one child.[67] Keller makes an exception for women from communities that have been targeted for genocide but fails to recognize that population policies are themselves often genocidal in intent.[68] It logically would follow from Keller's argument that only Europeans and Euro-Americans should reduce their population. In addition, this "one-child" recommendation implies that third-world, indigenous, and first-world women are all equally affected by giving birth to only one offspring. A White middle-class woman, however, stands to gain economically by such a decision, whereas a third-world woman may face a tremendous economic hardship as a result of such a policy. Gudorf does acknowledge this point but contends that it is a consequence that third-world women simply will have to suffer.[69]

Keller also erases the particularity of women of color when she says that "the rising global population rate is a catastrophic trend variously underplayed both by right-wing anti-abortionists and feminist combatting the misogyny implied by monofocal emphasis on population (often encouraging female infanticide and forced sterilization)."[70] She describes these population practices as "misogynist" but not racist as well, as though they have an impact on all women and not primarily women of color and third-world women. In addition, she implies that "feminists" are concerned only with "abuses" in population programs, rather than the fact that they are designed to serve as a smokescreen for perpetuation of larger structures of socioeconomic injustice—from which European and Euro-American middle-class women gain many privileges. Further, given that third-world women and women of color suffer the brunt of environmental destruction, it might be helpful for Keller to inquire of them what they believe the real "catastrophic trends" are.

All the previously cited authors discuss environmental destruction caused by Western consumption patterns. They also analyze how population growth is affected by colonialism. Keller, for instance, states:

> Justice-centered Christians speaking on behalf of the world of the poor make the irrefutable point that . . . it is the exploitation of the resources of the Third World for the sake of the First World and its client elites—not overpopulation—which deprives those "others" of the resources they need. Is not the focus on population control thus dangerously akin to genocidal policies which seek to rid the world of the troubling, potentially revolutionary masses of the poor?"[71]

Having asked the question, however, she then fails to address it in the remainder of her essay. If population is a symptom rather than a cause of other global trends, which these authors seem to say, why do they value the population paradigm so highly? Ruether and Keller, in fact, describe Overpopulation as one of the "four horsemen of doom," the others being Economics, War, and Environment.[72] In essence, they argue that the patterns of reproduction of third-world women and women of color that have developed as a result of colonization are as bad as colonization itself. A parallel argument would be if a man stood on a woman's toe causing her to scream and then complained that her screaming was diminishing his quality of life because of the noise level. Extending the metaphor, these feminists seem to say that the woman screaming is as responsible for causing damage to the general quality of life as the man standing on her toe. Ultimately, claiming that population is as great a problem as social injustice is little better than the argument that overpopulation is wholly to blame for the world's problems. In either case, it mitigates the responsibility of those in positions of privilege.

Gudorf lets the privileged off the hook when she grants a priority to population stabilization over social justice, arguing that "getting the rich to agree to any standard significantly below what they now receive seems . . . doubtful."[73] The implication is that we should focus on imperialistic population control policies because they will be easier to implement than economic justice. Furthermore, she states that "combatting hunger and . . . malnutrition must come primarily from population stabilization, not increased food production."[74] Apparently ending hunger through economic justice is ultimately not a primary consideration for her. Rosemary Ruether does not consider overpopulation and overconsumption equally to blame; rather, "the major cause of destruction of species comes *simply* from the expanding human population."[75] She goes on to say that overpopulation leads to "war, famine, and disease."[76] She calls for "the promotion of birth control," seemingly oblivious to the devastating health effects such "promotions" have had for third-world and indigenous women.[77] Her vision of "a good society" apparently entails population control, but it does not include redistribution of resources from North to South or anything that would significantly affect the privileges the dominant culture enjoys at the expense of the less developed.[78]

In addition, these scholars espouse other equally questionable ideas. Keller, Ruether, and McFague regard Malthusian orthodoxy as indisputably true despite its flawed assumptions.[79] As already noted, Ruether describes population in the Third World as rising independently from patterns of colonialism.[80] She also uncritically appropriates the formula of Paul Ehrlich, the author of *The Population Bomb*: population x consumption x technology = environmental impact (I = PAT). H. Patricia Hynes and Betsy Hartmann point out that this formula is problematic because it assumes that all population is the same, ignoring different peoples' differing impacts on the environment. It also views "all humans as takers from, rather than enhancers of, the natural environment. This truncated, culture-bound view of humans in their environment originates from an industrial, urban, consumerist society."[81] Affluence is conceived only as per capita consumption and does not include systemic inequities such as those caused by structural adjustment programs. It neglects the fact that the Third World sustains not only its own consumption but also that of the developed world.[82] All technology is assumed to be equally harmful. The effects of militarism are also ignored. As Hartmann states, "I = PAT obscures power relations at the global level; the precise dynamics of environmental degradation at the local, regional, and national level are also hidden behind a Malthusian veil."[83]

Probably most disturbing is Gudorf's approval of incentive and disincentive programs (such as paying women to use Norplant), as long as they "are as voluntary" as possible.[84] Given the oppressive conditions in which most third-world and indigenous women live, it is unclear how incentives can be considered in any sense "voluntary." If one is living hand-to-mouth, is the offer of financial resources in exchange for controlling one's population a genuine choice? The use of incentives in population control has been devastating for third-world women and women of color.[85] Even the *draft* Programme of Action from the United Nations' Cairo conference (before it was improved thanks to the lobbying of women's reproductive rights groups) condemns the use of incentives and disincentives.[86]

Finally, these writers speak quite eloquently of the responsibilities of the Western world to address environmental degradation by targeting consumption patterns. Ultimately, however, they contend that it should do so in order to encourage the Third World to reduce population. McFague states, "Unless and until we drastically modify our life-style, we are not in a position to preach population control to others." While this is true, it also suggests that the reason to modify one's lifestyle is to be able to preach population control convincingly.[87] This attitude motivates too many population-program planners. Many such policy makers attempt to determine the minimum amount of social and/or health reform necessary in order to reduce population. As Hartmann writes, "Once social reforms, women's projects, and family planning programs are organized for the explicit goal of reducing population growth, they are subverted and ultimately fail. . . . These basic rights are worthy of pursuit in and of themselves; they have far more relevance to the general improvement of human welfare than reducing population growth alone ever will."[88]

Liberal Christians, particularly feminists, focus their energies on countering claims made by the Vatican and "pro-life" forces. While this is important, it fosters a false dichotomy between being pro-population control and anti-choice. Consequently, the experiences of Third World and indigenous women become lost in these discussions. As Brazilian feminist Thais Corral reported about proceedings at the Cairo conference, population-control proponents insisted that third-world women *must* join them in combating fundamentalists and the Vatican. Anna Quindlen similarly argues, "It has become increasingly evident that Americans should not permit the Vatican to go unchallenged in its opposition to birth and population control. We can do this best by giving our own vocal support of U.S. funding of family planning as an important measure that can end unintended pregnancies, burgeoning population, and poverty."[89] This dichotomy, however, is a false one. While the Vatican rejected abortion and all forms of birth control other than natural planning at Cairo, it is important to recognize that it did not necessarily reject the premises of overpopulation. Vatican Secretary of State Cardinal Angelo Dodana has stated, "Everyone is aware of the complexity of the problem, but the urgency of the situation must not lead into error in proposing ways of intervening."[90] The Pontifical Academy of Sciences has recommended that couples have only two children in order to help curb "the world population crisis."[91]

Similarly, many "pro-life" Christians, including fundamentalists, wholeheartedly support population-control policies. Even some who consider abortion immoral support the use of incentives, long-acting hormonal contraceptives, and even coercion to stabilize population.[92] Many conservative Christians, however, who do *not* support population control do not take their position from a social-justice perspective. Some do so because they believe more Christians are needed to offset growing numbers of non-Christians.[93] Others argue against population control because they think that the earth has an endless capacity to sustain Western development models and needs nothing more than a free market in order to thrive.[94] Such Christians aver that we can trust in God not to allow the earth to deteriorate seriously.[95] Clearly, such "pro-life" positions are not "pro" women's lives, particularly the lives of third-world and indigenous women.

Meanwhile, as Mies and Shiva argue, the "pro-choice" population establishment is not necessarily asking about the quality of choices open to third-world and indigenous women. Population programs push "high tech," long-acting contraceptives that do more to pad profits of pharmaceutical concerns than they do to improve choices for women.[96] Programs vastly underplay low-tech methods, such as natural family planning, barrier methods, and means long used by indigenous peoples. In fact, AID deliberately has discouraged such methods.[97] Populationists do not question the Western medical model, which relies on invasive medical procedures and allopathic medicines rather than homeopathic and holistic remedies.[98] These pharmaceuticals then must be tested, often with disastrous side effects on "expendable" populations.

For instance, Mary Ann Mills and Bernadine Atcheson complain that most experimental vaccines given in the United States are administered to Native Alaskans, often without their consent and with a detrimental effect on their immune systems. Dr. William Jordan of the

U.S. Department of Health and Welfare confirms that virtually all field trials of new vaccines in the country are tested among the indigenous people of Alaska.[99] It is little wonder then that Native women, while overwhelmingly pro-choice, are generally absent from the mainstream pro-choice movement.[100] While in many ways the "pro-choice" populationists and the "pro-life" movement seem very different, as Hartmann states, they "share one thing in common: They are both anti-woman," and, in particular, anti-woman of color.[101]

Consequently, an ethic that takes seriously the lives of indigenous and third-world women must reject this false polarity and be truly pro-life *and* pro-choice. To do so, such an ethic must reject the population paradigm completely. Some women choose to work within this paradigm with the hope that they can reform the system. Others are concerned about population but, like the Christian feminists previously described, are working toward social and economic justice as well. Continuing to work within this paradigm, however, is problematic, given the manner in which reactionary forces attempt, usually successfully, to coopt the demands for social justice within the population movement, especially within the churches. Gudorf states, "There is a very real danger that religion, like . . . governments, will decide that (1) there is a population crisis that threatens the whole society; (2) the birthrate must be lowered; and (3) controlling women's bodies is necessary to lower the birthrate."[102]

Church leaders in both liberal and evangelical denominations came out in support of the Cairo conference, lauding its steps forward on women's reproductive health issues. The U.S. Department of State reported the "international consensus reached in Cairo" in which both industrialized and developing nations agreed on a comprehensive approach to population policy that included both family planning and development as means to slow population growth. This "unprecedented level of international agreement" stood in marked contrast to previous international population convocations in Bucharest (1974) and Mexico City (1984), when industrialized and third-world countries could not reach an accord.[103] In fact, this consensus largely has been manufactured. The issue of reproductive rights served as a smokescreen for the fact that issues of economic injustice were barely addressed. Contrary to the impression created in the media by the United States, many were highly critical of the Cairo Programme. Carol Benson Holst of the Ministry for Justice in Population Concerns, a nongovernmental organization participating in the conference, charged that the Programme was "nothing but an insult to women, men and children of the South who will receive an ever-growing dose of population assistance, while their issues of life and death will await the Social Development Summit of 1995."[104] Charon Asetoyer wrote in *Wicozanni Wowapi*: "Early into the conference, it became obvious that the issues

facing third-world countries such as development, structural adjustment, and capacity building were not high on the list of issues that the
'Super Powers' wanted to address. It was clear that the issues [of] world
population were going to be addressed from the top down with little
regard for how this may affect developing countries."[105]

While claiming not to "set demographic targets,"[106] the Programme
calls for nations to stabilize population at 9.8 billion by the year 2000.
While it denounces incentives and coercive measures, there are no
safeguards to ensure against them in implementation. Signatory nations covenanted to increase funding for population programs from $5
billion to $17 billion per year. And while some argue that this could
mean a diversion from military spending, there is nothing in the
Programme about redirection of spending.[107] More often, money for
population programs comes from funds that might otherwise go for
reproductive health or general healthcare. What proponents fail to
mention is that two-thirds of this increased funding is supposed to come
from *developing nations* themselves, thus further straining already
strapped budgets.[108]

What these trends suggest is that as long as we retain the population
paradigm in which *population* acts as a code word for third-world people
and people of color, such people will continue to be seen as "the problem." Because the structures of global injustice are decimating the earth
and its inhabitants, we must target these structures rather than population growth. A focus on population only serves to distract us from the
needed task of dismantling the "New World Order." As Mary Mellor
states, "The future of the planet [is] in the hands of a capitalist market
economy united with other powerful forces—feudalism, patriarchy, colonialism, imperialism, militarism and racism—to form a monstrous
global structure of economic, cultural, and political power."[109] Reducing population without taking the fate of the earth out of these hands
will not help us or the earth.

Notes

1. Glenn T. Morris, "Introduction," in Ward Churchill and Elizabeth
Lloyd, *Culture Versus Economism: Essays on Marxism in the Multicultural Arena*
(Denver: Fourth World Center for the Study of Indigenous Law and Politics,
1989), p. 2; cf., Donald A. Grinde, Jr., and Bruce E. Johansen, *Ecocide of Native
America: Environmental Destruction of Indian Lands and Peoples* (Santa Fe: Clear
Light Publishers, 1995), p. 266; see also, William Catton, *Overshoot: The Eco-
logical Basis for Revolutionary Change* (Urbana: University of Illinois Press, 1980).

2. Ward Churchill, *Struggle for the Land: Indigenous Resistance to Genocide,
Ecocide and Expropriation in Contemporary North America* (Monroe, Me.: Common Courage Press, 1993), p. 16.

3. Doug Hunt, "Theological Perspectives on Population and Consumption," *Earth Ethics* (Spring 1995), p. 10.

4. Ibid.
5. Morris, p. 2.
6. Hunt, p. 10.
7. Ibid., p. 11.
8. "A Forecast for 2050: Scarcities Will Force a Leaner U.S. Diet," *New York Times* (February 18, 1995), p. A8. American agriculture is heavily dependent on petroleum, using approximately 140 gallons for every acre of corn. About 120 million acres of cropland are projected to be lost through urbanization and erosion in the next sixty years (ibid.). Further, meat and dairy products are, as Smith points out, the most inefficient and expensive to produce (see, n. 44 below). United States diets are currently based 31 percent on animal products ("Forecast," p. A8).
9. See, Smith, n. 44 below; "Forecast," p. A8.
10. Churchill, p. 18; see, Smith, below.
11. Hopi Traditional Village Leaders, "Letter to President Richard Nixon" (August 4, 1970).
12. Zuñi People, *The Zuñis: Self Portrayals* (Albuquerque: University of New Mexico Press, 1972), quoted in Peter Nabokov, ed., *Native American Testimony*, exp. ed. (New York: Viking, 1991), pp. 439-440.
13. "Oklahoma: Sterilization of Native Women Charged to I.H.S.," *Akwesasne Notes* (Mid-Winter 1989), p. 30. Dr. Uri is the physician who discovered sterilization abuse of Native Americans in the 1970s.
14. Hannah Creighton, "Not Thinking Globally: The Sierra Club Immigration Policy Wars," *Race, Poverty and the Environment* 4 (Summer 1993), p. 25.
15. David Stannard, *American Holocaust* (New York: Oxford University Press, 1992), pp. 118-119. According to Stannard, control over women's reproductive abilities and destruction of women and children are essential to destroying a people. He points out that despite heavy Japanese losses during World War II, Japan's population actually increased 14 percent between 1940 and 1950 because a disproportionate number of those killed were men. Native women and children were deliberately targeted during the conquest in order to destroy Indian nations. Andrew Jackson recommended that troops systematically kill women and children after massacres in order to complete extermination. Similarly, Methodist minister Colonel John Chivington's policy at Sand Creek was to "kill and scalp all little and big" because "nits make lice" (ibid., pp. 121, 131). Conversely, the Spaniards encouraged Native reproduction as a means of supplying a labor force (ibid., p. 140).
16. Inés Hernández-Avila, "In Praise of Insubordination, or What Makes a Good Woman Go Bad?" in Emilie Buchwald, Pamela R. Fletcher, and Martha Roth, eds., *Transforming a Rape Culture* (Minneapolis: Milkweed, 1993), p. 386.
17. See, "The Threat of Life," *WARN Report*, pp. 13-16; Brint Dillingham, "Indian Women and IHS Sterilization Practices," *American Indian Journal* (January 1977), pp. 27-28; Brint Dillingham, "Sterilization of Native Americans," *American Indian Journal* (July 1977), pp. 16-19; Pat Bellanger, "Native American Women, Forced Sterilization, and the Family," in Gaya Wadnizak Ellis, ed., *Every Woman Has a Story* (Minneapolis: Midwest Villages & Voices, 1982), pp. 30-35.
18. "Survey Finds Seven in 10 Hospitals Violate DHEW Guidelines on Informed Consent for Sterilization," *Family Planning Perspectives* 11:6 (Nov./

Dec. 1979), p. 366; Claudia Dreifus, "Sterilizing the Poor," in *Seizing Our Bodies* (Toronto: Vintage Press, 1977), pp. 105-120.

19. Patricia Hill Collins, *Black Feminist Thought* (London: Routledge, 1991), p. 76; see also, Jean Sharpe, "The Birth Controllers," in Dreifus, pp. 57-72.

20. Debra Hanania-Freeman, "Norplant: Freedom of Choice or a Plan for Genocide?" *EIR* (May 14, 1993), p. 20.

21. "Oklahoma," p. 11.

22. "Taking a Shot," series of articles in *Arizona Republic* (November 1986).

23. Hanania-Freeman, p. 20; Kathleen Plant, "Mandatory Norplant Is Not the Answer," *Chicago Sun-Times* (November 2, 1994), p. 46.

24. "A Study of the Use of Depo-Provera and Norplant by the Indian Health Service," Native American Women's Health Education Resource Center, South Dakota (1993).

25. Gretchen Long, "Norplant: A Victory, Not a Panacea for Poverty," *The National Lawyers Guild Practitioner* 50:1, p. 11.

26. Walter Rodney, *How Europe Underdeveloped Africa* (London: Bogle l'Ouverture Publications, 1972), pp. 154-173; Gita Sen, *Development, Crises and Alternative Visions* (New York: Monthly Review Press, 1987), pp. 32-33.

27. Tom Barry and Deb Preusch, *The Central American Fact Book* (New York: Grove Press, 1986), p. 32; "Creating a Wasteland," *Food First Action Alert* (Winter 1993), pp. 1-2; "Structural Adjustment: Deadly Development," *Global Advocates Bulletin* (October 1994), pp. 1-2, 5, 7, 9.

28. Marcos Arruda, "Brazil: Drowning in Debt," in Kevin Danaher, ed., *50 Years Is Enough* (Boston: South End Press, 1994), p. 45.

29. *WARN Report*, p. 15.

30. Population Institute, *Annual Report* (1991).

31. Maria Mies and Vandana Shiva, *Ecofeminism* (London: Zed, 1993), p. 287.

32. Ibid., p. 288.

33. Rosemary Radford Ruether, *Gaia and God* (San Francisco: HarperSanFrancisco, 1992), p. 91.

34. Mies and Shiva, p. 284.

35. Bernadine Atcheson and Mary Ann Mills, speech at WARN Forum, Chicago, Illinois (September 1993).

36. "Bearing the Burden," Zero Population Growth Fact Sheet, Washington, D.C. (Spring 1992), p. 2.

37. Paula Gunn Allen, *The Sacred Hoop* (Boston: Beacon Press, 1986), p. 40.

38. Isis, *Women in Development* (Geneva: Isis, 1983), p. 79.

39. Sen, p. 75.

40. The term was coined by activist Betsy Hartmann, who identifies the group as including, among others, AID, the UN Fund for Population Activities, the World Bank, International Planned Parenthood, and various governments, consulting firms, foundations, and organizations such as Zero Population Growth, Population Action International, and the Sierra Club. Betsy Hartmann, *Reproduction Rights and Wrongs—Revised* (Boston: South End Press, 1995), pp. 113-124.

41. Ibid., pp. 29-30, 254; Ammu Joseph, "India's Population Bomb," *Ms. Magazine*, 3:3 (1992), p. 12.

42. "Mythoconceptions," *New Internationalist* (October 1987), p. 9.

43. Hartmann, p. 16.

44. The same land used to maintain livestock for 250 days could be used to cultivate soybeans for 2,200 days. Half of all water used in the United States is used for crops to feed livestock. One-third of the value of all raw materials consumed for all purposes in the United States is consumed in livestock feed (see, Carol Adams, *Neither Man nor Beast* [New York: Continuum, 1994], pp. 92-93). Thirty-eight percent of grain worldwide and 70 percent in the United States is used to feed livestock (Alan B. Durning and Holly B. Brough, *Taking Stock: Animal Farming and the Environment* [Washington: Worldwatch Institute, 1991], p. 14). By cycling grain through livestock, only 10 percent as many calories are available as would be if the grain were consumed directly (John Robbins, *Diet for a New America* [Walpole, N.H.: Stillpoint Publishing, 1987], p. 351). Livestock production accounts for 40-60 percent of U.S. imported oil requirements. In addition, cattle account for 85 percent of topsoil erosion (Adams, pp. 92-93).

45. Hartmann, p. 17.

46. Ibid., p. 235.

47. Ibid., p. 28.

48. Population Institute, *Annual Report* (1991). Zero Population Growth, and the Population Committee of the Los Angeles chapter of the Sierra Club have made similar claims.

49. Patience Idemudia and Kole Shettima, "World Bank Takes Control of UNCED's Environmental Fund," in Danaher, p. 108.

50. Margot Kässman, "Covenant, Praise and Justice in Creation," in David Hallman, ed., *Ecotheology* (Maryknoll, N.Y.: Orbis Books, 1994), p. 45.

51. Population-Environmental Balance, "Why Excess Immigration Damages the Environment," *Carrying Capacity Network Focus*, 2 (1992), pp. 31-32. Conservationists have often blamed species extinction on overpopulation. William Conway, president of the Wildlife Conservation Society in New York, stated, "We're at a time when population is growing so rapidly that the only wildlife we'll be able to save is the one we care about." Mireya Navarro, "Disney Announces Plans for a Wildlife Theme Park," *New York Times* (June 21, 1995), p. B9.

52. "A Proposed Principled Policy Statement Based on Fact, Not Fear," *Race, Poverty and the Environment* 4 (Summer 1993), pp. 39-40.

53. See, Creighton, pp. 24-29; see also, Ruth Conniff, "The War on Aliens," *Progressive* (October 1993), pp. 39-40.

54. Michael Novick, "Was Hitler an Ecologist? Racism, Environmentalism, and Environmental Racism," research report for People Against Racist Terror (310-288-5003), p. 2.

55. See, e.g., Cece Modupe Fadope, "U.N. Women's Health, Poverty, and Population Activities," *Vital Signs* 10 (November-December 1994), pp. 34-35; U.S. Women of Color Delegation to the ICPD, "Statement on Poverty, Development and Population Activities," *Political Environments* 1 (Spring 1994), pp. 28-29.

56. Celestine Bohlen, "Vatican Will Champion Role of Mothers at a U.N. Conference," *New York Times* (June 21, 1995), p. A5.

57. "A Call for a New Approach," reprinted in Hartmann, pp. 311-313.

58. Loretta Ross, "Why Women of Color Can't Talk about Population," *Amicus Journal* 15 (Winter 1994), p. 27.

59. Quoted from the First People of Color Environmental Leadership Summit, sponsored by the Commission for Racial Justice of the United Church of Christ, Washington, D.C. (October 1991). The event was attended by over 650 leaders from grassroots and national organizations and was a springboard for major environmental organizing by people of color across the U.S.

60. Dale Hathaway-Sunseed, "A Critical Look at the Population Crisis in Latin America," University of California, Santa Cruz (Spring 1979); see also, Hartmann, pp. 248, 250.

61. See, Arthur Dyck, "Religious View," in Robert Veatch, ed., *Population and Ethics* (New York: Halsted Press, 1977), pp. 277-323; Jürgen Moltmann, "The Ecological Crisis: Peace with Nature," *Scottish Journal of Religious Studies* 9 (Spring 1988), pp. 5-18; John Swomley, "Too Many People, Too Few Resources," *Christian Social Action* 5 (November 1992), pp. 10-12; Nancy Wright and Donald Kill, *Ecological Healing: A Christian Vision* (Maryknoll, N.Y.: Orbis Books, 1993), pp. 7-9, 119-121; Roger Shinn, *Forced Options* (San Francisco: Harper and Row, 1982), pp. 85-105; James Nash, *Loving Nature* (Nashville: Abingdon, 1991), pp. 44-50; John Carmody, *Ecology and Religion* (New York: Paulist Press, 1983), pp. 140-142.

62. Ruether, p. 88; Catherine Keller, "Chosen Persons and the Green Ecumenacy: A Possible Christian Response to the Population Apocalypse," in Hallman, p. 301; Christine Gudorf, *Body, Sex and Pleasure* (Cleveland: Pilgrim Press, 1994), p. 43.

63. Keller, p. 301.

64. Ruether, p. 47.

65. Sallie McFague, *The Body of God* (Minneapolis: Fortress, 1993), p. 4.

66. Hartmann, p. 6.

67. Keller, p. 307; Gudorf, p. 48. Two children per couple is replacement-level reproduction. Thus one child would lead to declining population.

68. See, Art. II(d), United Nations Convention on the Prevention and Punishment of the Crime of Genocide. The section condemns imposing measures to prevent births within a targeted group.

69. Gudorf, p. 48.

70. Catherine Keller, "Talk about the Weather," in Carol J. Adams, ed., *Ecofeminism and the Sacred* (New York: Continuum, 1993), p. 31.

71. Keller, "Chosen Persons," p. 301. Dianne Moore notes that there is a relationship (albeit a complex one) between the eugenics movement of the 1930s and the first statements coming from churches supporting birth control (Dianne Moore, "Gender, Essentialism and the Debate over Reproductive Control in Liberal Protestantism," Ph.D. diss., Union Theological Seminary, 1995).

72. Ruether, p. 111; Keller, "Chosen Persons," p. 307.

73. Gudorf, p. 42.

74. Ibid., p. 59.

75. Ruether, p. 101. Emphasis mine. See, n. 51, above.

76. Ibid., p. 263.

77. Ibid., p. 264.

78. Ibid., pp. 258-268.

79. Keller, "Chosen Persons," p. 302; Ruether, p. 263; McFague, p. 56.

80. Ruether, p. 95.

81. Hartmann, p. 24.

82. Mies and Shiva, p. 283.

83. Hartmann, p. 26.

84. Gudorf, p. 50.

85. See, Hartmann, pp. 66-72.

86. See, Draft Programme of Action of the International Conference on Population and Development, ¶ 7.20.

87. McFague, pp. 4-5; see also, Keller, "Chosen Persons," p. 309.

88. Hartmann, pp. 40, 235-240.

89. Swomley, p. 12.

90. Ibid., p. 11. For other papal statements on the urgency of population stabilization, see, Dyck, p. 316.

91. "Vatican Contradiction on Population Control," *Christian Century* 111 (September 7-14, 1994), p. 809.

92. Loren Wilkinson, "Are Ten Billion People a Blessing?" *Christianity Today* 37 (January 11, 1993), p. 19; Wendy Steinberg, "The Population Problem," *Christianity Today* 38 (December 12, 1994), p. 6; Nigel M. de S. Cameron, "Cairo's Wake-Up Call," *Christianity Today* 38 (October 24, 1994), pp. 20-21; Andrew Steer, "Why Christians Should Support Population Programs," *Christianity Today* 38 (October 3, 1994), p. 51; Loren Wilkinson, ed., *Earthkeeping in the '90's* (Grand Rapids: Eerdmans, 1991), pp. 51-86; Ronald Fasano, "A Biblical Perspective on Ecology," *Christianity Today* 38 (June 20, 1994), pp. 7-8; Susan Bratton, *Six Billion and More* (Louisville: Westminster, 1992), pp. 178-198.

93. Cindy Rollins, "Don't Limit the Size of the Family," *Alliance Life* 123 (November 23, 1988), p. 21.

94. See, Michael Coffman, *Saviors of the Earth?* (Chicago: Northfield Publishing, 1994); see also, Tim Stafford, "Are People the Problem?" *Christianity Today* 38 (October 3, 1994), pp. 45-60. Stafford suggests that there are two positions one can have on the population issue: either one can support Ehrlich's radical Malthusianism and his oppressive population policies or one supports Julian Simon's cornucopianism, which holds that the earth is in better environmental shape than ever.

95. E. Calvin Beiser states, "From the Christian perspective of faith in a God of providence we can be confident that human population will never be an insuperable problem" (quoted in John W. Klotz, "Review of *Prospects for Growth*," *Concordia Journal* 18 [April 1992], p. 218).

96. See, Hartmann, pp. 176-179.

97. Ibid., p. 65.

98. See, e.g., Susan Rennie, "Breast Cancer Prevention: Diet vs. Drugs," *Ms. Magazine* 3 (May/June 1993), pp. 38-46.

99. Traditional Dena'ina Health Committee, "Summary Packet on Hepatitus B Vaccinations" (Sterling, Alaska, November 9, 1992).

100. According to a 1991-1992 Women of Color Reproductive Health poll, 80 percent support a woman's right to choose.

101. Hartmann, p. xvii.

102. Christine Gudorf, "Population, Ecology, and Women," *Second Opinion* 20 (January 1995), p. 63.

103. See, U.S. Department of State, "Bringing Cairo Home: Peace, Prosperity, and Democracy, Conference Discussion Guide" (Washington: Government Printing Office, 1994). In discussing the Programme of Action, the State Department acknowledged that "unwanted fertility is only one cause of rapid population growth, and that many social and economic factors contribute to the desire for large families. For example, high fertility is associated with poverty, high rates of infant and child mortality, lack of education, and the low status of women" (ibid.).

104. Ramona Morgan Brown and Carol Benson Holst, "IPCD's Suppressed Voices May Be Our Future Hope," *Ministry for Justice in Population Concerns* (October-December 1994), p. 1.

105. Charon Asetoyer, "Whom to Target for the North's Profits," *Wicozanni Wowapi* (Fall 1994), pp. 2-3.

106. U.S. Department of State, "Bringing Cairo Home."

107. Jane Hull Harvey, "Cairo–a Kairos Moment in History," *Christian Social Action* 7 (November 1994), p. 15.

108. Hartmann, p. 139; Brown and Holst, p. 1.

109. Mary Mellor, "Building a New Vision: Feminist, Green Socialism," in Richard Hofrichter, ed., *Toxic Struggles* (Philadelphia: New Society, 1993), p. 39.

9.

TEK Wars

First Nations' Struggles for Environmental Planning

DUANE GOOD STRIKER

EDITOR'S INTRODUCTION: Although there are basic similarities between the experiences and history of Natives in Canada and the United States, there are also marked differences. These range from the superficial–"reserves" rather than "reservations" and "residential schools" rather than "boarding schools"– to the substantial. Though the general policy in Canada, as Dennis McPherson (Anishinaabe) and J. Douglas Rabb make clear, was the same as that in the United States–namely, destruction of indigenous cultures and assimilation of Natives–there were in Canada no genocidal campaigns of extermination such as characterized the Indian Wars during and following the American Civil War.[1] Instead, the history of Canadian-Indian relations has been one of a peaceful, though not wholly voluntary, cession of Native lands by means of a long series of treaties, some negotiated long after the end of treaty-making in the United States in 1871.

Following the Treaty of Paris, which ended hostilities between the British and French, vast territories in North America previously controlled by France were handed over to Great Britain. On October 7, 1763, King George III issued a Royal Proclamation concerning the governance of British North America. The Royal Proclamation became the basis of Indian law in Canada. It recognized aboriginal title to a large portion of North America and set out a treaty process for extinguishing that title and ceding land. It also established the basis for the reserve system.[2] Though several treaties were signed in the ensuing years, many of these were merely expressions of peace and friendship. The Confederation in 1867, whereby much of the responsibility for governing Canada was transferred to the federal government, however, gave treaty-making "new momentum and new significance," making "more specific demands upon the Indians."[3]

Between 1871 and 1929, thirteen "numbered" treaties were executed, ceding large areas of Canada west of the Ontario border and creating reserves for the displaced indigenes. About half of Canada's Indians are covered by these treaties, which, in boilerplate language, opened much of the prairies of Alberta, Manitoba, and Saskatchewan to settlement.[4] Both the lands covered by these treaties and the Indian tribes that are party to them are still referred to by the number of the treaty involved. Thus in the following essay, Duane Good Striker, a Blood, refers to the southern Alberta home of his people as the Treaty 7 area.

Canadian courts and parliaments took a "dim view of the status of [these] treaties and the rights they supposedly secured to tribal Indians."[5] In fact, the Indian Act was amended in 1927, making it a federal crime to pursue Native land claims in court, to raise money to prosecute such claims, or even to organize to do so. As a result, for many years "treaty rights lay largely dormant and unenforced."[6] Since 1978, however, and particularly since the repatriation of the constitution in 1982, First Nations have parlayed their supposed "citizen plus" status within Canada into a significant position in Canadian constitutional negotiations.[7]

The extent to which Natives should rely on treaties to enforce their rights has become a bone of contention among Canadian Natives in recent years. Many would agree with non-Native sociologist Menno Boldt that treaties form the best basis for preserving Native peoples and their rights.[8] Others, however, would concur with Howard Adams (Métis). Adams has declared: "A tragic consequence of the treaties was that Indians later accepted them as a kind of legal Bible which they felt gave them special rights and privileges. This attitude persists with most Indians today. Not only do the treaties represent cruel thefts of aboriginal rights, but they are also contracts of continuing oppression. When Indians hold the treaties as sacred testaments, the process of colonization is indeed complete."[9] Alberta First Nations have, in fact, broken with the Assembly of First Nations (AFN), a representative body for Canadian Natives, because of a perception that AFN is insufficiently committed to the treaty system on the prairies.[10]

Disputes on treaty status aside, the Blood Tribe of southern Alberta has been in the forefront of environmental management for several years. A successful and expanding Agricultural Project, despite the problems limned by Good Striker, seeks to enable tribal members "to participate in the modern world on an equal footing while maintaining much of their traditional lifestyle."[11] The Blood Tribe Irrigation Project uses the tribe's substantial water resources to irrigate reserve lands.[12] With the retaining of Good Striker to conduct an environmental assessment on the reserve and to head the tribe's environmental initiative, the groundwork was laid for the assumption by the tribe of its own comprehensive environmental responsibilities.[13]

Many tribes in the United States have environmental programs and departments. Provisions of many environmental laws permit tribes to assume responsibility for regulation on their lands in lieu of the federal government.[14] First Nations in Canada, however, have lagged behind. Nothing as ambitious as the program envisioned by the Bloods and Good Striker has been attempted previously. Perhaps the most innovative feature of the Blood proposal is the inclusion of traditional environmental knowledge (TEK) in any environmental considerations. Unfortunately it also has led to TEK wars, discussed by Good Striker in the following essay.

The Creator put all peoples on this earth, each with a unique culture and language, to occupy a specific territory in order to fulfill his purpose for creation. I am a Blood. The Kainaawa, or Blood tribe, has existed as a nation from time immemorial.[15] It is a member of the Blackfoot Confederacy. The Blood Reserve lies between the St. Mary's and Belly Rivers in Alberta. Covering approximately 350,000 acres, it is the largest Indian reserve in Canada. It possesses a large agricultural base and substantial natural resources, including oil and gas, semi-precious minerals, and timber. It also contains much of the headwaters of the United States, with numerous river systems that flow into Hudson's Bay, the Gulf of Mexico, and the Pacific Ocean beginning on, or flowing through, the reserve. It comprises the largest part of the five bands that make up the Treaty 7 area.

Two years ago I was approached by my tribe to undertake an assessment of environmental problems on our reserve. The inventory was necessitated by an initiative of the Department of Indian Affairs and Northern Development (DIAND), the Canadian equivalent of the Bureau of Indian Affairs in the United States. The goal was to identify all ecological problems and then proceed with cleanup operations. Following this remedial action, DIAND intended to develop an environmental management framework for each reserve. When the Blood assessment was completed, it revealed some toxic dumping and problems associated with open-pit mining and oil and gas exploration. It also disclosed damaging farming practices by outside agricultural concerns that lease much of the crop land on the reserve. DIAND had just moved to clean up sites in Alberta, British Columbia, and a few locations in Manitoba and British Columbia when the law changed.

On January 19, 1995, the Canadian Environmental Protection Act (CEPA) was replaced by the Canadian Environmental Assessment Act (CEAA). Under provisions of the new legislation, land-based Indian bands can formulate and adopt their own environmental policies. Shortly after the law's passage, negotiations commenced between DIAND, Environment Canada (the counterpart of the United States' Environmental Protection Agency [EPA]), and Alberta Environmental Protection (the provincial regulatory agency), on one side, and the Horse Lake Band, on the other, to develop protocols for a comprehensive devolution of environmental regulatory authority to the Indian bands. Subsequently an invitation was extended to the other bands and tribes in the Treaty 6, 7, and 8 areas to participate in the project to create a province-wide environmental organization to be called the Alberta Treaty Nations Society for Environmental Protection (ATNS).[16]

The immediate objective was to create a First Nations Environmental Assessment Manual. With the impending devolution of assessment responsibilities from the federal government to First Nations, development of the manual was a critical step in assisting First Nations to increase their ability to conduct such assessments. In the future, as First Nations also assume regulatory and compliance authority, it also would provide the framework for comprehensive environmental regulation on participating reserves. A three-person focus group, composed of one representative from each of the three treaty areas, was established. I was appointed as the member for Treaty 7.

The focus group quickly determined that the manual would incorporate the most stringent standards of the EPA, CEAA, and Alberta Environmental Protection. A fourth component would be the traditional environmental knowledge of the First Nations, to which we gave the somewhat ironical acronym TEK. We were clear that TEK needed to be included in the assessment and decision-making process. We were no less certain that it should play a role equal to scientific and technical data. From the beginning TEK emerged as the largest of many sticking points in our discussions with the federal and provincial governments.

Although all First Nations in the ATNS will use the manual, the TEK portion will vary from area to area and be geared to the specific tribes using it. Thus, the Treaty 7 version of the volume will reflect a Blackfoot understanding of TEK. For the Treaty 6 area, it will contain Cree knowledge. And for the Treaty 8 area, it will include a Dene view. We considered this to be crucial. Every people must govern itself according to customs given to it by the Creator and maintain itself under the Creator's guidance.[17] One cannot simply mix the ways of different cultures indiscriminately. The Lakota way is the Lakota way. The Blackfoot way is the Blackfoot way. And so it is meant to remain.

DIAND, however, failed to grasp this basic point. Initially, it insisted on a single, homogenized version of TEK, reflecting a single, homogenized image of Native peoples. In our first TEK war, I threatened to resign and go to fight, turning the various bands against the entire project. Reluctantly, DIAND capitulated.

A second and related battle occurred over the meaning of TEK and how it was going to be gathered. In writing the manual, we thought of TEK as relating to ecological knowledge at the time of first contact with Europeans. In camp two hundred to five hundred years ago, how did an individual interact with the environment? At the community level, what was the people's understanding of where they fit in Creation? How did they conceive of the cosmos, the earth, and other creatures? What rules and practices did they have in place for conservation to ensure sustainable supplies of crops and animals to hunt? Once again DIAND objected, contending that such beliefs, practices, and attitudes could not be determined after so many years of interaction with Euro-Canadian society and the resultant changes in Native communities. We, in turn, argued that TEK could be gathered by interviewing our elders. While it is true that residential schools took away most of our people for generations, a few always were held back.[18] We are rich in resources for learning traditional knowledge because these people carry encyclopedias in their heads.

Once it was conceded that elders were the appropriate source (rather than some alternative source, such as nineteenth-century ethnographies of questionable accuracy), yet another point of contention in our ongoing TEK wars arose as to the manner in which their knowledge would be collected. DIAND, as a prerequisite to the provision of funding, demanded that it be in written form. This posed a serious and immediate logistical problem. Our cultures are oral cultures. Our Native languages are still the first language of many of our elders. Those languages carry within them our thoughtworlds and our cultures, and the differences in worldview between these cultures and the West often make concepts difficult to render into English. An additional difficulty arises because our languages have been reduced to written form only within the last twenty years. Though these transliterations are reasonably advanced, they are far from perfect. I finally told DIAND that, in order to get the TEK portion for the manual, it had to supply us with enough money to videotape the interviews with elders. After the interviews were taped, we would have time to worry about problems of translation. The videos will have the added advantage that they will be available for use in informational and training programs for First Nation peoples.

The focus group completed a draft of the manual in May 1995 and circulated it to the bands participating in the ATNS for comment. A final version is scheduled for release in August. Though the impact of this manual in Indian Country will be significant, it is by no means the end of the environmental issue. Each band must still adopt it. We hope that it will serve as a model for First Nations not part of the ATNS, who may adapt it to create their own programs. The alternative is to do nothing and continue to be governed by CEAA. It is up to the chiefs and the band councils whether they will have a policy with teeth. I travel to other reserves and tell them, "I don't have to live here–you do. Do something. Don't just lie down." We're using the manual to create a consciousness. Even for the ATNS, however, the manual is just a beginning.

Our ultimate goal is the assumption of complete regulatory and compliance jurisdiction over our own reserves. Though none of the problems uncovered in my initial assessment on the Blood Reserve was disastrous, several were still in need of remedial action. DIAND has initiated action on the identified sites. Once their reclamation is complete, the tribe will assume responsibility. Once jurisdiction has been assumed fully by the tribe, anyone who operates on our land in the future will have to abide by our rules and go by our procedures.

CEAA will have no consequence on the reserve. It is a part of sovereignty and self-government. When any enterprise operates on our reserve, we want there to be 100 percent mitigation. We want to see the land in better condition than it was before they conducted their operation. We want to see more gophers and grass there than before they arrived. If there is an environmental problem, we will demand that it be remedied promptly to our satisfaction, or we will seize all the responsible party's assets on our reserve. Once the manual is in place and we assume jurisdiction, we want to be part of any environmental review or assessment board affecting not only our reserve and migratory resources, such as water or wildlife that pass through our reserve, but also having an impact on our traditional territory that was ceded by treaty. Then an entirely new campaign in the TEK wars undoubtedly will begin.

As indicated earlier, besides natural resource production, another potential problem area on our reserve involves agriculture. Many of our members are "rocking chair" farmers. They lease their land to outside agricultural concerns, typically for an average term of five years. In exchange for the lease, they receive one-third of the crop produced. These outside agro-combines plant canola and other cereals for export. They do not practice crop rotation and do not allow fields to lie fallow to renew themselves. Potent pesticides and fertilizers are used at high levels. They are interested only in obtaining the highest yield of cash crops for the term of the lease. Once the tribe assumes environmental jurisdiction, it will have the power to regulate agricultural practices as well. No longer will a lessee in the last year of a five-year lease be able to poison the ground with ever-increasing amounts of fertilizer to maximize the crop and then simply disappear. Ideally, we would move away from the current sharecropping system of export crops to production of our own food–corn, potatoes, beets.

Before we can assume full jurisdiction, however, we need to increase our environmental assessment and compliance capabilities. Recognizing this, the focus group initiated discussions with DIAND, Environment Canada, and Alberta Environmental Protection concerning the creation of an internship program. Under this program two representatives from each of the treaty areas in the ATNS will undergo an environmental internship, working on a rotating basis in each of the participating departments. This will occur in three phases. During the first phase, interns will spend six to eight months in government offices, where they will become familiar with existing environmental legislation and regulation and enforcement/compliance methods. Following this, they will return to their reserves to work on environmental issues and put what they have learned into practice. The second phase will involve another work rotation through government departments. This will provide an opportunity for interns to get further guidance concerning implementation of environmental practices on reserves and to report to government officials their experiences in implementing their learnings from the first phase of the internship. When appropriate, during a third phase, interns may receive specialized training in specific fields, such as wildlife or water management. Environment Canada has agreed to participate in the intern program. DIAND and Alberta Environmental Protection are still determining the extent and timing of their involvement. Following implementation of the manual, environmental assessment training also will be needed to train a core of First Nation representatives who will, in turn, train band members from across the province. The focus group has begun discussions with DIAND concerning such a program.

Most First Nations will not have the capability to implement fully comprehensive environmental regulations on their reserves, nor will they have enough demand for services to warrant the hiring of a highly skilled environmental professional full-time. We are therefore proposing a central environmental resource center that could supplement resources available to bands and provide technical assistance and delivery of environmental services. To be known as the Alberta Treaty Nations Environmental Protectorate, the center also would act as a clearinghouse for information on environmental legislation, standards, and practices; serve as a central registry for information related to environmental assessment and compliance on reserve lands; provide advice on collection and documentation of TEK and serve as a repository of TEK; develop environmental assessment and compliance tools and procedures; serve as a point of contact between government departments and First Nations; advise bands in the hiring of providers of environmental services; provide information concerning sources and collection methods of environmental baseline data; facilitate First Nation involvement in governmental environmental reviews; and conduct and facilitate public hearings on behalf of chiefs and band councils.

We are also moving ahead in the exploration of alternative energy resources. The Piegan (another Blackfoot tribe), for example, have begun an experimental wind farm. Using the Chinook, wind could become an important source for generation of electricity.[19] Solar energy could also prove a major resource in the future, as we harness large amounts of the sunlight we enjoy.

Of course, any environmental program as ambitious and comprehensive as the one being discussed by the ATNS will be costly. Besides some start-up funding from DIAND, we have begun discussions with Environment Canada. Environment Canada has been in existence for seventeen years. The vast majority of funds it has expended has gone to off-reservation projects. It is our contention that the federal government owes us seventeen years' worth of retroactive funding.

The process has not been easy, and it will not be easy. But our elders have declared that our leaders must ensure our inherent right to govern ourselves and to protect our lands.[20] When I was drafted two years ago to perform an environmental assessment of our reserve, I went up to the high places that are sacred to our people and asked for help. I did not ask for help for myself but for my people and for future generations. We can always sell our land and its resources for short-term gain, but if we do, it is our children and grandchildren who will suffer. And if we act in keeping with our TEK, it is they who will benefit.

Notes

1. Dennis McPherson and J. Douglas Rabb, *Indian from the Inside: A Study in Ethno-Metaphysics* (Thunder Bay, Ont.: Center for Northern Studies, Lakehead University, 1993), pp. 38-47.

2. Ibid., pp. 27-29.

3. Ibid., p. 40.

4. Augie Fleras and Jean Leonard Elliott, *The Nations Within: Aboriginal-State Relations in Canada, the United States, and New Zealand* (Toronto: Oxford University Press, 1992), p. 31.

5. David H. Getches, Charles F. Wilkinson, and Robert A. Williams, Jr., *Cases and Materials on Federal Indian Law*, 3d ed. (St. Paul: West Publishing, 1993), p. 987.

6. Ibid.

7. Sally M. Weaver, "Political Representivity and Indigenous Minorities in Canada and Australia," in Noel Dyck, ed., *Indigenous Peoples and the Nation-State* (St. John's, Newfoundland: Institute of Social and Economic Research, Memorial University of Newfoundland, 1985), p. 133; Douglas E. Sanders, "The Indian Lobby and the Canadian Constitution, 1978-1982," in Dyck, p. 151; Pauline Comeau, *Elijah: No Ordinary Hero* (Vancouver: Douglas & McIntyre, 1993).

8. E.g., Menno Boldt, *Surviving as Indians: The Challenge of Self-Government* (Toronto: University of Toronto Press, 1993), pp. 42-43; but cf., Daniel N. Paul, *We Were Not the Savages: A Micmac Perspective on the Collision of European and Aboriginal Civilization* (Halifax: Nimbus Publishing, 1993), and James Burke, *Paper Tomahawks: From Red Tape to Red Power* (Winnipeg: Queenston House Publishing, 1976).

9. Howard Adams, *Prison of Grass: Canada from a Native Point of View*, rev. ed. (Saskatoon: Fifth House Publishers, 1989), p. 67. Adams terms "citizen plus" status an illusion and notes that Indians did not become citizens until 1961 (ibid.).

10. Duane Good Striker, North American Native Workshop on Environmental Justice, Iliff School of Theology, Denver, Co. (March 18, 1995). According to Good Striker, the Alberta tribes chose the name Alberta Treaty Nations Society for Environmental Protection for their environmental organization because Alberta First Nations would have produced the initials AFN (ibid.).

11. "Blood Tribe Successfully Working with Mother Earth," *Native Journal* (November 1992), pp. 1-2.

12. Ibid.

13. See, Tom Russell, "Creating Our Own Stuff–from Our Own Designs," *Native Journal* (February 1995), p. 7; "Environmental Disputes Can Be Worked Out through Mediation," *Native Journal* (September/October 1993), p. 16.

14. See, Jace Weaver, "Triangulated Power and the Environment: Tribes, the Federal Government, and the States," herein.

15. "Kainayassini," Declaration of the Elders of the Blood Indian Nation (1995).

16. Treaty 6 covers central Alberta and most of southern Saskatchewan. Treaty 7 covers southern Alberta. Treaty 8 covers northern British Columbia, northern Saskatchewan, and northern Alberta.

17. "Kainayassini."

18. *Residential school* is the Canadian term for what Americans would call *boarding school.* Forced attendance at such institutions, usually run by the government or by Christian religious denominations, was a common feature of both the Canadian and American Native experience in the latter part of the nineteenth and first part of the twentieth centuries.

19. The Chinook is a powerful, warm, moist wind that blows across the Northwest. See, Peter Watts, *A Dictionary of the Old West* (New York: Alfred A. Knopf, 1977), p. 86. As the author himself characterized it at the North American Native Workshop on Environmental Justice, "We have wind like you wouldn't believe!"

20. "Kainayassini."

10.

An American Indian
Theological Response to Ecojustice

GEORGE E. TINKER

By now readers of this volume should be relatively aware of the extent to which modern ecological devastation has put the lives and well-being of American Indian peoples at risk. Indeed the bulk of this volume has used particular cases studies from illustrative Indian communities in order to demonstrate the range and intensity of ecojustice concerns among Indian people in general: land, water, mining, toxic waste deposit sites, and the like. It is ironical that those who have the deepest cultural connection to American soil would be among those most deeply affected by the modern, technological devastation of the land.[1] Yet it is the painful truth that ecological devastation, while it eventually affects the well-being of everyone, initially and most particularly affects American Indians and people of color on this continent and two-thirds-world people in general more directly and adversely than it affects White Americans, especially those of the middle and upper classes.[2] As Ward Churchill implies, genocide seems all too often to accompany ecocide.[3]

There are those in the world today who regularly espouse an environmental consciousness predicated on American Indian belief systems, summoning images of a simpler existence with a built-in concern for the whole of creation. This common notion that American Indian peoples and other indigenous peoples have some spiritual and mystical insight on environmental issues confronting the world today is usually an instinctive if unstudied recognition of the differentness of those cultures. It thus tends to be a relatively intuitive truth-claim based on little research and an overabundance of romanticization. Even those who have had the opportunity to witness the poverty of our poorest reservations, evidenced by the rusting hulks of worn-out automobiles parked in various states of abandonment around reservation homes, continue to recite their own facile version of Native concern for the environment.

On the other hand, there are others who have a more openly racist concern for protecting the privilege of White power and discourse in North America and who find ways to use their position and prestige to deprecate American Indian environmental consciousness. Sometimes this perspective is packaged in the clothing of modern academic research, typically by White scholars who use "Native American Studies," as Gerald Vizenor would remind us, as a "trope to power."[4] Namely, many White scholars who specialize in Native American studies feel so threatened by the emergence of Native scholars that they have used their academic positions and their manipulation of the discourse more to empower themselves than in the quest for truth. Other commentators in the largely White liberal ecology movement, as Jace Weaver has already noted in the Introduction to this volume, seem to have their own racist power agenda.[5] Namely, there seems to be a lingering self-defense (or defensiveness) among many in the more reactionary environmentalist set, like *Earth First!*, that other peoples have also abused the natural world–they just lacked the resources and technology to do it as exhaustively as Europeans and Americans have done.[6]

The truth of the Native world is far more complex and sophisticated than either of these sides would allow. This essay is, then, an attempt to begin a process of theological reflection that must finally be inclusive of many more voices than that of this author alone. The immediate need is to begin to delineate some of the complexity and sophistication of Indian beliefs in general, while paying attention to the specifics of different tribes along the way.

What follows is one Indian scholar's attempt to reflect theologically on the relationship between American Indian peoples and what Western theologians would call creation and the contemporary ecological devastation of that creation. The occasion for this essay, obviously enough given the context of this book, is the continuing program of the World Council of Churches' program unit called Justice, Peace, Creation (JPC) and the particular case study designed by the JPC unit around the topic "Creation as Beloved of God." It was around this assigned topic that we assembled nearly two dozen Indian persons from nearly as many tribal traditions for conversation in March 1995.

I want to move beyond the mere reporting on how ecojustice issues uniquely affect the indigenous peoples of the Western hemisphere. Rather, I want to suggest that these examples are indicative of a systemic problem that is pervasively political and intellectual. The modern "world system," driven by the economics and politics of domination, functions primarily on the basis of maximizing profits with only minimal regard for environmental concerns. In turn, this world system is sustained intellectually in no small part by the prevailing theologies of

the powerful churches of Europe and North America and the philosophies taught in their universities. If the European and Euro-American
churches do not pay particular attention to these philosophical and
theological foundations, which underlie modern technology, economics, and international politics, and their resulting contexts of
ethno-ecojustice, then the political realities of interethnic and international injustice and ecological devastation have little chance of changing
for the better.

"CREATION AS BELOVED OF GOD"

The first step in this theological reflection has to do with language
and culture, and with the inappropriateness of typical Euro-Christian
cultural language for referencing American Indian cultural realities.
Three words in the assigned program title will pose problems for Indian peoples linguistically, culturally, and theologically—namely, *creation*,
beloved, and *God*. If Christianity is to make any legitimate claim to uni-
versality, it must struggle to overcome the cultural limitations of its
traditional categories of theological analysis in order to better accommodate peoples with radically different cultures and languages.
Otherwise, the Christian enterprise is forever condemned to perpetrate imperialist acts of colonization and conquest.

Beloved

"Creation as Beloved of God" is actually very strange language for
an American Indian community to consider. Of course, it makes sense
in the context of the World Council of Churches, especially given the
scriptural tradition that understands God as typified by love in terms
of the New Testament Greek word *agape*. But this is a relatively technical linguistic-cultural phenomenon that only works universally for
Christianity with careful translation from the Greek and ongoing education. In a cultural world that has been consistently abused by
Christianity,[7] and one that has also struggled to maintain its own cultural and spiritual identity, the technicality of Greek language translation
is almost completely irrelevant or even antagonistic. This imposition
of meaning is then heightened by the fact that no Indian community I
know of refers to God's relationship with creation as characterized by
love. Of course, Indian peoples have nouns and verbs to describe emo-
tive-bonding relationships between people, but we do not, as a rule,
impute these same human emotive states, like love, to God. God and
the spiritual realm can be happy or upset with things that humans do;
they even have expectations for our continued participation in maintaining the balance in the world. There is no sense, however, that God

or the spiritual realm has any different regard for human beings than for the rest of creation, and there is certainly no notion of God's relationship with the whole of creation as marked by the human emotion of love.

This is in sharp contrast with Euro-Christianity and its consistent interpretation of its sacred texts. For instance, most commentators on the gospel of John insist that God's love for the world (Jn 3:16: "God so loved the world. . .") must be understood as love for human beings. The Greek word *cosmos*, translated "world," is usually interpreted in this context as referring only to the world of human beings. God's salvific act in Christ Jesus is thought of as efficacious only for human beings, and, hence, God's salvific love for the world must imply logically that the world is here limited only to those who are most privileged in creation and are the proper object of God's affections. The danger of such privileging of human beings should be obvious. It runs the risk of generating human arrogance, which too easily sees the world in terms of hierarchies of existence, all of which are ultimately subservient to the needs and whims of humans.

In any case, the imposition of the word *beloved* functions necessarily to negate or at least to falsify the traditional Indian understanding of God and God's relationship to creation. If we are to insist that *agape* actually refers to "acting in the best interests of another," rather than to the emotion of love, then we need to inquire seriously about the effectiveness of translating the Greek into a language like English and then having to translate the translation before sense can be made of the original. Thus if one wants to affirm that God always "acts in the best interests" of human beings and of the whole of creation, why must we use the emotive word *love* as the only suitable language for articulating the concept, especially when that language usage proves to be foreign to specific cultural communities?

God

God is yet another problem for Indian people except to the extent that we have already been colonized by past missionaries to assume that the word is an adequate gloss for our own naming of the Sacred Other. To begin with, the word *God* is a difficult word in modern theological and philosophical discourse. The givenness of its meaning for European and Euro-Americans has long since given way to a modernist and postmodernist angst that leaves the word without an immediately agreed-upon sense. Much more important in this context, there is a facile assumption that languages are merely codes for one another, and that a simple translation settles all difficulties. Hence, the question too often asked of Indian peoples is: What is the word for God in your language?

Christianity and its sacred texts regularly impute to God attributes that are intrinsically human-like, even if these attributes are seen as somehow more than human in God's case. Hence God is indeed identified not only as having emotions such as love and anger, but God is identified as the personification of love itself. The intense sophistication of Indian tribal spiritualities takes a different tack. Namely, what Christians would refer to as God is understood as a spiritual force that permeates the whole of the world and is manifest in countless ways in the world around us at any given moment and especially in any given place.[8] *Wakonda*, who is ultimately an unknowable mystery that is only knowable in particular manifestations, makes itself manifest first of all as Above and Below, *Wakonda Monshita* and *Wakonda Udseta*, symbolized as sky and earth, and called upon as Grandfather and Grandmother, he and she. *Wakonda*, which has no inherent or ultimate gender, is knowable only in the necessary reciprocal dualism of male and female. Thus, to assume that the simplistic gloss *God* somehow is adequate to translate and classify *Wakonda* (or *Wakan Tanka, Gitchy Manitou*, etc.) into English immediately falsifies the internal, cultural meaning of *Wakonda* for Osage peoples (or Lakota or Ojibwe, in the case of the other examples). As a result of extensive colonization and missionization, Indian people who would never do so in their own language have become perfectly comfortable in referring to God as "he" in English.

Creation

Finally, the word *creation* presents problems insofar as it assumes either the Judeo-Christian creation story or something like it. While every tribe has several creation stories, they simply are not valorized the way the Judeo-Christian accounts are in Christianity. To begin with, the word *creation* is not a common usage in very many tribes, and when it is used it almost always represents a convenient English signifier that has no immediate referent in the speaker's own language. Moreover, when the word is used in a Christian context, it seems to Indian peoples to connote a heavy dose of reification that is completely lacking in any Indian intellectual tradition. That is, in the Euro-American context, creation is objectified as something that is quite apart from human beings and to which humans relate from the outside.

Another pronounced difference between Euro-American and Indian traditions is the usual assumption in the Indian of the pre-existence of the world in some form. Thus most Indian story-telling begins with the givenness of the world of which we are an integral part. Rather, then, than conceiving of an initial creation that was long ago and has little continuing relevance in a world in which only human redemption is in process, Indian intellectual traditions conceive of the world in constant creative process that requires our continual participation.

If the words *creation* and even *createds* have a distinctly borrowed flavor in an Indian context, there is no easy alternative for articulating *what is*, or *that which we are a part of.* Some sense of what is at stake is apparent in a Lakota phrase that may be illustrative. *Mitakouye oyasin* can be translated as a prayer "for all my relations." As such it is inclusive not only of immediate family or even extended family, but of the whole of a tribe or nation; of all the nations of two-leggeds in the world; and particularly of all the nations other than two-leggeds—the four-leggeds, the wingeds, and the living-moving-things. It is this interrelatedness that best captures what might symbolize for Indian peoples what Euro-Americans would call creation. More to the point, it is this understanding of interrelatedness, of balance and mutual respect among the different species in the world, that characterizes what we might call Indian peoples' greatest gift to Euro-Americans and to the Euro-American understanding of creation at this time of ecological crisis in the world.

HUMAN PRIVILEGE AND COMMUNITIES OF RESPECT

In the biblical creation story and in the ensuing Christian tradition, human beings are significantly privileged over against the rest of creation. Indeed the relationship stipulated at the beginning of the book of Genesis, as it is too commonly interpreted by Euro-American readers, is one of subjection and domination:

> And God said to them [the humans], "Be fruitful and multiply, and fill the earth and subdue it; and have dominion over the fish of the sea and over the birds of the air and over every living thing that moves upon the earth" (Gn 1:28).

In American Indian cultures there is no similar privileging of human beings in the scheme of things in the world. Neither is there any sense in which somehow humans are external to the rest of the world and its functions. To the contrary, humans are seen as part of the whole, rather than apart from it and free to use it up. Yet there are expectations of human beings. We do have particular responsibilities in the scheme of things, but, then, so do all our other relatives in the created realm— from bears and squirrels to eagles and sparrows, trees, ants, rocks, and mountains. In fact, many elders in Indian communities are quick to add that of all the createds, of all our relations, we two-leggeds alone seem to be confused as to our responsibility toward the whole.

I have long suspected that European Christianity has undergone a millennia-long transformation that eventually put humans in opposition to the rest of creation. At the very least, this is signified in the theological, philosophical, scientific, and economic struggle for control over the world, its environment, and its "resources." This may have begun as early as the time of Aristotle, with the birth of so-called objective observation and description, an incipient scientific method. It continued its development during the European Renaissance with its neo-Aristotelian project of emerging taxonomic systems and the control over the world that seems to come from naming and categorizing. The philosophical and scientific basis for control of nature was initially rooted in the acts of naming. Perhaps the modern Euro-American need for exerting control over the world was most explicitly founded by Descartes in a logical extension of both Aristotle and the Renaissance. Descartes most clearly announced the ultimate knowability of the world and the human responsibility to do the knowing (and hence, exert control).

This philosophical movement toward greater and greater human control over the environment was paralleled by an ever-increasing importance granted philosophically and theologically to the individual in European cultures. This shift toward the ascendancy of the individual necessarily included a concomitant displacing of community values. I would argue that this shift meant not only the displacing of the importance of human communities, implicitly devaluing notions of the common good, but that it also meant displacing any lingering sense of the importance of a community inclusive of nonhuman entities in the created realm. In the Indian intellectual tradition and in cultural practice human beings are not privileged over the rest of the world, nor are individuals privileged over the good of the whole community.

BALANCING THE WORLD FOR LIFE

If we allow for a full translation of the Euro-Christian, cultural-linguistic metaphor of creation, we are left with a substantial thought of extreme importance to Indian peoples. What is clear to all American Indian peoples is that respect for creation, that is, for the whole of the created realm, or for all our relations, is vitally important to the well-being of our communities. While respect for all our relations in this world is critical for all Indian education, it is perhaps most readily apparent in the general philosophy of balance and harmony, a notion adhered to by all Indian communities in one form or another. Respect for creation emerges out of our perceived need for maintaining balance in the world around us. Thus Indian spirituality is characteristically oriented toward both the everyday and the ceremonial balancing of the world and our participation in it. When the balance of existence is disturbed, whole communities pay a price that is measured in some lack of communal well-being.

Once we have clarified the place of human beings in the ongoing processes of world balancing and world renewal, there are two aspects of what might be considered a general Indian theology that Christians and other Euro-Americans might do well to note. They can be initially categorized as reciprocity and spatiality. My contention will be that attention to these two important spiritual aspects of Indian cultures and what I am calling Indian theology can become radically transformative for the Euro-American system of values and structures of social behavior.

Reciprocity: A Foundation for Balance

The general American Indian notion of reciprocity is fundamental to the human participation in world-balancing and harmony. Reciprocity involves first of all a spiritual understanding of the cosmos and the place of humans in the processes of the cosmic whole. It begins with an understanding that anything and everything that humans do has an effect on the rest of the world around us. Even when we cannot clearly know what that effect is in any particular act, we know that there is an effect. Thus, Indian peoples, in different places and in different cultural configurations, have always struggled to know how to act appropriately in the world. Knowing that every action has its unique effect has always meant that there had to be some sort of built-in compensation for human actions, some act of reciprocity.

The necessity for reciprocity becomes most apparent where violence is concerned, especially when such violence is an apparent necessity, as in hunting or harvesting. Violence cannot be perpetrated, a life taken, in a Native American society, without some spiritual act of reciprocation. We are so much a part of the whole of creation and its balance that anything we do to perpetrate an act of violence, even when it is necessary for our own survival, must be accompanied by an act of spiritual reciprocation intended to restore the balance of existence. It must be remembered that violence as a technical category must extend to *all* one's relatives. Thus, a ceremony of reciprocity must accompany the harvesting of vegetable foods such as corn or the harvesting of medicinals such as cedar, even when only part of a plant is taken. The ceremony may be relatively simple, involving a prayer or song and perhaps a reciprocal offering of tobacco. Many tribes maintained very extensive and complex ceremonies of reciprocation to ensure continuing balance and plentiful harvests. Likewise, there is a tradition of mythic stories that accompany such ceremonies and function to provide the theoretical foundation for the ceremonies. Ultimately, all of these stories function further to insure the continuing respect of the communities who tell the stories for all the parts of the created world, all the relatives, upon which the people depend for their own well-being. Even gathering rocks for a purification ceremony (sweat lodge ceremony) calls for care and respect, prayers and reciprocation.

In the same manner, ceremonies involving self-sacrifice (typically called "self-torture" or "self-mutilation" by the missionaries and early ethnographers) also come under this general category of reciprocation. In the Rite of Vigil (vision quest), which is very widespread among Indian peoples of North America, as well as in the Sun Dance, the suffering the supplicant takes upon himself or herself is usually thought of as vicarious and as some sort of reciprocation. Since all of a person's so-called possessions are ultimately not possessions but relatives that live with that person, an individual is not giving away a possession when he or she gives a gift to someone else. In actuality, the only thing a person really owns and can sacrifice is his or her own flesh. Thus, these ceremonies of self-sacrifice tend to be the most significant ceremonies of a people. While missionaries typically thought of these ceremonies as vain human attempts to placate some angry deity, Indian communities know that these ceremonies are much more complex than that. Rather, they are much more often thought of as vicarious sacrifices engaged in for the sake of the whole community's well-being. Moreover, they are believed to be ceremonies that came to the community as a gift from the Sacred Mystery in order to help the community take care of itself and its world. Thus, the Sun Dance is considered a ceremony in which two-leggeds participate with the Sacred in order to help maintain life, that is, to maintain the harmony and balance of the whole.

Hence, hunting and war typically involved a complex ceremonial preparation before a contingent of warriors left their home. The Osage War Ceremony, for instance, involved an eleven-day ritual, allowing enough time to affirm the sacredness of life, to consecrate the lives that would be lost in war, and to offer prayers in reciprocation for those potentially lost lives.[9] In the hunt most Indian nations report specified prayers of reciprocation involving apologies and words of thanksgiving to the animal itself and the animal's spirit nation. Usually this ceremonial act is in compliance with the request of the animals themselves as the people remember the primordial negotiations in mythological stories. Thus, formal and informal ceremonies of reciprocation are a day-to-day mythic activity that has its origin in mythological stories in which human beings were given permission by the animal nations to hunt them for food. The resulting covenant, however, calls on human beings to assume responsibilities over against the perpetration of violence among four-legged relatives. Even after the hunt or battle, those who participated must invariably go through a ceremonial cleansing before re-entering their own village. Not to do this would bring the disruption of the sacred caused by the perpetration of violence right into the middle of national life and put all people at risk.[10]

Animals, birds, crops, and medicines are all living relatives and must be treated with respect if they are to be genuinely efficacious for the people. The ideal of harmony and balance requires that all share a respect for all other existent things, avoiding gratuitous or unthinking acts of violence. Maintaining harmony and balance requires that even necessary acts of violence be done in a sacred way. Thus nothing is taken from the earth without prayer and offering. When the tree is cut down for the Sun Dance, for instance, something must be offered, returned to the spirit world, for the life of that tree. The people not only ceremonially and prayerfully ask its permission but ask for its cooperation and help during the four days of the dance itself.

No model of development, involving modern Western technologies, as far as I know, embodies or incorporates an indigenous ethic of reciprocity as is found in Indian communities. It is not enough to replant a few trees or to add nutrients to the soil. These are superficial acts to treat the negative symptoms of development. The value of reciprocity, which is a hallmark of Indian ceremonies, goes to the heart of issues of sustainability, which is maintaining a balance and tempering the negative effects of basic human survival techniques. Moreover, as far as I know, there is no ceremony for clear-cutting an entire forest.

Spatiality: Place vs. Time

That there is and has been historically a fundamental difference between Euro-American and American Indian worldviews emerging from different priorities of space and time has been long recognized by American Indian observers of Euro-American cultures, even if it has not been regularly noticed or granted by the academic specialists or Euro-American observers of Indian cultures. These American Indian observations were first codified by Vine Deloria, Jr., the dean of American Indian academics, in his 1973 book *God Is Red*.[11] As I have also argued,[12] it is not a case of one culture being marked solely by temporality and the other by spatiality. Rather, it appears that either space or time has become the primary category of existence around which all other categories are arranged. For Euro-American peoples temporality has been a primary category for many centuries, while space has been a secondary category of existence, subordinate in all respects to the priority of temporality. The sacred is measured in temporality, with a seven-day cycle requiring the repetition of a ceremonial event (mass or liturgies of worship), most typically on the first day of the cycle, the cycle itself being a relatively arbitrary, human designation. For American Indians, on the other hand, spatiality has been the primary category and temporality the secondary.

In Euro-American (and European) philosophical and theological history it is more common to see intellectual reflections on the meaning of time; it is far less common to see intellectual reflections on space. Hence, progress, history, development, evolution, and process become key notions that invade all academic discourse in the West, from science and economics to philosophy and theology. Thus the Western worldview has an inherent blind spot that prevents any comprehensive or deep understanding of the scope of ecological devastation which is, in fact, accelerating despite our best efforts at "sustainable development." To do no more than propose "solutions," such as reforestation projects, without acknowledging this blind spot is only to address the superficial symptoms of maldevelopment.

In contrast, cultural values and social and political structures in Indian communities are rooted in a worldview shaped by reciprocity and spatiality. Indian ceremonial existence, for instance, is inevitably spatially configured with place taking precedence over the question of when a ceremony will happen. Even in the case of annual or periodic ceremonial cycles, spatial configurations involving spatial relationships between sun or moon and the earth are determinative. The spatial relationship between the community and the sun at solstice or equinox, or the spatial appearance or nonappearance of the moon at full or new moon is more important than calendar dates and Julian months.

This foundational metaphor of spatiality in Indian cultures also begins to clarify the extent to which Indian spirituality and Indian existence are deeply rooted in attachment to the land and to specific territories in particular. Each nation has some understanding that it was placed into a relationship with a particular territory by spiritual forces outside of itself and thus has an enduring responsibility for that territory, just as the earth, especially the earth in that particular place, has a filial responsibility toward the people who live there. Likewise, the two-leggeds in that place also have a spatially related responsibility toward all others who share that place with them, including animals, birds, plants, rocks, rivers, mountains, and the like. With such extensive kinship ties, including a kinship tie to the land itself, it should be less surprising that Indian peoples have always resisted colonial pressure to relocate them to different territories, to sell their territories to the invaders, or to allow the destruction of their lands for the sake of accessing natural resources. Historical conquest and removal from our lands and contemporary ecological destruction of our lands have been and continue to be culturally and genocidally destructive to Indian peoples as peoples.

There is, however, a more subtle level to this sense of spatiality and land rootedness. It shows up in nearly all aspects of our existence–in our ceremonial structures, our symbols, our architecture, and in the symbolic parameters of a tribe's universe. The land and spatiality are the basic metaphor for existence and determine much of a community's life. In my own tribe, for instance, every detail of social structure–even the geographic orientation of the old villages–reflected a reciprocal duality of all that is necessary for sustaining life. Thus the *Hunka* or earth moiety situated to the south of the village and the *Tzi Sho* or sky moiety situated to the north represented female and male, matter and spirit, war and peace, but they only functioned fully because they were together and together represented wholeness. Spirit without matter is motion without substance; matter without spirit is motionless and meaningless. Once again we see reciprocity in a symbiotic dualism, this time clearly configured spatially.

We should not think here of the oppositional dualism of good and evil that we have learned to identify as typically Western (that is, ancient mid-Eastern). American Indian duality is a necessary reciprocity, not oppositional. They are different manifestations of the *same Wakonda*, not of two *Wakonda*, even though they carry personality specificity just as traditional Christian trinitarian doctrine would assert. While they are manifestations of the same *Wakonda*, they are different manifestations, both of which are necessary in order to have some balanced understanding of the Otherness that is the Sacred Mystery. Indeed, *Wakonda* has manifested itself in a great many other ways, all of which help our people to better understand the Mystery, our world, ourselves, and our place in the world. At this point it may also be clearer why the European word *God* is inadequate to express the full complexity of what we have only begun to explore in the Osage word.

Even the architectural geography of our spirituality functioned politically to give the village group cohesion; it functions at a deeply spiritual level that still pertains for a great many Indian people today. While an Osage person may be either *Tzi Sho* or *Hunka*, he or she is a child of parents who come from each of the divisions. Each individual recognizes himself or herself as a combination of qualities that reflect both sky and earth, spirit and matter, peace and war, male and female; we struggle individually and communally to hold those qualities in balance. These value structures begin with spatial designs of existence and are rooted in those spatial metaphors as fundamental mores of communal behavior and social organization.

This is not the only spatial symbolic paradigm of existence that determines Native American individuality and community. The fundamental symbol of plains Indian existence is the circle, a polyvalent symbol signifying the family, the clan, the tribe, and, eventually, all of creation. As a creation symbol, the importance of the circle is its genuine egalitarianness. There is no way to make the circle hierarchical. Because it has no beginning and no end, all in the circle are of equal value. No relative is valued more than any other. A chief is not valued above the people, nor are two-leggeds valued above the animal nations, the birds, or even trees and rocks. In its form as a medicine wheel, with two lines forming a cross inscribed vertically and horizontally across its whole, the circle can symbolize the four directions of the earth and, more important, the four manifestations of *Wakonda* that come to us from those directions. At the same time those four directions symbolize the four cardinal virtues of a tribe, the four sacred colors of ceremonial life, the sacred powers of four animal nations, and the four nations of two-leggeds that walk the earth (Black, Red, Yellow and White). That is, in our conception of the universe, all human beings walk ideally in egalitarian balance. Moreover, Native American egalitarian proclivities are worked out in this spatial symbol in ways that go far beyond the classless egalitarianness of socialism. In one of the polyvalent layers of meaning, those four directions hold together in the same egalitarian balance the four nations of two-leggeds, four-leggeds, wingeds, and living-moving things. In this rendition human beings lose their status of "primacy" and "dominion." Implicitly and explicitly American Indians are driven by their culture and spirituality to recognize the personhood of all "things" in creation. If temporality and historicity lend themselves implicitly to hierarchical structures because someone with a greater investment of time may know more of the body of temporally codified knowledge, spatiality lends itself to the egalitarian. All have relatively similar access to the immediacy of the spatially present.

ECOJUSTICE, SOVEREIGNTY, AND A THEOLOGY OF LIBERATION

Given the fundamental differences between American Indian cultural values and those of Euro-American peoples, it should be no mystery that the relationship between the two has been consistently one of conquest, colonization, and finally the eco-devastation of our territories. Our theological reflection must now move toward a sharper assessment of the systemic causes of this ethno-eco-devastation from an Indian perspective and toward the development of possible solutions. We have already begun to argue that we must understand the connection between ecological and social injustice in the world if there is to be significant transformation from the current global crisis to a healthy and sustainable future. Hence, it becomes empty quixotism to think of treating ecological devastation apart from treating issues of racism and ongoing colonialism, including especially those new forms of colonialism some have called neo-colonialism.

In particular, I am arguing that the twofold problem of ecological and social justice is systemic in character, and that the concerns of ethno-ecojustice must move beyond the mere naming of ecological devastations that are affecting Indian peoples and other indigenous and poor peoples today. This is a point I can begin to illustrate with a simple example. Over the past ten to twenty years many of us have been converted to the ecojustice vocation of *recycling*, a calling that has piqued our consciences as individual consumers to an extent that our kitchens and garages have become dangerous labyrinths of plastic, aluminum, and glass repositories as we have committed ourselves to a new lifeway behavior. Yet our national situation with respect to garbage disposal and landfill capacity has gotten consistently worse. In spite of our committed new behavior as socially conscious individuals, the United States generated more landfill garbage during the decade of the 1980s (the decade we began actively and broadly recycling) than all the garbage generated during the first two hundred years of its existence. Changing individual patterns of behavior has failed us as a strategy. We need more holistic and systemic solutions, and systemic solutions call for theological and philosophical foundations.

It needs to be said here that by a theological response to the systemic I do not have in mind just another individualistic intellectual exercise of the sort that has plagued our universities and seminaries too much, but rather a theological reflection that is far more communal. Theology must become an exercise in expressing the self-identity of whole communities. For this sort of theology we need stories rather than treatises, essentialist discourse, problem-resolution, or structuralist puzzle-solving. Not even some post-structuralist deconstruction that never seems to emerge from the text will finally be able to touch the hearts and minds of whole communities. For theology of this magnitude, we must have stories.

The Euro-Americans have stories, of course, but they tend to be stories of conquest. For instance, Columbus is the quintessential all-American culture hero, the perfect exemplar for the righteous empire, the "discoverer" and conqueror who knew no sin. Even Jesus, the most important culture hero of America, has become a conqueror in Western storytelling. The sacrificial cross of Jesus has become a symbol of conquest that seems to encourage more conquest.[13] Thus the myth of Columbus and the stories of conquest continue to play themselves out with disastrous consequences in the lives of modern Indian peoples, as the case studies in this volume all too well attest.

What Euro-Americans do not yet have is a story that accounts for their history of systemic violence in the world and their easy proclivity for rationalizing any act of military or economic colonization and conquest as somehow good. Instead, Euro-Americans and their elected officials seem to engage in a behavior pattern well-known in alcohol and drug addictions therapy: denial. Too many churches and too many politicians have lived out such a denial, like ostriches with their heads in the sand, as if such eco-devastation and national injustice and immorality cannot possibly affect them, living in the protected comfort zones of American society.[14] Easy answers that reflect some level of denial are too often given: It is too late to rectify injustices perpetrated against Indian nations; too much water has gone under that bridge. Or it is sometimes insisted that Indians are too small a percentage of the population to merit attention. We are forced, they claim, to concentrate on the vast majority of Americans, to maximize the good (and wealth) for the most people. This old Euro-American philosophical tradition of utilitarianism continues to exert its powerful influence on political practice to such an extent that abject racism can thrive, rationalized as being "in the best interests of the state." It becomes all too easy to think of Indian reservations as "national sacrifice areas."[15] Stories of conquest are complemented by stories of utilitarian rationalization.

Even in those cases in which we have begun to address ourselves to community well-being and ecojustice, we seem to do so with isolated strategies and a much too narrow focus. Especially at the level of theological reflection, the churches have not yet begun to deal with ecojustice, let alone ethno-ecojustice and racism, as a systemic whole, as a system of oppression rooted in structures of power that touch every part of our lives. At the level of liberal political action and theoretical reflection in the United States, solutions have still dealt typically with "them" and "their" problems rather than with the "us" of the United States and "our" participation in the ongoing story of world injustice. As long as the liberal Euro-American story only includes Euro-Americans in the role of moral conquerors providing solutions to others' problems, the real root causes of the problem will never go away. That is to say, even our proposed solutions have not been comprehensive enough to address the problem genuinely.

In this analysis I want to argue two correlative points addressing what I see as a key systemic aspect of the problem, focusing on the rise of Western individualism and the systematic destruction of indigenous communities worldwide. Further, I want to insist that the dismantling of indigenous communities has happened at a philosophical as well as political level. To put it another way, I am arguing that modern ecological devastation is in no small part generated by the Western, European shift that devalued communal interests in favor of the increasing prominence of the individual and that this shift can be measured in the lack of political and economic respect and the lack of theoretical recognition given to the legitimacy of self-governing, autonomous, long-lived indigenous communities. Let me state the argument as provocatively as possible.

Individualism and Western Development

First, the Western commitment to individualism colors all of the West's intellectual and theoretical posturing, whether theology, philosophy, political theory, politics, or law. For Euro-Americans in particular, the corporate level of denial is rooted in a cultural flaw that emerges from a trajectory that has its beginning in the later philosophies of the Hellenistic period and continues through the European reformations to modern notions of American hegemony in the "New World Order." From the Stoics in particular, but also the Epicureans and Skeptics of the third century BCE, the shift to the prominence of the individual can be traced through philosophic and religious movements. While the Stoics shifted their discourse from a search for the common good to a search for the wise individual, religious movements of the first century BCE began a similar shift toward concern for the individual. As the focus of the old Mediterranean cults shifted away from communal well-being, the so-called mystery religions introduced a newly developing concern for individual salvation. This theological shift eventually also won the heart of Greco-Roman Christianity.

Modern theologies of all of our churches continue this overweening concern for the individual and the individual's need for, and impediments to, salvation and well-being. Thus, our systemic interpretations tend likewise to emphasize individualistic analyses: The problem is identified as original sin or, in its secularized version, the individual failings of human beings. Even our interpretations of sacred texts—themselves far less invested in the West's individualism—are regularly interpreted from the individualist perspective. For instance, the synoptic gospels' metaphoric paradigm for the good—the goal of all life, the *basileia tou theou* (usually translated as the "kingdom of God")—is consistently interpreted in individualistic terms. The *basileia*, we are told, has to do with the individual's relationship with God or with the individual's call to decision. Any notion of it being many people together, or all peoples, or all of creation, is little mentioned.[16]

Moreover, this problematic is not exclusive to theological education but extends to all academic disciplines in the humanities and social sciences, such as political theory, international law, economics, and the like. The culture of the West (European and Euro-American) is a culture of the individual, and, through modern colonialist institutions (such as the World Bank and the International Monetary Fund), the imposition of this culture of individualism is quickly being extended throughout the colonized (Two-thirds) world via economic and political development policies. In the ongoing discourse about human rights, for instance, most would argue for understanding such rights in terms of individual rights while vehemently denying extension of the category to groups. Human rights are, by definition, the inherent rights of individuals and not rights of culturally discrete, indigenous national communities. Hence, the cultures of these communities can be destroyed with impunity.[17]

Statism and Indigenous Sovereignty

Second, I want to argue that the very emergence and eventual dominance of the modern state and the concomitant degradation of indigenous national entities contribute significantly to our situation of ecological injustice and devastation.[18] It should not be surprising that indigenous cultural groups, being fundamentally defined by their communitarian values and communal coherence, have been consistently attacked and destroyed by colonial intruders who usurp their lands and resources. Yet it needs to be said that the conquest of indigenous peoples has not been merely a military, political or economic colonization, but that the conquest has been equally engaged at the intellectual and philosophical level. Natural, self-governing national entities have given way to new larger and more centralized, but artificial, government structures identified in common parlance as the "modern state."

It is symptomatic that modern political theory has little interest in defining the appropriate place of indigenous nations in relationship to nation-states. To the contrary, it is assumed that the states have some natural sovereignty over their defined territories, even if their territorial claims wholly include ancient indigenous nations that have never relinquished their own sovereignty to that state. In general in our critical analyses and in our imagination of solutions, we Natives tend to concede too much to modern state systems and institutions. We assume too readily the authenticity and validity of the state and the broad bureaucratic institutions formally and informally associated with it—including our modern denominational structures.

The systemic nature of the problem as it relates to American Indians becomes apparent in the continual and progressive erosion of Indian national sovereignty and self-determination over the past five hundred years. This erosion began the moment that Columbus first claimed Indian land as the property of his Spanish monarchs. It was unabated as the liberal Bartolomé de Las Casas insisted on the peaceful conquest of Indian peoples as the rightful subjects of those same monarchs. And it continued in nineteenth-century U.S. jurisprudence and legislation that legally canonized the "domestic" and "dependent" nature of Indian sovereignty, wholly dependent on and accountable to the plenary power of the U.S. Congress.[19] Today, Indian sovereignty has become a shadow of its former self that invariably shrinks with each new incursion of the U.S. government and multinational corporate power brokers interested in wresting natural resources away from one

Indian nation or another at unreasonably cheap prices to themselves and equally unreasonably high long-term costs to those nations in terms of their environmental well-being.[20]

To extend the analysis of the problem a step further, the poverty that has consistently plagued Indian peoples since the onslaught of conquest is a natural result of colonization experienced by the colonized throughout the world. And postmodernist deconstruction seems to have little creative effect on the colonizer or on the colonized—except that we, the colonized, continue to experience the deconstruction of our cultures, our ecosystems, whatever is left of our Native economies and our internal sustainability.

With a poverty level that puts American Indians at the bottom of nearly every social indicator, we suffer a resulting level of community dysfunctionality that increases our lack of sustainability and makes us all the more susceptible to external political and economic power. Indian unemployment is stuck chronically at more than 50 percent across the continent.[21] Per capita income is the lowest of any ethnic community in the United States. Indian longevity figures are twenty years less than the American average. The infant mortality rate is the highest of any group in the United States. And diseases like tuberculosis (nearly eradicated for most of the U.S. population) and diabetes occur at seven and six times the average U.S. rates.[22] In some states (like Montana or South Dakota) Indian inmates number more than half of the state's prison population, even though Indians in the state account for less than 10 percent of the total population in the state.

Given statistics such as these, we have precious few political, legal, or even intellectual resources on which to capitalize or for controlling our immense natural resources.[23] Of course, the cultural-economic question for Indian nations may be not only how we develop natural resources but whether we feel that they can be respectfully developed and exploited at all. The continuing reality of our oppression, however, leaves this a moot point, because our poverty leaves us with few defenses against the pressures brought to bear on our communities from the outside. Hence, the prior question is one of Indian sovereignty, for the sake of reclaiming Indian community sustainability, first of all, but, so I shall argue, for the sake perhaps even for the health and sustainability of the world community as well.

Indians want life. We do not just want mere existence, that is, life in the sense of simple biological survival. What we want is life in the sense of self-sufficient, cultural, spiritual, political, and economic sustainability—on our own terms. At this late date, the question is not whether Indian peoples should have the right to self-determining autonomy, but how our communities can regain this rightful heritage without the continuing colonial pressure to feed the consumptive habits of White America. We believe that the larger justice issue involved is one of both political hegemony and ecological survivability. The answer to this systemic problem may contain part of the answer to sustainability for all people on this earth.

My suggestion that we take the recognition of indigenous sovereignty as a priority is an overarching one that involves more than simply justice for indigenous communities around the world. Indeed, such a political move will necessitate a rethinking of consumption patterns in the North, and a shift in the economics of the North will cause a concomitant shift also in the Two-thirds World of the South. The relatively simple act of recognizing the sovereignty of the Sioux Nation and returning to it all state-held lands in the Black Hills (for example, National Forest and National Park lands) would generate immediate international interest in the rights of indigenous, tribal peoples in all state territories. In the United States alone it is estimated that Indian nations still have legitimate (moral and legal) claim to some two-thirds of the U.S. land mass.[24] Ultimately, such an act as return of Native lands to Native control would have a significant ripple effect on other states around the world where indigenous peoples still have aboriginal land claims and suffer the ongoing results of conquest and displacement in their own territories.

American Indian cultures and values have much to contribute in the comprehensive reimagining of the Western value system that has resulted in our contemporary ecojustice crisis. The main point that must be made is that there were and are cultures that take their natural environment seriously and attempt to live in balance with the created whole around them in ways that help them not overstep environmental limits. Unlike the West's consistent experience of alienation from the natural world, these cultures of indigenous peoples consistently experienced themselves as part of that created whole, in relationship with everything else in the world. They saw and continue to see themselves as having responsibilities, just as every other creature has a particular role to play in maintaining the balance of creation as an ongoing process. This is ultimately the spiritual rationale for annual ceremonies like the Sun Dance or Green Corn Dance. As another example, Lakota peoples planted cottonwoods and willows at their campsites as they broke camp to move on, thus beginning the process of reclaiming the land humans had necessarily trampled through habitation and encampment.

We now know that indigenous rainforest peoples in what is today called the state of Brazil had a unique relationship to the forest in which they lived, moving away from a cleared area after farming it to a point of reduced return and allowing the clearing to be reclaimed as jungle. The group would then clear a new area and begin a new cycle of production. The whole process was relatively sophisticated and functioned in harmony with the jungle itself. So extensive was their movement that some scholars are now suggesting that there is actually very little of what might rightly be called virgin forest in what had been considered the "untamed" wilds of the rainforest.

What I have described here is more than just a coincidence or, worse, some romanticized falsification of Native memory. Rather, I am insisting that there are peoples in the world who live with an acute and cultivated sense of their intimate participation in the natural world as part of an intricate whole. For indigenous peoples, this means that when they are presented with the concept of development, it is *sense-less.* Most significantly, one must realize that this awareness is the result of self-conscious effort on the part of traditional American Indian national communities and is rooted in the first instance in the mythology and theology of the people. At its simplest, the worldview of American Indians can be expressed as Ward Churchill describes it:

> Human beings are free (indeed, encouraged) to develop their innate capabilities, but only in ways that do not infringe upon other elements—called "relations," in the fullest dialectical sense of the word—of nature. Any activity going beyond this is considered as "imbalance," a transgression, and is strictly prohibited. For example, engineering was and is permissible, but only insofar as it does not permanently alter the earth itself. Similarly, agriculture was widespread, but only within norms that did not supplant natural vegetation.[25]

Like the varieties of species in the world, each culture has a contribution to make for the sustainability of the whole. Given the reality of eco-devastation threatening all of life today, the survival of American Indian cultures and cultural values may make the difference for the survival and sustainability for all the earth as we know it. What I have suggested implicitly is that American Indian peoples may have something of value—something corrective to Western values and the modern world system—to offer to the world. The loss of these gifts, the loss of the particularity of these peoples, today threatens the survivability of us all. What I am most passionately arguing is that we must commit to the struggle for the just and moral survival of Indian peoples as the peoples of the earth, and that this struggle is for the sake of the earth and for the sustaining of all of life. It is now imperative that we change the modern value of acquisitiveness and the political systems and economics that consumption has generated. The key to making this massive value shift in the world system may lie in the international recognition of indigenous political sovereignty and self-determination. Returning Native lands to the sovereign control of Native peoples around the world, beginning in the United States, is not simply just; the survival of all may depend on it.

We have suggested that an appropriate theological response must emerge from communities rather than from the minds of individual intellectuals, and that these theological responses to the modern crises of ecological and social devastation must thus begin as a story of existence that can move us beyond the West's usual stories of conquest. Yet having said this much, a word of caution must be added. Any emergent story or theological response must be careful not to fall into the trap of becoming just another layer of the conquest motif. Even the "common" creation story, currently in vogue among many in the ecological movement, runs the risk of being conquest-oriented. It is *common* only insofar as it has been able to impose itself on others, to conquer the stories of others.

Imagine two Indian communities separated by a mountain ridge. While each considers its council fire, located in the center of its valley, to be the center of the universe and tells stories of creation to verify its reality, they know one another quite well. When visitors from one community visit the other community, they also recognize the truth of their neighbors' stories and their claim. Sometimes a single truth is not enough to explain the balance of the world around us.

Yet we need communal stories that can generate "functional" theologies, or, better yet, functional mythologies, that will undergird the life of the community (the lives of communities) in new and vibrant ways. The contemporary crisis calls for imagining new stories that can generate life and not conquest—whether cultural, military, economic, or intellectual!

Notes

1. Donald A. Grinde, Jr., and Bruce E. Johansen, *Ecocide of Native America: Environmental Destruction of Indian Lands and Peoples* (Santa Fe: Clear Light Publishers, 1995): "In a world full of profound and sometimes cruel ironies, one stands out: Native Americans, who held the lands of the Western Hemisphere in a living trust for thousands of years, have been afflicted by some of the worst pollution of an environmental crisis that has reached planetwide proportions" (p. 1).

2. Benjamin F. Chavis, Jr., and Charles Lee, eds., *Toxic Wastes and Race in the United States: A National Report on the Racial and Socio-Economic Characteristics of Communities with Hazardous Waste Sites* (New York: Commission for Racial Justice, United Church of Christ, 1987); and Benjamin A. Goldman and Laura Fitton, *Toxic Wastes and Race Revisited: An Update of the 1987 Report on the Racial and Socio-Economic Characteristics of Communities with Hazardous Waste Sites* (Washington, D.C.: Center for Policy Alternatives, 1994). I find Gregg Easterbrook's popular news essay on two-thirds-world pollution problematic, especially in what I see as his short-sighted proposal for resolving two-thirds-world ecojustice concerns (Easterbrook, "Forget PCB's. Radon. Alar: The World's Greatest Environmental Dangers Are Dung Smoke and Dirty Water," *The New York Times Magazine* [September 11, 1995], pp. 60-63).

3. Ward Churchill, *Struggle for the Land: Indigenous Resistance to Genocide, Ecocide and Expropriation in Contemporary North America* (Monroe, Me.: Common Courage Press, 1993); Mark Zannis, *The Genocide Machine in Canada: The Pacification of the North* (Montreal: Black Rose Books, 1973).

4. Gerald Vizenor, *Manifest Manners: Postindian Warriors of Survivance* (Hanover, N.H.: Wesleyan University Press, 1994).

5. Jace Weaver, "Notes from a Miner's Canary," herein.

6. This rather absurd and patently "Eurosupremicist" hypothesis is argued, for instance, by George Weurthner, who ultimately reduces pre-contact Indian peoples to environmental pillagers ("An Ecological View of the Indian," *Earth First!* 7 [1987]). For an Indian critique of the position, see Ward Churchill, *Struggle for the Land,* pp. 420, 447f.; and M. Annette Jaimes, "The Stone Age Revisited: An Indigenist Examination of Labor," *New Studies on the Left* 14 (1991).

7. See, George Tinker, *Missionary Conquest: The Gospel and Native American Cultural Genocide* (Minneapolis: Fortress Press, 1993).

8. This sense is much more than Paul Tillich's notion of panentheism.

9. See, Francis La Flesche, *The War and Peace Ceremony of the Osage Indians,* Bureau of American Ethnography, Bulletin 101 (1939).

10. Leslie Silko's famous novel *Ceremony* (New York: Viking, 1977) is precisely about such a situation. The whole of the novel deals with the healing and cleansing of a World War II veteran for whom a new ceremony had to be devised. The social and spiritual complexities of disintegration and alienation had made it much more difficult for the Laguna people and for himself. Thus, his healing has to do with the healing of the whole community and not just of himself.

11. The book was recently republished in a significantly revised edition: Vine Deloria, Jr., *God Is Red: A Native View of Religion* (Golden, Co.: Fulcrum, 1992).

12. George Tinker, "Spirituality and Native American Personhood: Sovereignty and Solidarity," in K. C. Abraham and Bernadette Mbuy-Beya, eds., *Spirituality of the Third World* (Maryknoll, N.Y.: Orbis Books, 1994), pp. 119-132; "An American Indian Reading of the Bible," in Leander E. Keck, et al., eds., *New Interpreter's Bible* (Nashville: Abingdon, 1994), pp. 174-180.

13. See, George Tinker, "Columbus and Coyote: A Comparison of Culture Heroes in Paradox," *Apuntes* (1992), pp. 78-88.

14. See, Jace Weaver, "Introduction" to Andrea Smith, "Malthusian Orthodoxy and the Myth of ZPG," herein.

15. This term seems to have been coined in a study commissioned by the National Academy of Science on resource development on Indian lands. It was submitted to the Nixon administration in 1972 as input toward a national Indian policy. See, Thadis Box, et al., *Rehabilitation Potential for Western Coal Lands* (Cambridge: Ballanger, 1974), for the published version of the study. Churchill, *Struggle for the Land,* pp. 54, 333, 367; also, Russell Means, "The Same Old Song," in Ward Churchill, ed., *Marxism and Native Americans* (Boston: South End Press, 1983), p. 25; and Ward Churchill and Winona LaDuke, "Native America: The Political Economy of Radioactive Colonialism," in M. Annette Jaimes, ed., *State of Native America* (Boston: South End Press, 1992), pp. 241-266.

16. George Tinker, "The Integrity of Creation: Restoring Trinitarian Balance," *Ecumenical Review* (1989), pp. 527-536; and "Gerechtigkeit, Frieden und die Integrität der Weinachtsbäume," *Ökumenische Rundschau* 28 (1989), pp. 169-180.

17. See, Richard Falk, "The Rights of Peoples (In Particular Indigenous Peoples): A Non-Statist Perspective," pp. 17-37; and Ted Robert Gurr and James R. Scarritt, "Minority Rights at Risk: A Global Survey," *Human Rights Quarterly* 11 (1989), pp. 375-405.

18. Many identify the eighteenth century with the emergence of the modern state (see, Cornelia Narari, "The Origins of the Nation-State," in Leonard Tivey, ed., *The Nation State: The Formation of Modern Politics* [New York: St. Martins, 1981], pp. 13-38). It seems more useful and accurate to date the emergence to the sixteenth century with the strong move toward centralization and bureaucratization during the reign of Henry VIII in England, or even the late fifteenth century with the formation of a "modern" Spanish state in the merging of Castile and Aragon with the marriage of Ferdinand and Isabela (see, Robert Williams, *American Indians and Western Legal Thought* [Oxford: Oxford University Press, 1990]; and Stephen L. Collins, *From Divine Cosmos to Sovereign State: An Intellectual History of Consciousness and the Idea of Order in Renaissance England* [New York: Oxford University Press, 1989]).

19. See, Jace Weaver, "Triangulated Power and the Environment," herein; Ward Churchill, *Struggle for the Land*, pp. 42-45; Howard R. Berman, "The Concept of Aboriginal Rights in the Early Legal History of the United States," *Buffalo Law Review* 28 (1978), pp. 637-667; and Felix S. Cohen, "Original Indian Title," *Minnesota Law Review* 32 (1947), pp. 28-59. On the "plenary power" of the U.S. Congress over Indian "sovereignty" and the Congress's resulting fiduciary or trust responsibilities, see, C. Harvey, "Constitutional Law: Congressional Plenary Power over Indian Affairs–A Doctrine Rooted in Prejudice," *American Indian Law Review* 5 (1977), pp. 117-150.

20. Obviously, I have distinguished between nation and state in this essay. For the scholarly critique of statist doctrines, see, Bernard Nietchmann, "Militarization and Indigenous Peoples: The Third World War," *Cultural Survival Quarterly* 11 (1987), pp. 1-16; Russell L. Barsh, "The Ethnocidal Character of the State and International Law," *Journal of Ethnic Studies* 16 (1989), pp. 1-30; Gurr and Scarritt, "Minority Rights at Risk"; and Falk, "The Rights of Peoples."

21. George Tinker and Loring Bush, "Native American Unemployment: Statistical Games and Cover-ups," in *Racism and the Underclass in America*, George W. Shepherd, Jr., and David Penna, eds. (Greenwood Press, 1991).

22. U.S. Bureau of the Census, Population Division, Racial Statistics Branch, *A Statistical Portrait of the American Indian Population* (Washington, D.C.: U.S. Government Printing Office, 1984); U.S. Department of Health and Human Services, *Chart Series Book* (Washington, D.C.: Public Health Service HE20.9409.988, 1988). The 1990 census has not testified to an abatement of these statistical horrors in any category for Native Americans (see, Glenn T. Morris, "International Law and Politics: Toward a Right to Self-Determination for Indigenous Peoples," in *State of Native America*, pp. 71, 84n; Ward Churchill, *Struggle for the Land*, pp. 54f., 79).

23. For an official U.S. government indication of the vast mineral resources of American Indian tribes, see, U.S. Department of the Interior, *Indian Lands*

Map: Oil, Gas and Minerals on Indian Reservations (Washington D.C.: U.S. Government Printing Office, 1978). Churchill comments with a bitter irony: "With such holdings, it would seem logical that the two million indigenous people of North America . . . would be among the continent's wealthiest residents. As even the government's own figures reveal, however, they receive the lowest per capita income of any population group and evidence every standard indicator of dire poverty: highest rates of malnutrition, plague, disease, death by exposure, infant mortality, teen suicide, and so on" (*Struggle for the Land,* p. 262).

24. See, Churchill, *Struggle for the Land.*
25. Churchill, *Struggle for the Land,* p. 17.

Afterword

Where Do We Go from Here?

THOM WHITE WOLF FASSETT

PRELUDE

The Pomo sacred basket has an important place in the moral and cultural development of Pomo children. These water-tight, bright-plumed baskets provided a schooling for young girls that could be obtained in no other manner. Working with sedge, willow, pine root, cedar root, redbud, feathers, and other materials, the California Pomo Indian woman produced what anthropologists and ethnologists have acknowledged as the finest basket made by any people in the world. European observers noted the method of construction and commented on the brilliance of the plumes and the complexity of the patterns. Many of the descriptions were recorded as a scientific measure designed to preserve in the memory of history the wonderful craft and the women who made them. In their documentation, however, they were never able to capture the essence of Pomo basketry.

Few observers know that the Pomo creation story tells of the birth of the people coming to earth in a basket. The infant Pomo girl even lived in a basket which was probably the same one used by her mother and grandmother. For Indian girls to learn how to weave a basket was to learn about the Creator and all of creation. First, she learned to distinguish among various plants; some were used for baskets, others for food and medicine. As she learned about food plants, she also learned about baskets used in food preparation. Because it took nearly a year to gather the materials for the construction of the basket, the young girl learned about the seasons and her place in relation to her family, her tribe, other people, the natural world, and her Creator.

Perhaps the most important lesson she learned was that the earth was Mother to us all, provided by a great Creator for all of the people.

From the earth came not only the materials for her basket but lessons available nowhere else. Plants must be gathered carefully and precisely to coincide with life's cycles. Gentleness must be employed in preparing the plants for weaving. Patience must be exercised to ensure that each strand is in its place. A task begun must be continued to completion. A partially finished or poorly made basket served no purpose. Therefore, through large baskets and small ones, through flat ones and fat ones, through baskets used every day and those used only on special occasions, the young Pomo girl learned about life and her role in creation.[1]

THE LAND WAS OURS

When persons travel from one culture to another, they often find it difficult to reconcile what they feel and experience with what their own culture has taught them. The crafting of the Pomo basket and its subsequent decline is but one of many examples illustrating the introduction of European society and its effect on Native lifestyles. Baskets are now made in shrinking numbers. They are no longer associated with power and prophecy. They are largely a memory, the story a collective recollection.[2]

This story could be recited repeatedly about other Native cultures and nations. Each time it would leave its own images of pathos as history recalls days, years, and centuries of European/Christian settlement of the Americas and the subsequent collection of reports, artifacts, and bones stored in archives and museums gathered by ethnocentric anthropologists and ethnographers who, like the culture they represented, needed to preserve the history of the "children of the forest," the "Noble Savage," the original American. Little care or thought was given to the survival of the Native cultures themselves, since they were considered to be obstacles to the spread of "civilization" and the quest for land and riches. The church and its missions played a major role in this process and, indeed, supplied Adam Smith with the perceptive observation that the pious purpose of converting Indians to Christianity was to sanctify the injustice of colonization and economic development.

The advance of the cross provided the ingredients to a process that would see European/Christian values competing for dominance over Native cultures, which were held in contempt. The birth of the British Missionary Society in London in 1795 gave impetus to the project and added special urgency while addressing the "serious and zealous professors of the Gospel of every denomination respecting an attempt to evangelize the heathen."[3] This new mission society set the stage for a renewed effort and a new order that more directly placed immigrants and their deities in contention with Native faith systems. In spite of their solemn declaration to "utterly and sincerely disclaim all political views and party design; abhorring all attempts to disturb order and government . . . vigorously united . . . sending ministers of Christ to preach the Gospel among the heathen,"[4] missionaries and their churches would soon be entering into collusion with governments to achieve mutually agreed-upon goals concerning destruction of Native cultures.

Probably the finest definition of Manifest Destiny was provided, albeit unwittingly, by Robert Frost when he recited his poem, "The Gift Outright," at the inauguration of President John Kennedy. The poignant line, "The land was ours before we were the land's" provides definition for a phrase that scholars and historians have been unable to capture quite so clearly. The immigrants to the North American continent surely believed that the land was theirs long before they set eyes upon it. They were thus permitted to launch an assault on indigenous America that has brought us to our current state of emergency.

According to the work of D'Arcy McNickle (Flathead/Métis) at the Newberry Library over twenty years ago, when Europeans seriously set about the task of colonizing the Americas in the late fifteenth century, the nations and societies already populating the North American continent numbered perhaps 100 million. How do we explain, then, the fact that there are only five to ten million Native American people left today in the United States?[5] How do we explain to our children and the ensuing generations the disappearance of these nations of people? How do we explain the parallel destruction of the earth and the nations of birds, animals, trees, insects, plants; the leveling of mountains; the poisoning of the water and the air; and the attendant disasters plaguing humankind?[6]

Not only are the surviving Native people crying out for justice—as witnessed in the above case studies—but the Natural World people, the rest of creation, are pleading for mercy and justice from modern technological civilization. This civilization's roots do not grow in first-century Christian justice paradigms—or any other paradigms of spirituality—and they forsake the sanctity of creation and the nations of people who belong to it.

When we speak of "defending Mother Earth" today, we will, more likely than not, incur the wrath of Christian fundamentalists for adhering to some kind of animist pagan devotion. Such a reaction discredits the seriousness of our pleas and the cause of justice implicit in our arguments. Few give consideration to the consequences of the disappearance of Native people. Fewer still will understand Jace Weaver's "miner's canary" analysis as the dominant culture continues to eradicate thousands of life forms in its insatiable appetite for material prosperity. This dominant culture seems intent on the annihilation of Native peoples to complete its work. The catalogue of past historical atrocities has already been well documented. It is important to note, however, that those same historic depravities continue today in modern garb, oppressing those who will fight for their right to exist while struggling to adhere to the original instructions provided by the Creator.

THE "INDIAN PROBLEM"

In 1541 the Spanish Council of the Indies debated the humanity of the Indians of the Americas. If Indians were considered beasts of burden, they would be assigned to the control of the military. If, however, they had souls, they would fall under the tutelage of the church. Either decision promoted the exploitation of American Indians as inferior beings.

The past is easily forgotten or explained away, but the mentality of those who sat on the Council of the Indies persists today in many forms. Colonial philosophies belonging to days gone by are still operative today in dominant cultural behavior and public policy initiatives. United States federal policies of the past 220 years continue to work their judgments on Native peoples. The so-called Contract with America does not recognize the validity of the many treaties and agreements reached between the United States and sovereign tribal entities through this long history. In fact, the Contract, through its ten-point program, may well provide that "final solution" for Native Americans that has been long sought by parliamentarians and economic policy makers.

We must not forget that it was precisely these motives that, in the 1970s, spawned the birth of anti-Indian backlash organizations such as Montanans Opposed to Discrimination and Interstate Congress on Equal Rights and Responsibilities. In that decade more than half of the states in the United States had local chapters related to such organizations, whose memberships were composed of ranchers, sportsmen, fishermen, and others. These groups and others like them were the precursors of today's militia movement. Today, their visibility, coupled with Congressional machinations, lends credence to Native expectations that even greater effort will be made to wrest away the estimated 35 percent of America's energy resources now in the hands of tribal nations.

National and international communities of conscience must clearly define their roles in relationship to the oppression of Native and Natural World people and consider ways to bring an end to oppressive practices. Native and Natural World peoples have a right to exist as unique life forms. Therefore, hard political and moral questions must be addressed in these precarious times concerning the right of people to adhere to their original ways of life and the conditions necessary for this to occur.

The Denver meeting of the North American Native Workshop on Environmental Justice was an important step, among a progression of events, in decrying the heretical and denying the ongoing colonial view that established the Western priority of solving what has always been termed the "Indian problem." Coming together as Native people provided us with strength. We are one. We are people of the same experience, and the sense of solidarity and mutual purpose and the resulting sense of self-worth provided us with evidence of our ongoing viability. If there had been a sub-theme for our proceedings, it would have declared our rejection of participation in tribal and global suicide. Sovereign Native territories will not be declared "national sacrifice areas"; neither will Native peoples become "national or global sacrifice peoples."

Although most non-Natives are isolated from the issues of justice for America's Native people by the lapse of time, the remoteness of reservations or Native territories, the comparative invisibility of Natives in the urban setting (despite the fact that 63 percent of Natives now live in urban areas), the distortions in historical accounts, and accumulated prejudices, Native and Natural World voices must be heard in the national forum, as well as in the global arena.[7] The responsibility for the continued destruction of Native peoples should weigh heavily on the world community and its religious leaders, who must institute measures that will enable them to speak in spiritual language above nation and state. This, of course, assumes a radical shift in current practices and belief structures. We live in days when national chauvinism precludes commitment to spiritual ideals. Perhaps it is more accurate to say that the so-called spiritual ideals espoused today are merely expressions of secular values based on concepts of nationalism and partisan ideology.

Racism in the United States finds its origin in materialistic acquisitiveness serving the dominant culture's needs and greeds. It has become ever more acceptable as Native Americans, Hispanics, African Americans, and Asians are made the scapegoats of a plummeting economy. The economics of racism are clear. While it is easy to talk about institutional racism, it is more difficult to comprehend that behind the institutions are individuals connected to industry, banks, and commerce who benefit from racism. Taking notice of the fact that the International Monetary Fund and the World Bank were fifty years old in 1995 should give us little comfort, as they continue to institute policies destructive of the world's marginalized people. It was the economic motive exercised by these same classes of persons and their quest for wealth and empire that were responsible for the first genocidal assault on the Indians of the Americas. Genocidal practices of the 1990s differ little from those employed over the past few hundred years: resettlement, sterilization, forced assimilation, cultural and physical extermination, economic exploitation, environmental devastation, natural resource development. These are but a few of the ways in which racism directed at Native peoples manifests itself today. On the grand, global scale we could easily be describing the impact of these same measures on other indigenous peoples—Native Hawaiians, the Maoris of New Zealand, the Loita Pastoralists of Kenya, Orang Asli of Malaysia, the Batwa of Rwanda, and others too numerous to mention.

Racism lies at the foundation of "natural resource development" in Indian Country and is now proving earlier predictions correct as other racial and ethnic minorities in the United States come to understand that the same strategies employed to oppress Natives are now being utilized to oppress them. It wasn't until other racial and ethnic minority peoples discovered toxic waste dumps being planned for their neighborhoods that the phrase *environmental racism* found its way into the environmental movement with sharp, descriptive accuracy. It should be pointed out that the phrase also applies to Natural World peoples as well.

THE EARTH AS A LIVING ORGANISM

Analysis of racism also provides the means of enabling us to understand the process of genocide as it applies to all life forms beyond humankind—the Natural World people. We can see clearly from early colonial agricultural and horticultural practices that the immigrants not only attempted to colonize Native peoples but the life forms of the earth as well. Some life forms were acceptable. These were organized and colonized, as crops, to harness their usefulness for the new arrivals and their communities. Others were unimportant and even noxious to the new settlers and were eliminated to the point of extinction. Animals and other non-plant life forms were also treated in a similar manner. Some were domesticated. Others were exterminated or relegated to distant "wilderness" reservations where they struggle to survive even today.

Since 1492 Christians have told Native people that Christians have a superior or "correct" understanding of God. Christians believed that Native people worshiped the things of creation. They told the indigenes that the mountains were not sacred, nor were the streams, the forests, the birds, the animals, the plants. The immigrant population immediately set about proving that these life forces of creation were not sacred by despoiling, colonizing, and eliminating them. Is it any wonder that Mother Earth is in such a state of emergency?

Our old stories teach us lessons poignantly valuable today for our self-understanding. We were told in the Creator's original instructions that we have been provided with all the things necessary for life. We were instructed to show great respect for all the beings of the earth. We were taught that our life exists beside the Tree life and that our well-being depends upon the well-being of the Vegetable life. We are close relatives of the Four-legged beings. All living things are spiritual beings. The Creator enters into and sustains the acts of creation. The spiritual universe, then, is manifest to us as creation–the creation that produces and supports life. We are a part of that creation, and our duty is to support all life in its relationship with all other living beings.

It is in the teachings of the elders from the longhouse of the Six Nations Iroquois (Haudenosaunee) that we learn that human beings are to walk about on the earth in a manner that expresses great respect, affection, and gratitude toward all the manifestations of the Creator. We give a greeting and thanksgiving to the many supporters of our lives–the corn, beans, squash, winds, water, sun, and all living beings who work together on this land. When people cease to respect and express gratitude for these many things, then all life will be destroyed and human life as we know it on this planet will come to an end.

Our roots are deep in the lands where we live. The elders say that the soil is rich from the bones of thousands of our generations. All of us were created in these territories and on these lands, and it is our duty to take great care of them, because from these lands will spring the future generations. Defending Mother Earth is not a project. Defending Mother Earth is a way of life; it is a call for the radical transformation of nations, societies, and individuals.[8]

CHANGES IN MOTHER EARTH

For over five hundred years Native Americans have been subjected to raids of extermination from France, England, Spain, and the United States. These incursions have driven the people from their lands, deprived them of their way of life, and persecuted them for their customs. As a result, our children have been taught to despise their ancestors, their culture, their religions, and their traditional values. The Native stewards of the earth were estranged from her as ever more insidious measures were undertaken by military, governmental, and economic forces to subdue the people and, with them, the earth.

Clearly the exploitative forces initiated measures so severe as to produce startling case histories of environmental degradation, economic instability, and social disintegration, some of which we now confront in this volume. It is equally clear that American society does not revere the earth as a living organism to be preserved for future generations of human beings as do traditional Native peoples. For non-Natives the earth is simply a "resource," and it is this difference that distinguishes between peoples who live in a sacred world and those who do not. We have learned bitter lessons by separating the people from the land. Such a divorce kills both people and land.

Toxic waste dumps, uranium poisoning, destructive mining practices, emission of fluorocarbon gases, destruction of the ozone shield protecting the earth from excessive doses of ultraviolet rays, multibillion dollar "Star Wars" programs, and disposable products are but a few of the threats that characterize our current dilemma. The litany of American ills reads badly and superficially manifests itself in beer-can-strewn highways and public landfills stuffed with the artifacts of a culture never celebrated in the spiritual ceremonies of Native peoples. But it all somehow is supposed to be redeemed by the provocative, blinking television image of Iron Eyes Cody tearfully standing in garbage as a crude commercial reminder of what the world once was and could be again (offered as a public service message squeezed between evening news and late-night programming). Perhaps, after all, Iron Eyes symbolizes spiritual despair in an age of material hope.

If the circle of life is, ultimately, to remain unbroken, the teachings of our Creator and the wisdom of our elders must pass from generation to generation. But America's circle is very small and does not embrace all of creation. It cycles every two or four years–from one election to the next–and would ruin the whole world to get from the first year to the fourth. That is the extent of our public vision, and it is all accentuated by the focus of the television cameras and further detailed through op-ed pieces published in the *New York Times* or the *Washington Post.* America gives thanks for the next world, having forgotten how to walk in a sacred manner in the present one.

WINNING THE WEST

People are like trees, and groups of people are like forests. While the forests are composed of many different kinds of trees, these trees intertwine their roots so strongly that it is impossible for the strongest winds which blow on our Islands to uproot the forest, for each tree strengthens its neighbor, and their roots are inextricably entwined.

In the same way the people of our Islands, composed of members of nations and races from all over the world, are beginning to intertwine their roots so strongly that no troubles will affect them.

Just as one tree standing alone would soon be destroyed by the first strong wind which came along, so it is impossible for any person, any family or any community to stand alone against the troubles of this world.

–Haida Chief Skidegate (Lewis Collinson)
March 1966[9]

Disney's "Pocahontas" may be a box-office success story in movie houses, but there is little resemblance between this environmentally correct fairytale and the continuing struggles of today's Native peoples to secure redress or halt the movement of history toward certain ecological Armageddon. We cannot depend on elections or victory at the polls. Our numbers are too small, and those who would sympathize with even part of our agenda are too few. In 1968 the Native struggle emerged as spiritual and political militancy manifesting itself, subsequently, in the creation of the American Indian Movement; the takeover of the Bureau of Indian Affairs building in Washington; sojourns at spiritual holy places; actions at Alcatraz, Ft. Lawton, and Wounded Knee. Later, in Canada, it produced the stand-off at Oka. It was a time that also marked the return of throngs of young Natives to the longhouse, Sun Dance, round house, and other tribal spiritual practices.

More than twenty years later, we see that those efforts were simply a prelude to addressing a survival crisis of massive human and natural world proportions. It is easy to agree with George Tinker's suggestion that "American Indian culture and values have much to contribute in the systemic reimagining of the West."[10] We currently have no comprehensive or systematic methodologies with which to affect such a process. Certainly neither the United States nor Canadian governments are contemplating entering into partnership with Natives to initiate any sort of reimagining process. The United Nations is, perhaps, a more appropriate and viable candidate for such an alliance.

It was not until 1992 that the United Nations directly entertained the moral and ethical imperatives presented by indigenous peoples that ultimately resulted in the International Year of the World's Indigenous People in 1993. We need only to recall the rejection of the Hopi messengers who were sent from the kiva to the "House of Mica" to deliver a message of warning and salvation soon after the chartering of the United Nations, fifty years ago, to understand how long it has taken for the world's indigenous people to be recognized. Thomas Banyacya, Hopi elder, finally completed his mission by delivering the Hopi message to the General Assembly on December 10, 1992.[11]

We must understand, however, that we are still categorized as *nongovernmental* entities (NGOs)—regardless of our own sovereign nation self-understanding and the validity of our constitutionally and internationally recognized treaties. Prior to 1992 our access was limited to the Commission on Human Rights in Switzerland and a few additional relationships with other United Nations entities. The United Nations Charter, article 63, for example, provides that the Economic and Social Council "may make suitable arrangements for consultation with nongovernmental organizations which are concerned with matters within its competence." All other United Nations units deal with NGOs as well. Close to 1250 NGOs now compete for agenda time with all

United Nations entities. We find ourselves vying for attention with other NGOs ranging from the International Association of the Soap and Detergent Industry to the International Organization of Consumers Unions or from Amnesty International to the International Association of Chiefs of Police.

It is important to note that NGOs–now understood as representing "civil society"–are making a greater impact on the deliberative process of the United Nations. Although we bear no resemblance to the ancient Greeks, the 1992 breakthrough for indigenous people does offer a Trojan Horse model which worked–at least this time. There is now, presumably, an openness to deal with the implications of indigenous status as the United Nations implements the International Decade of the World's Indigenous People while adopting the United Nations Declaration of Indigenous Peoples' Rights. Although this declaration is not uniformly embraced by all members of the United Nations, its very formulation offers hope. However, in an institution where nearly every written word must be documented and footnoted, the United Nations process may move exceedingly slowly. Equally hopeful is the recently announced collaboration between the Haudenosaunee Confederacy and the United Nations. On July 18, 1995, chiefs and clan mothers of the Six Nations of the Iroquois met with representatives of the UN Environmental Program and other agencies. Meant to signal a new kind of "coalition politics" among indigenous nations, governments, and the United Nations, the summit could, according to Oneida Chief Chez Wheelock, provide "a model. As we develop relationships with other Indigenous people throughout the hemisphere, we're hopeful we can help them avoid some of the environmental problems we have today and assist other Indigenous people in applying their perspective to their situations." That Natives have something important to bring to the table was dramatically illustrated by Oren Lyons (Onondaga) when he showed a satellite photograph of the earth that revealed that "the only area being protected in anything close to its original and life-giving state" was an Indian reservation. Dare we hope that this new cooperation between Natives and the United Nations might begin to provide a basis to defend Mother Earth?[12]

In contrast to the United Nations, other world forums are instrumental in mobilizing support and encouraging solidarity and could effectively carry momentum to various segments of the world community, although they have no direct impact on political or legislative processes because of their ad hoc nature. The Global Forum on Environment and Development for Human Survival held in Moscow in January of 1990 is one such extraordinary example.[13]

Representing eighty-three countries, a thousand participants joined together in Moscow to share concerns about the future of the planet and its inhabitants. This global forum of spiritual and parliamentary leaders included indigenous delegates, who drafted a statement reflecting the unique perspectives of indigenous communities:

> We have jeopardized the future of our coming generations with our greed and lust for power. The warnings are clear and time is now a factor. . . . We speak of our children, yet we savage the spawning beds of the salmon and herring, and kill the whale in his home. We advance through the forests of the earth felling our rooted brothers indiscriminately, leaving no seeds for the future. We exploit the land and resources of the poor and the indigenous peoples of the world. We have become giants, giants of destruction, and now we have gathered here to acknowledge this and to see what we must do to change. . . . Indigenous peoples possess many different habits and lifestyles but all recognize they are children of Mother Earth and that we receive from Her our life, our health, the air we breathe, the water we drink, our everyday food, and our energy. Earth suffers ill treatment because of lack of respect. All of us can understand the importance of the health of Mother Earth and all have a potential to enjoy our lives in greater harmony with the forces which create life.[14]

The recommendations emanating collectively from the larger forum called for the planting of a "global survival forest," convening a council of spiritual leaders, encouraging the development of a center for religion and culture in Moscow, converting military enterprises, supporting various United Nations initiatives, endorsing a global environmental monitoring network, and convening a world-wide conference for educators on global survival issues and strategies.[15]

Events such as the Moscow forum can be helpful in strengthening international will and assisting in the interpretation, implementation, and monitoring of international agreements. Because the United Nations has no enforcement mechanisms, it is incumbent upon various international humanitarian organizations to secure governmental support and cooperation related to covenants and declarations supporting indigenous people and the survival of Mother Earth.

In launching the International Year of the World's Indigenous People in 1993, the General Assembly of the United Nations chose the theme of "Indigenous People–A New Partnership." Does this new partnership signal the beginning of a time that will give definition to and further detail the steps required to allow us to foreclose on the destructive incursions of corporations, governments and other predators on creation and Native civilizations? One must doubt that members of the General Assembly had fully formulated or even anticipated the dimensions of this partnership or where it would take them. Perhaps the Haudenosaunee summit shows the way forward.

The implications for North America are profound. Although intended as a projection of a new partnership between North and South, Mahbub ul Haq of the United Nations Development Programme could just as easily have applied his analysis to relations between North American governments and Native peoples:

> A new partnership . . . will also demand a new ethics of mutual responsibility and mutual respect. The North does not realize yet that, through its constant advocacy, it may have unleashed forces of change which will not only change other nations but also its own lifestyles. In particular, democracy is rarely so obliging as to stop at national borders. Its vast sweep will change global governance in the 21st century. The real choice is either to accept the evolution of such a global civil society and to speed up its arrival—or to resist it in the name of old-fashioned power balances and to plunge the world into utter confusion.[16]

As ul Haq testifies, the North fears that it may lose some of its previous privileges and cites recent evidence:

- While the poor nations are beginning to open up their economies, the rich nations are beginning to close theirs.
- While the poor nations are undergoing a structural adjustment at such a low level of income, the rich nations are resisting any such adjustment in their own lifestyles.
- While the rich nations preach democracy to the poor nations, they resist such democracy in international institutions and in global governance.[17]

Are there alternatives to embracing the potential of this new partnership with the United Nations? Do we have the means available to create a democratic counterinsurgency, an environmental counterinsurgency, an ecojustice counterinsurgency? Do we have the collective capacity to organize a North American Native Front to negotiate agreements, sign accords, and institute policies to ensure survival and protection for Mother Earth?

Although desirable, such action would be formidable and far exceed expectations of most North American Natives. The fundamental issues would call us to reestablish our traditional territories and gain recognition of our historic rights; exercise autonomy and self-determination; and gain collective property rights over our forests, lakes, rivers, and streams, as well as usufructuary rights over the subsoil and sea resources. We would institute complete freedom of movement and organization inside and outside the borders of the United States and Canada, as well as the continent, and develop Native self-defense mechanisms by commissioning Native troops to assume responsibility for the order and security of our communities and traditional territories. We might also ask for the release of political prisoners, indemnification for communal goods destroyed in wars since, shall we say, 1868, and the voluntary return and resettlement of displaced persons in their traditional communities of origin.[18]

If the United Nations has the potential for partnership so hopefully heralded December 10, 1992, it has been further strengthened by the Haudenosaunee summit and World Summit for Social Development (WSSD) in Copenhagen, March 6-12, 1995. Unfortunately, the Indigenous Caucus did not materialize in the preparatory meetings until January 24, 1995, and in Copenhagen there were but a handful of participants, who soon joined in the work of other issue caucuses. This is not to say that Native participants were absent in the WSSD; there simply was no visible coalition either before or during the meeting. This is important to note if we are to utilize the world's nation-states as a means of advancing our goals. We cannot absent ourselves from international discussions so critical to the survival issues that brought us together at the workshop in Denver.

The Copenhagen summit was an extraordinary time for recasting the important discussions of human and natural world viability. The intention of the summit was clear, and it was articulated in strong language recognizing the importance of people-centered development, equitable and sustainable use of our environment, broadly based economic policies, protection of family (in a variety of cultural contexts), observance and protection of all human rights, equality and equity between women and men, and protection of the rights of children.[19] While recognizing and supporting indigenous people in their pursuit of social and economic development and valuing indigenous identity, traditions, forms of social organization, and cultural values,[20] it came as no surprise that two major principles were in contention until the end of the summit. These reservations related primarily to issues of equitable distribution and the reaffirmation and promotion of the right to self-determination of people under colonial or foreign occupation.[21] Through the efforts of certain member nations and nongovernmental organizations, these goals were ultimately sustained in the final document.

It is clear that a strong, visible, identifiable, collective, and cohesive Native alliance with the United Nations is imperative to fulfill our principles and goals. That strategy is now fragmented and seriously wanting. The energy and cost of such an effort, however, can be staggering for Native people, who have little or no resources for plane tickets and hotel rooms. A multilevel approach must be taken, collectively, to tap currently financially strapped foundations and appropriate civil organizations for the economic means to pursue this process. The issues of justice for Native peoples are at risk and will be compounded in the United States by the politics of the Contract with America and the elimination of forty years of progressive social legislation in favor of benefits for the rich and powerful.

It is overwhelmingly evident to us—if to relatively few others—that Native peoples have approaches to and methods for considering ultimate questions that a materialistic world profoundly needs. Only by rediscovering the simplest and most basic values and virtues of the spirit and engaging in creative discourse on the meaning of hope and the nature of the common good will we be able to provide moral precepts and agreements of conduct necessary to create restorative measures for the continued viability of Mother Earth. The concluding four paragraphs of a historic document authored by the Dine, Lakota, and the Haudenosaunee provide us with an abiding theme for our labors together:

> The traditional people recognize that the injustices perpetuated upon our people, and indeed upon many of the peoples of the world, are the major factor destroying the Spirituality of the Human Race. Peace and unity are the foundations of the Spiritual Way of Life of our peoples. But peace and unity are not companions to justice.
>
> We call upon all the peoples of the world to join with us in seeking peace, and in seeking to ensure survival and justice for all indigenous peoples, for all the Earth's creatures, and all nations of the Earth.
>
> We will take whatever steps necessary in the protection of our Sacred Mother Earth, and the rights and well-being of our peoples.
>
> We will continue our efforts before the World Community to regain our inherent Human and Sovereign Rights.[22]

Notes

1. As retold in a narrative from the oral tradition transcribed by Martha E. Baker for the Northern California Indian Education Project, unpublished (1973).

2. Greg Sarris, *Keeping Slug Woman Alive* (Berkeley: University of California Press, 1993), pp. 51, 57.

3. *Respecting an Attempt to Evangelize the Heathen* (London: British Missionary Society, 1795), Fassett Collection, Washington, D.C.

4. Ibid.

5. The United States Bureau of Census officially counts fewer than three million Native people. Native nations and organizations are well aware that this is an inaccurate count, and the Bureau of Census acknowledges it as well. Conversation between Thom White Wolf Fassett and Dr. Martha Farnsworth Richie, Director, U.S. Bureau of the Census, in Copenhagen, Denmark (March 1995).

6. Oren Lyons, a faithkeeper of the Haudenosaunee, reminds us that the passenger pigeons once blanketed the sky for hours at a time; the buffalo (bison) would take days to pass by. And then he asks, "Where did they go, and who took them away?"

7. "The United Methodist Church and America's Native People," adopted by the 1980 General Conference of The United Methodist Church.

8. Supreme Court Justice William Douglas wrote a dissenting opinion in *Sierra Club v. Morton*, declaring that Nature has the right to be defended as though it were a human being. For the text and a discussion of this important opinion, see, Vine Deloria, Jr., *God Is Red*, rev. ed. (Golden, Co.: Fulcrum Publishing, 1992), pp. 293-296.

9. Haida Chief Skidegate (Lewis Collinson), *Communique No. 12*, Traditional Circle of Indian Elders and Youth, Haida Gwaii, Queen Charlotte Islands, Skidegate-Massett (June 14, 1989).

10. George Tinker, "An American Indian Theological Response to Ecojustice," herein.

11. Thomas Banyacya, in Alexander Ewen, ed., *Voice of Indigenous Peoples: Native People Address the United Nations* (Santa Fe: Clear Light Publishers, 1994), pp. 112-118.

12. Gil Stevenson, "Haudenosaunee Nations and United Nations Begin Historic Environmental Collaboration," *Indian Country Today* (July 27, 1995), p. A2.

13. See, "Moscow Plan of Action of the Global Forum on Environment and Development for Human Survival," forum paper (Moscow, January 15-19, 1990).

14. Partial quotation from the "Statement of Indigenous Delegates to the Global Forum on Environment and Development for Survival," forum paper (Moscow, January 15-19, 1990). See, *Indigenous Economics: Toward a Natural World Order*, (Ithaca, N.Y.: Akwekon Journal, 1992), pp. 106-107, for complete text.

15. "Moscow Plan of Action."

16. Mahbub ul Haq, *New Imperatives of Human Security* (New York: United Nations Development Programme, 1995), p. 10.

17. Ibid.

18. As suggested by the Indigenous Initiative for Reconciliation in Yapti Tasba (Republic of Nicaragua, February 2, 1988).

19. *Report of the World Summit for Social Development*, (Copenhagen: United Nations, 1995).

20. Ibid., p. 10.

21. Ibid., pp. 9-10.

22. *Hypocrisy and Outrage: Human Rights from a Native Perspective*, "Statement to the People of the United States and the World" (Washington, D.C.: July 1978), from the original document prepared for "The Longest Walk" by representatives of the Dine, Lakota, and Haudenosaunee, the first position paper ever to be presented in Washington by these three nations.

Resources

ORGANIZATIONS

The following is a listing of a few of the organizations in the Americas that are working on indigenous environmental issues:

Canadian Porcupine Caribou Management Board; Site 20, Comp. 116, R.R. #1; Whitehorse, Yukon Territory Y1A 4Z6; Canada

Colorado People's Environmental and Economic Network; c/o Cross Community Coalition; 2332 East 46th Ave.; Denver, CO 80216-3914
Ph: (303) 292-3203   Fax: (303) 292-3341

Confederación de Nacionalidades Indígenas del Ecuador; Casilla 17171235; Los Granados 2553 y 6 de Diciembre; Quito, Ecuador
Ph: (593-2) 248930   Fax: (593-2) 442271

Council for Yukon Indians; 11 Nitsulin Dr.; Whitehorse, Yukon Territory Y1A 3S4; Canada
Ph: (403) 667-7631   Fax: (403) 668-6577

Council of Energy Resource Tribes; 1999 Broadway, Suite 2600; Denver, CO 80202-5726
Ph: (303) 297-2378   Fax: (303) 296-5690

Greenpeace Native Lands Toxics Campaign; P.O. Box 701796; Tulsa, OK 74170
Ph: (918) 743-6530   Fax: (918) 743-6495

Indigenous Environmental Network; P.O. Box 485; Bemidji, MN 56601
Ph: (218) 751-4967   Fax: (218) 751-0561

Indigenous Women's Network; P.O. Box 174; Lake Elmo, MN 55042
Ph: (612) 777-3629   Fax: (612) 770-3976

InterTribal Sinkyone Wilderness Council; 190 Ford Road, #333; Ukiah, CA 95482
Ph: (707) 485-8744

National Environmental Coalition of Native Americans; 2213 West 8th Street; Prague, OK 74864
Ph/Fax: (405) 567-4297

Native Environmental Justice Advocacy Fund; Four Winds Project; 215 West 5th Ave.; Denver, CO 80204
Ph: (303) 629-0224   Fax: (303) 629-0622

READINGS

Below is a selected list of readings related to indigenous environmental perspectives and the concerns discussed in this volume:

Carol J. Adams, ed., *Ecofeminism and the Sacred* (New York: Continuum, 1993)
   Collection of essays by feminists from around the world, including Andy Smith's "For All Those Who Were Indian in a Former Life."

John Bierhorst, *The Way of the Earth: Native America and the Environment* (New York: William Morrow, 1994)
   Problematic discussion of Native environmental teachings and ethics by a scholar whose primary focus is Mesoamerica.

Ward Churchill, *Struggle for the Land: Indigenous Resistance to Genocide, Ecocide, and Expropriation in Contemporary North America* (Monroe, Me.: Common Courage, 1993)
   Collection of twelve essays focusing on land rights and environmental issues. Topics include nuclear waste, toxic dumping, water, and resource development.

Mary Davis, ed., *Native America in the Twentieth Century: An Encyclopedia* (New York: Garland Publishing, 1994)
   Invaluable resource that deals with the panoply of Native tribes and issues in this century. Includes numerous articles on related topics by both Native and non-Native scholars.

Vine Deloria, Jr., *God Is Red*, 2d edition (Golden, Co.: Fulcrum Publishing, 1992)
   Important early work (1973) by a Native American scholar, now thoroughly revised and updated. It deals with Native American worldviews and also discusses ecological and environmental issues.

Dene Nation, *Denedeh: A Dene Celebration* (Toronto: McClelland and Stewart, 1984)
   Compilation related to the Dene Nation of western Canada includes much material on the Dene view of the environment. The title is the word for the Dene land in their own language.

John Elder and Hertha Wong, eds., *Family of the Earth and Sky: Indigenous Tales of Nature from around the World* (Boston: Beacon Press, 1994)
   Similar to *Story Earth*, from which some of the pieces are drawn, this anthology contains traditional and contemporary myths and essays on Natives and nature.

Donald Fixico, *The Invasion of Indian Country in the Twentieth Century: American Capitalism and Tribal Natural Resources* (forthcoming)

Deals with the history of natural-resource struggles in this century, including the Osage Reign of Terror, water and fishing rights, and timber management.

Donald A. Grinde, Jr., and Bruce E. Johansen, *Ecocide of Native America: Environmental Destruction of Indian Lands and Peoples* (Santa Fe: Clear Light, 1995)
Up-to-date study of traditional environmental teachings and selected environmental issues, including toxic contamination, fishing rights, and resource exploitation.

David G. Hallman, *Ecotheology: Voices from South and North* (Maryknoll, N.Y.: Orbis Books, 1994)
Collection of theological reflections on North/South environmental issues includes two pieces by North American Natives: Stan McKay, "An Aboriginal Perspective on the Integrity of Creation," and George Tinker, "The Full Circle of Liberation: An American Indian Theology of Place."

Dieter T. Hessel, ed., *After Nature's Revolt: Eco-Justice and Theology* (Minneapolis: Fortress Press, 1992)
Collection of essays on environmental justice by ethicists and theologians, including an essay by George Tinker, "Creation as Kin: An American Indian View."

Dieter T. Hessel, ed., *Theology for Earth Community: A Field Guide* (Maryknoll, N.Y.: Orbis Books, 1996)
Collection of essays that examines state-of-the-art scholarship and pedagogy in ecological theology, including an essay by George Tinker, "EcoJustice and Justice."

Inter Press Service, comp., *Story Earth: Native Voices on the Environment* (San Francisco: Mercury House, 1993)
Collection of eighteen essays by indigenous scholars and activists around the world, including articles by Indians from the United States, Canada, Guatemala, Brazil, and Peru.

M. Annette Jaimes, ed., *The State of Native America* (Boston: South End Press, 1992)
Collection of essays by Native scholars and activists on a wide variety of contemporary Native issues, including land and water rights.

Geoffrey R. Lilburne, *A Sense of Place: A Christian Theology of the Land* (Nashville: Abingdon, 1989)
Although Australian Lilburne focuses primarily on that nation's aboriginal population, he also draws parallels to North American Natives in attempting to formulate his land-centered theology.

Jay B. McDaniel, *With Roots and Wings: Christianity in an Age of Ecology and Dialogue* (Maryknoll, N.Y.: Orbis Books, 1995)

Contains a chapter entitled "Communion with Spirits and Ancestors: Selected Lessons from North American Native Traditions for Remembering Our Roots in the Earth."

Dennis H. McPherson and J. Douglas Rabb, *Indian from the Inside: A Study in Ethno-Metaphysics* (Thunder Bay, Ont.: Lakehead University, 1993)
   Important new study of Native worldviews by a Native and a non-Native scholar includes a chapter, "Values, Land and the Integrity of Person."

Calvin Martin, *Keepers of the Game: Indian-Animal Relationships and the Fur Trade* (Berkeley: University of California Press, 1978)
   Historian Martin, focusing on the Micmac and Ojibwa, argues that Euro-Americans cannot assess Native actions by Western frames of reference because of the differences in worldview.

John Joseph Mathews, *Talking to the Moon* (Norman: University of Oklahoma Press, 1945)
   Autobiographical account of Osage author Mathews's time spent among the blackjacks of Osage country in Oklahoma. Structured around the seasons and the Osage names for individual months, the volume is rich in detail about the land and its flora and fauna.

Don Monet and Skanu'u (Ardythe Wilson), *Colonialism on Trial: Indigenous Land Rights and the Gitksan and Wet'suwet'en Sovereignty Case* (Philadelphia: New Society Publishers, 1992)
   Chronicle of *Delgam Uukw v. the Queen*, one of the most important and controversial Native lands-rights cases in Canadian history, decided in 1991.

Norman Myers, *The Primary Source: Tropical Forests & Our Future*, revised edition (New York: W. W. Norton, 1992)
   Classic treatment on importance of tropical rainforests to the health of the planet and its people.

Richard K. Nelson, *Make Prayers to the Raven: A Koyukon View of the Northern Forest* (Chicago: University of Chicago Press, 1983)
   Anthropologist discusses the traditional worldview of the Koyukon people of Alaska.

Paul A. Olson, ed., *The Struggle for the Land: Indigenous Insight and Industrial Empire in the Semiarid World* (Lincoln: University of Nebraska Press, 1990)
   Includes "American Indian Land Wisdom" by J. Baird Callicott, a non-Native philosopher who, like historian Calvin Martin, has investigated the worldviews and environmental ethics of the Algonkian cultures of eastern North America.

David Sukuzi and Peter Knudtson, *Wisdom of the Elders: Honoring Sacred Native Visions of Nature* (New York: Bantam Books, 1992)
   This discussion of indigenous views of ecology and nature around the world includes much anthologized material from Native cultures in the Americas.

Christopher Vecsey and Robert W. Venables, eds., *American Indian Environments: Ecological Issues in Native American History* (Syracuse: Syracuse University Press, 1980)

Largely historical essays by non-Native scholars, the volume also contains two brief contemporary pieces by Native leaders Peter MacDonald and Oren Lyons.

Jace Weaver, *Then to the Rock Let Me Fly: Luther Bohanon and Judicial Activism* (Norman: University of Oklahoma Press, 1993)

Biography of prominent Oklahoma lawyer and jurist discusses important Native land- and water-rights decisions, including the first case to deal with compensability for aboriginal rights not based on treaty.

Participants

North American Native Workshop on Environmental Justice

Margaret Sam-Cromarty (Cree) is a poet who has held readings and lectured throughout the United States and Canada on Cree life and the issues surrounding hydroelectric development at James Bay. She is the author of *James Bay Memoirs: A Cree Woman's Ode to Her Homeland* and two other volumes of poetry. She currently lives in Fort George on James Bay.

William Cromarty (Ojibway) lives a traditional life with his wife, Margaret, in Fort George on James Bay.

Josh DiNabaugh (Cheyenne River Sioux) works at Living Waters Indian Church in Denver, Colorado.

Thom White Wolf Fassett (Seneca) is General Secretary of the General Board of Church and Society of The United Methodist Church. He splits his time between Washington, D.C., and Valois on the Seneca Reservation in upstate New York.

Donald Fixico (Shawnee/Sac and Fox/Muscogee/Seminole) is professor of history at Western Michigan University. He is the author of *Termination and Relocation: Federal Indian Policy, 1945-1960* and the forthcoming *The Invasion of Indian Country in the Twentieth Century: American Capitalism and Tribal Natural Resources.*

Duane Good Striker (Blood) is director of the Blood environmental program. He was previously employed by the Department of Indian Affairs and Northern Development in Canada.

Norma Kassi (Gwich'in) is Arctic Environmental Strategy Coordinator for the Council for Yukon Indians in Whitehorse, Yukon Territory.

Anne Marshall (Muscogee) is Associate General Secretary of the General Commission of Christian Unity and Interreligious Concerns of The United Methodist Church. She divides her time between New York City and her home in Oklahoma.

Russell Means (Oglala Lakota) was a co-founder of the American Indian Movement in 1968. Since then, he has played a major role in such events as the

1972 AIM take-over of the Bureau of Indian Affairs offices in Washington, the 1973 occupation of Wounded Knee, and the 1980 establishment of Yellow Thunder Camp in the Black Hills. He has appeared in numerous motion pictures. He currently resides in Porcupine, South Dakota.

Glenn Morris (Shawnee) is associate professor of law and politics at the University of Colorado at Denver where he is director of the Fourth World Center for the Study of Indigenous Law and Politics. He is chair of the Colorado chapter of the American Indian Movement and has been involved in numerous indigenous and human rights causes.

Gabina Pérez Jiménez (Mixtec) has been an advocate for the Mixtec language and for other indigenous and human rights causes for many years. She currently resides in Rijswijk, Netherlands.

Sage Douglas Remington (Southern Ute) is director of the Native Environmental Justice Advocacy Fund and the Four Winds Project. He is a long-time activist for Indian rights.

Dale Ann Frye Sherman (Yurok/Karok/Tolowa/Hupa) is a master's candidate at the University of Denver.

Andrea Smith (Cherokee) is a master's candidate at Union Theological Seminary in New York. She is a founder of the Chicago chapter of Women of All Red Nations. She is the author of the widely anthologized article "For All Those Who Were Indian in a Former Life," which deals with New Age appropriation of Native religion.

Justine Smith (Cherokee) is a director of the Midwest Treaty Network and is active in the Indigenous Environmental Network. She was formerly with the Lake Michigan Federation.

Grace Thorpe (Sac and Fox) is a tribal judge for the Sac and Fox Nation and president of the National Environmental Coalition of Native Americans. She is the daughter of legendary Native athlete and Olympic gold medal winner, Jim Thorpe.

George E. Tinker (Osage/Cherokee) is associate professor of crosscultural ministries at the Iliff School of Theology in Denver. He is the author of *Missionary Conquest*, which discusses the history and effects of Christian mission work on Native Americans.

Jackie Warledo (Seminole) is the Native Lands Campaigner for Greenpeace USA in the organization's Toxics Campaign. She works in Tulsa.

Jace Weaver (Cherokee) is an attorney and earned a Ph.D. at Union Theological Seminary in New York, where he also teaches Native American studies. He is the author of *Then to the Rock Let Me Fly: Luther Bohanon and Judicial Activism*, which deals in part with Native land claims.

Phyllis Young (Standing Rock Sioux) has been an activist for Native American causes on the national and international level for more than twenty years. She previously worked as a tribal intern with the Environmental Protection Agency in Denver.

Index

Indian Health Service (IHS),
124, 125
Insecticides, 79-80
Irrigation: Indian, 145; land
damage caused by, 89, 91;
western water rights and, 86-
87

James Bay Memoirs (Margaret
Sam-Cromarty), 101
Johansen, Bruce, 3, 7, 10, 14, 15,
17, 18, 107, 195

Keller, Catherine, 131-33
Kennecott Copper, 60, 66, 67
Kennedy, John F., 89, 179
Kenny-Gilday, Cindy, 20, 73,
107
Kinship. *See* Community

Lakota Nation. *See* Sioux Nation
Land, Indian: colonization and,
3, 4, 19-20, 41, 163, 171, 183-
84; female representations of,
9-10, 102, 104; guardianship
concept of, 16-19; irrigation
and, 89; legal jurisdiction
over, 19-20, 108-17, 144-45,
169; religion and, 4, 8, 9, 12-
14, 37, 163-64; rituals of
respect for, 74-75
Law: land rights under, 19-20,
108-17, 144-45, 169; treaty
rights under, 61-62, 63, 67,
110, 144-45; water rights
under, 85-87, 95
Lilburne, Geoffrey, 4
Lyons, Oren, 16, 19, 36, 186

Martin, Calvin, 5-6, 196
Mathews, John Joseph, 1, 30, 196
McDaniel, Jay, 4
McFague, Sallie, 131, 133, 134
McPherson, Dennis, 6-7, 144,
196
Means, Russell, 54, 60, 92

Medicine: food contamination
and, 80; herbal, 34, 127;
Indian Health Service (IHS)
and, 124, 125; land and, 76;
obtaining wisdom through,
35; Western, 127, 135-36
Menominee Nation, 62, 67, 68
Military sites, pollution from, 78,
79
Mills, Mary Ann, 127, 135
Mining: of coal, 3, 109; colonization and, 59-60; cultural
values concerning, 31;
environmental impact of, 63-
65, 68, 78, 81, 95-96, 109-10,
146; of gold, 78, 94; in
"national sacrifice areas," 60;
reclamation and, 60, 66, 95,
109; sovereignty issues and,
63; sulfide waste in, 64-65;
takings concept and, 94-96;
treaty rights and, 61-62, 63,
67; of uranium, 47-49, 50, 54,
66
Missionaries, 76-77, 156, 157, 161,
178-79
Momaday, N. Scott, 2
Mother Earth: An American Story
(Sam Gill), 9

NAFTA, 3
National Environmental Coalition of Native Americans
(NECONA), 51, 53, 54, 55
"National sacrifice areas," 60,
167, 181
Natural resources: cultural value
systems and, 30-31, 41-42,
182; increasing destruction
of, 41-42, 43, 80; Indian
control over, 32, 42, 59-60,
170, 180
Nature: equality in, 36; European categorization of, 159;
Indian lifeways and, 7-9, 16,
172; religion and, 11, 13, 34